W9-CUZ-258

Planning for the
quality of life in aging...
To Bernie
from Ursula
Haloween 1992

Who Is Responsible for My Old Age?

Robert N. Butler, M.D., is Brookdale Professor and Chairman of the Department of Geriatrics and Adult Development at Mount Sinai Medical Center in New York City, the nation's first medical school to establish such a department. The founding director of the National Institute on Aging, Dr. Butler won the Pulitzer Prize in 1976 for his book, *Why Survive? Being Old in America*. He is Editor-in-Chief of the journal, *Geriatrics*, serves as Co-Director of the International Leadership Center on Longevity and Society (U.S.), and sits on the boards of many of the country's leading associations.

Kenzo Kiikuni, Managing Director of the Sasakawa Memorial Health Foundation, is also a Professor at the Institute of Community Medicine at the University of Tsukuba. He obtained his B.A. from International Christian University and did graduate work and obtained an advanced degree at Northwestern University, Chicago, as a Fulbright Scholar. Professor Kiikuni is a past president of the Japanese Society on Hospital Administration and is currently on its board of trustees. He is also science councilor for the Japan Medical Education Foundation.

Who Is Responsible for My Old Age?

Robert N. Butler, M.D.
Kenzo Kiikuni

Editors

SPRINGER PUBLISHING COMPANY
NEW YORK

Copyright © 1993 by Springer Publishing Company, Inc.

All rights reserved

No part of this publication may be reproduced, stored in a retrieval system, or transmitted in any form or by any means, electronic, mechanical, photocopying, recording, or otherwise, without the prior permission of Springer Publishing Company, Inc.

Springer Publishing Company, Inc.
536 Broadway
New York, NY 10012

93 94 95 96 97 / 5 4 3 2 1

Library of Congress Cataloging-in-Publication Data

Who is responsible for my old age? / Robert N. Butler & Kenzo Kiikuni, editors.
    p. cm.
    Includes bibliographical references and index.
    ISBN 0-8261-8140-6
    1. Aged—Care—United States—Congresses. 2. Aged—Care—Japan-
Congresses. 3. Aged—Government policy—United States—Congresses.
4. Aged—Government policy—Japan—Congresses. I. Butler, Robert N.,
1927– . II. Kiikuni, Kenzo, 1933–
HV1461.W495 1992
362.6′0973—dc20   92-25181
                                                          CIP

Cover design by Holly Block
Printed in the United States of America

Contents

Contributors

Mariko Sugahara Bando graduated from Tokyo University's Faculty of Literature in 1969 and in 1980–1981 was a Fellow at the Bunting Institute of Radcliffe College. In 1969 she joined the Prime Minister's Office of the Government of Japan, where she assumed positions in the Policy Office for the Aged, Headquarters to Improve the Policies Relating to Women, and the Youth Bureau. Since 1985 she has been councilor of the Prime Minister's Secretariat. Among Ms. Bando's writings are: *Scenario for the 21st Century—The Future of Babyboomers, Era of the New Family,* and *Managerial Women in Japan.*

James E. Birren, Ph.D., D.Sc., is Director of the Borun Center for Gerontological Research at the University of California (Los Angeles). Dr. Birren's career includes being past president of the Gerontological Society of America, the Western Gerontological Society, and the Division on Adult Development and Aging of the American Psychological Association. Currently, he is a member of the World Health Organization's Expert Advisory Panel on Health of Elderly Persons. He is Series Editor of the internationally renowned *Handbooks on Aging* and has over 250 publications in academic journals and books.

Rosalynn Smith Carter, wife of the 39th President of the United States, Jimmy Carter, has been a tireless participant in numerous humanitarian efforts since 1971 and has received many honors and awards for her work in mental health, women's rights, and human rights. Mrs. Carter has become recognized in this country and abroad as an advocate in the mental health field and as an activist on behalf of the mentally ill and disadvantaged. In addition to her autobiography, *First Lady from Plains,* published in 1984, she co-authored with her husband, *Everything to Gain: Making the Most of the Rest of Your Life,* a critically acclaimed and inspirational review of the Carters' past achievements and future plans.

Betty Friedan's 1963 book, *The Feminine Mystique,* ignited the women's movement, which she helped found. Her more recent books, *The Second Stage* and *It Changed My Life,* track the social evolution that followed. Now turning her attention to older women, Ms. Friedan, who is currently Distinguished Visiting Professor at the University of Southern California, is writing about the "mystique of age" in her upcoming book, *The Fountain of Age.*

Lauren Goldberg, M.D., was a third-year medical student at the Mount Sinai School of Medicine at the time of the "Who Is Responsible for My Old Age?" symposium.

Yoshio Gyoten, M.D., is Japan's leading television commentator on public health issues. He was born in Tokyo in 1926 and graduated from Chiba Medical College. In 1949 he joined NHK (Nihon Broadcasting Station), where, for the next 35 years, he produced, directed, and anchored health-related programs, including those on heart transplants, in vitro fertilization, and aging. Dr. Gyoten is the recipient of numerous broadcasting awards, including the National Public Health Award (Hoken Bunka Sho).

Keiko Higuchi was born in 1932. After a long and successful career as a social critic and author, she joined the faculty of the Tokyo Kasei University in 1986. As Japan's leading commentator on women's and aging issues and a well-known media personality, Ms. Higuchi is founder and president of Japan Older Women's Association and leads the National Women's Group for the Improvement of the Aging Society.

Toshiyuki Kato has been involved with Japanese trade unions for much of his career. After graduating from Niihama Technical College with a degree in electrical engineering, he joined the Mitsubishi Electric Corporation in 1969. He began his association with the Mitsubishi Electric Workers' Union in 1974, becoming president of the communication equipment works branch in 1982. He became Executive Director of the Research and Legal Affairs Bureau, JPTUC–RENGO (Japanese Private Sector Trade Union Confederation) in 1987. Since 1989 Mr. Kato has been Executive Director of the Legal Affairs Bureau of JTUC–RENGO (Japan Trade Union Confederation), Executive Committee Member of DENKI–ROREN (Japanese Federation of Electrical Machine Workers' Unions), and Executive Committee Member of Mitsubishi Electric Workers' Union. Since 1990 he has been the Workers' Representative of the Homework Council of the Labor Ministry.

Eugene M. Lang founded and has been Chairman since 1952 of REFAC Technology Development Corporation, a company specializing in the negotiation and administration of international manufacturing licenses and joint ventures. He is widely recognized for his entrepreneurship, public service contributions, and philanthropic activities, many of which have benefited educational institutions as well as individual students. Mr. Lang's name came to public attention with the founding of the "I Have a Dream" education program, a model philanthropic effort through which disadvantaged young people who graduate from high school are granted support for their college education. The program has become nationwide, with 145 individual projects in 43 cities that include over 10,000 children. Mr. Lang is Chairman Emeritus of

Swarthmore College, Vice-Chairman of the New School for Social Research, and a Managing Director of the Metropolitan Opera Association in New York City.

The Honorable Claude D. Pepper (1900–1989), Democrat of Miami, Florida, was elected to the U.S. Senate in 1936 and remained Senator from Florida until 1951. In 1962, he was elected to the House of Representatives and reelected to each succeeding Congress. Representative Pepper's dedication, perseverance, and imagination led to the passage of the amendments to the Age Discrimination in Employment Act of 1967, virtually bringing an end to mandatory retirement. His long service in Congress established him as a conscientious, knowledgeable, and productive member who worked across a broad spectrum of legislative fields. As Chairman of the House Rules Committee, a position he held until his death in 1989, he was in a pivotal position to advance legislation in health and social welfare for Americans of all ages. One of the outstanding legislators of the 20th Century, Representative Pepper was recognized after his death by his colleagues in Congress, who arranged for his body to lie in state in the Capitol Rotunda and who created an endowment for the Mildred and Claude Pepper Foundation.

Alan Pifer was educated at Harvard College and Cambridge University, and he holds honorary degrees from some of the nation's leading universities. From 1967 to 1982 he was President of Carnegie Corporation of New York. Since 1987 he has been Chairman and President of the Southport Institute for Policy Analysis in Connecticut. Throughout his career he has been actively involved in issues in social policy, including education, private philanthropy and public needs, social welfare, and aging. He is author of *Government for the People* (W. W. Norton, 1987) with Forrest Chisman.

Ryoichi Sasakawa was born in 1899 in a suburb of Osaka Prefacture in Japan. Shortly after World War II, Mr. Sasakawa vowed to work toward saving humanity from the tragedy of war and establishing world peace. Believing that peace can be achieved only when life is free from want, illness, and injustice, Mr. Sasakawa has contributed, through the Japan Shipbuilding Industry Foundation and the Sasakawa Memorial Health Foundation, billions of dollars to a number of health, social, and public works projects within and outside of Japan, as well as the United Nations, particularly the World Health Organization. Mr. Sasakawa's gifts have helped to eradicate smallpox worldwide, combat leprosy, and develop strategies to prevent famine in Africa, among many other worthy projects.

Takako Sodei did her graduate work in sociology at the Tokyo Metropolitan University in 1970. She is currently Professor in the Department of Home Economics at Ochanomizu University in Tokyo. Professor Sodei is on the editorial staff of the *Journal of the Japan Social Gerontological Society* and has written extensively on the topics of aging, the status of women, and family relations, and has been a member of several local and national committees that reported on the special problems of women and the aged. In 1980 and 1981 she was a visiting scholar at the National Council on Aging as a senior researcher of the Japan–U.S. Educational Commission.

John L. Steffens is Executive Vice President, Private Client, of Merrill Lynch & Company, Inc. Before assuming his present post in November 1990, Mr. Steffens had served as President of Merrill Lynch Consumer Markets since July 1985 and was a member of Merrill Lynch & Company's Board of Directors from April 1986 to April 1991. A native of Cleveland, Ohio, he graduated from Dartmouth College in 1963 with a B.A. in Economics and attended the Advanced Management Program of the Harvard Business School in 1979.

Daiseku Teraguchi was a high school student at the United Nations International School at the time of the "Who Is Responsible for My Old Age?" symposium.

Foreword

I am now 92 years old—93 counting the Japanese way—and I continue to enjoy good health. I work 365 days a year, and some years 366 days, for a better, healthier, and more peaceful world. People from all over ask me, "What is the secret of your health?" There are several secrets, and I will disclose some of them here.

First, it is necessary to lead a simple lifestyle. And second, we must practice healthy habits. According to Oriental philosophy, moderation is wisdom: avoidance of overeating, overdrinking, speeding while driving and so on contributes to a moderate lifestyle. At the age of 93 I continue to practice such moderation and to engage in physical activity. I still jog every morning and use the stairs instead of the elevator.

The third secret involves appreciating one's own health, and when I use the word "health," I mean it in the World Health Organization sense, which includes physical, mental, and social well-being. I would add here that good health comes in part from a peaceful mind, and a peaceful mind comes from knowing that one is contributing to society. Consequently, social contribution is a necessary ingredient in achieving good health. But older people will not be able to live according to this principle if the larger context in which they live does not allow them to do so.

I believe that we have to develop an environment in which all people, young and old alike, can live healthier and happier lives. As far as older people are concerned, society must encourage their self-reliance, because self-reliance is an essential ingredient in older people's well-being, as well as in the well-being of society in general.

Positive self-reliance, or positive individual responsibility, comes from feeling satisfied with one's daily life, and this satisfaction is often realized through continuation of meaningful, responsible work. Unfortunately, there are few opportunities for most people to continue working well into their later years. The elderly have gained wisdom through a lifetime of experience, but their wisdom is not being fully utilized by our societies. Finding ways to allow older people to share their wisdom, on paid and voluntary bases, should be one of our top priorities. My point is that we should put the elderly on the "givers" side, not merely on the passive "receivers" side.

Japan, like other developed countries, is worried about the escalating costs of medical care for the elderly. Rising costs in the care of this segment of the population may in part be due to the customary emphasis on treating disease once it is detected, instead of trying to prevent it in the first place. Both self-reliance and control of medical costs would be better served by health promotion and disease prevention. Even some older people who are disabled can be relatively self-reliant once they learn how to live with their disability.

By now it must be clear that self-reliance cannot be achieved without the active participation of the entire community. Self-reliance for older people does not mean leaving them to their own devices. It means all of us working together to create societies in which young and old help each other to live productive, healthy, and fulfilling lives.

RYOICHI SASAKAWA

Acknowledgments

The "Who Is Responsible for My Old Age?" symposium, on which this book is based, was sponsored by the Japan Shipbuilding Industry Foundation and organized by the Department of Geriatrics and Adult Development of the Mount Sinai Medical Center, New York City.

We would like to thank the following collaborating organizations: Brookdale Center on Aging, Hunter College; Hunter–Mount Sinai Geriatric Education Center; The Jewish Home and Hospital for the Aged; and the Page and William Black Post Graduate School of Medicine of the Mount Sinai School of Medicine. We would like to thank the following supporting organizations as well: Alliance for Aging Research; American Association for International Aging; American Association of Retired Persons; American Medical Association; The Brookdale Foundation; Comprehensive Center for Local Autonomy, Japan; Economic Planning Agency of the Japanese Government; Japan External Trade Organization; Permanent Mission of Malta to the United Nations; Permanent Mission of Japan to the United Nations; Tokyo Metropolitan Institute of Gerontology; U.S. House Select Committee on Aging; U.S. National Institute on Aging; U.S. Senate Special Committee on Aging; Well-Aging Association of Japan; and the World Health Organization.

We are also grateful to the following organizations whose generosity and support contributed to the success of the symposium: Alliance for Aging Research; American Association of Retired Persons; Permanent Mission of Malta to the United Nations; Merrill Lynch and Company, Inc.; and the Sandoz Pharmaceutical Company.

The preparation of this book was made possible through a grant from the Brookdale Foundation. We would like expressly to thank Stephen Schwartz, President of the Brookdale Foundation, and Danylle Rudin, Program Officer and Assistant Vice President, for their generous support.

Finally, we wish to thank Masako Osako for her valuable assistance in translation and coordination during this symposium. We also wish to acknowledge and thank Debra Di Piazza and Mia Oberlink for their help in the preparation of this book.

Introduction
The Longevity Revolution: Sharing Responsibility for Old Age

Robert N. Butler

The new longevity—the increase of over 25 years in average life expectancy throughout the industrialized world—creates new challenges and opportunities for the human family. This triumph of survivorship is a terrific advertisement for scientific and economic growth and progress and promises to transform our social and cultural values. It is a product of the great industrial and scientific revolutions that have taken place over the past 150 years, which have brought us the separation of the family from the workplace; changes in family structure and relationships; the privileges of the individual over the community; postindustrial developments, such as the information boom; and, more recently, the rise of the entrenched welfare state.

But this new longevity, while it is a historically unprecedented social achievement, also poses very real challenges to us, its beneficiaries. We must secure the economic resources and cultural framework that are necessary to support the old age of great numbers of people. We ask, "Who is responsible for *my* old age?" Note the stress on *my*. Within this question a host of other questions is submerged, only one of which is, "how should we allocate responsibility among individuals, the family, the community, the economic enterprise, and the government at every level?"

The title of this book, *Who Is Responsible for My Old Age?*, and the title of this introductory chapter were selected to convey the urgent need for all of us to recognize the extraordinary socially transforming geopolitical force that population aging represents. It is most certainly the goal of our two great societies, Japan and the United States, to protect our older persons, to sustain their economic security and their health security. We gathered in New York in 1988* to see what we might learn, each from the other, via the wonderful contrasts and sharp distinctions that can emerge as people begin to think about these two societies, very different and yet united by universal human experience. One society is much more ancient, much more enriched by a long past. The other society is really very new, barely 200 years old as an independent republic. We considered many things at this conference: the impact of culture, including its impact on savings and consumption; the role of women in society and in issues surrounding aging; the role of government versus the role of the individual and the community; the experience of aging as a transformative process; and intergenerational relations.

The new longevity is not merely a function of biological evolution. Rather, it is a social achievement, a triumph of medical, legislative, and technological progress. A long, healthy life, once the privilege of a wealthy few, is now available to many. This century can rightly be called the century of old age. We've witnessed, in less than 100 years, the democratization of longevity. Unfortunately, there is still a very strong correlation between socioeconomic status and longevity. There is a much lower average life expectancy in the so-called Third World nations. Clearly, we have a lot of work to do to provide some equality of longevity within our societies and throughout the world.

Despite this great achievement of widespread longevity, there are many fears that haunt societies. One is the fear that somehow the increasing number and proportion of older persons in the population may lead to economic stagnation and

*Symposium held in New York City, November 28–30, 1988.

may impose a greater burden upon our societies than they can reasonably withstand. There are also fears that the rapid aging of populations will lead to intergenerational conflict. We must address these fears and recognize that longevity has always been a relative concept. At the time of the Declaration of Independence, the average life expectancy was just 35 years. We have more than doubled that life expectancy since then, a mere two centuries later. So what one considers "old" is really quite relative. The age structure of any society is a function of three elements: The birthrate, which has declined markedly in both Japan and the United States through aggressive family planning and an increase in delayed marriage and childbearing; mortality rates, which have also declined in both nations; and net migration. It is in this third element, in patterns of migration, that we see a real difference between the United States and Japan. Japan is a much more homogeneous and cohesive society than the United States. Indeed, in the United States, immigration alone could help counter some of the fears about population aging, since immigrants are usually young, often only in their teens or twenties, and the United States has an estimated 500,000 to 1 million new immigrants each year.

Why did this symposium, "Who is Responsible for My Old Age?," focus so particularly on Japan and the United States? These two countries are characterized by rapidly aging populations; Japan is the most rapidly aging nation in the world, with the most long-lived people in the world. A valuable book, prepared by the Japan Economic Planning Agency and titled *Japan in the Year 2000*, identifies the three great issues that will confront Japanese society as it moves into the next century. These issues are the maturing of its economy, increasing internationalization, and the aging of the population. Japanese men have an average life expectancy of 76 years, compared to 72 for American men, while Japanese women can expect to live to be 81 years old, compared to 79 years for American women. The United States is projected to reach the same point in terms of median age of the population and the proportion of the population that is 65 or older 10 years later than Japan. Besides the "graying" of our populations, there are other reasons for the United States and Japan to join together to share ideas and concerns about population aging: We are important trading partners—the Pacific Rim nations now account for 60% of the world's commerce.

What are some of the opportunities for comparative study that present themselves to us, especially with respect to aging? We might, for example, study family life. In Japan, many more older persons live with family members, compared to elders in the United States. We might also compare savings rates in the two nations. In the United States, people save, on average, only 8% of their net income. In Japan, the rate is 15%. There are also some very interesting differences in the attention paid to individual self-responsibility, sometimes referred to as health promotion and disease prevention. For example, the Health Care Act in Japan has actually legislated the availability of health diaries for people to use to build health habits that will protect them and preserve their good health in the future.

Comparisons raise some interesting questions for us to consider. It has been argued, for instance, by former Treasury Secretary Donald Regan, that savings rates in the United States do not factor in home purchases, which are a major form of saving in this country. Are we then miscalculating when we examine savings rates? In Japan, workers receive semiannual bonuses designed to stimulate saving. The Nobel Prize–winning economist Franco Modiglioni has suggested that as we grow older, we begin to *dis*-save. Since the 1930s, workers in the United States have been encouraged to spend and consume to stimulate the economy, and *not* to save. Our society sends mixed messages, and it is important in our considerations of the apparent differences between Japan and the United States to examine some of the details more closely. Do the reductions in maternal, infant, and childhood mortality fully account for the increased longevity we have seen? Not entirely, though they do, of course, contribute. But it is estimated that up to 20% of the gain in average life expectancy in this century is a consequence of a decline in mortality after the age of 65. In the United States alone, we've experienced a 40% drop in deaths from stroke and a 30% drop in deaths from heart attacks. Similar declines have been recorded in Japan.

But people do not want to live long lives merely for the sake of living. Everyone wants to live a high-quality life. We all would like to live both long and well. A recent survey revealed that some 45% of United States citizens would like to live to be 100 years old. And in fact, centenarians comprise the fastest-growing age group in the United States. There are now about 25,000 people aged 100 years or older in the United States; and by the year 2000, if current trends persist, that number is projected to rise to over 100,000.

So we know that people are indeed living longer. And there is gratifying evidence that they are also living better. There are increasing numbers of elderly people, on both sides of the Pacific Ocean, who are living vigorous, productive, *effective* old ages. This longevity revolution is a scion of the industrial revolution. Better nutrition, improved sanitation, higher standards of living, socioeconomic progress—all account for this new longevity. Advances in medical practices per se are certainly not unimportant factors, but behind the broad changes in public health are *ideas*, and *ideas* spur social change. One of those ideas involves the sophistication that grew out of the end of the last century with regard to nosology, the study of the cause of disease, and specifically the germ theories of Robert Koch and Louis Pasteur. Medicine, and science in general, have played a great role in prolonging our lives, and therefore we must hold them accountable. Medicine and science have a responsibility in helping societies and individuals adapt to this socially transforming increase in life span.

We hear a great deal these days about the global economy and the internationalization of national economies. Science has long been international, universal in its methodology and in its application. It is fitting, therefore, that a great American medical establishment, Mount Sinai Medical Center, and two great Japanese institutions, the Japan Shipbuilding Industry Foundation and the Sasakawa Memorial Health Foundation, have been working in concert to consider the issues involved in population aging.

In 1987 we held our first joint symposium, "The Promise of Productive Aging," at the United States Senate. We looked at both the physiological and behavioral bases of our ability to perform and function in our later years, and we also looked at some of the social, political, and cultural obstacles to the realization of productivity throughout the life course. The purpose of that symposium was to promote the triangle of health, aging, and productivity. With the increase in health and in longevity, we have seen a concomitant increase in productivity in our societies. The economic distress of the Third World countries certainly illustrates the problems that plague developing nations, where 20% of the lifetimes of people is marred by disease and disability, which sap their energy, strength, and productive potential.

Perhaps I have, up to this point, painted too rosy a picture of the new longevity. We must not forget that there is poverty and illness in both the United States and Japan. Individuals in both societies must share the responsibility for these social failures. There is much debilitating illness that is preventable and curable. We seem, however, to lack the will and determination to invest in medical and behavioral research and application. There is a great deal of poverty, particularly, and sadly, in the United States. These are problems that deserve broad-based attention on the individual, community, and federal levels. We came together at this symposium to promote a new triangle, the triangle of responsibility among individuals and families, government, and the economic enterprise.

The individual can do a great deal to prepare for a high-quality old age. I have already referred to self-responsibility, which I regard as a stronger term than "health promotion/disease prevention." The classic example is tobacco use, which probably accounts for one-third of the extraordinary "gender gap" in life expectancy. In short, each one of us must develop an individualized life plan. People still underestimate their potential for longevity. They have not yet developed any real sense of the life cycle. By and large, people have not been able to translate our contemporary medical knowledge into good health habits.

We are, all of us, plagued by denial and fear of old age, and that is one of the greatest obstacles to change with regard to life planning and social planning for old age. It is not necessary to have a morbid preoccupation with aging, but the truth is that the future belongs to those who prepare for it, to those who have realistically examined their options. Admittedly, there are few guidebooks, at least in Western culture, for making a plan for one's entire life. Here is where we might learn a great deal from Japan, and from Eastern philosophy in general, about how to live, how to age, and how to die. The philosophy of aging is one we sorely need to revive here in the West. One example I can think of is the work of Ludovico Cornaro, a 16th-century Italian who wrote what in his time might be the analogue of our present-day American Heart Association Prudent Diet. But his work is a little short on suggestions for what to do with our intellectual and spiritual selves as we grow older. We really don't know how to use our newly won time, so much of which can be leisure time. How can we use these years, literally snatched from the jaws of death, for personal growth and development and for recreation and fulfillment?

We need real mutuality among the generations, beyond the intergenerational social contracts of Social Security in the United States and the National Pension System in Japan. We need new contexts, new contracts, and new intergenerational arrangements. We need ways of effectively enabling older persons to mentor and sponsor the young. We need ways of making sure that older persons are more productive, both through paid labor and personal voluntary service.

Society has not provided for all of life's contingencies with full and wise measures to protect us from those social, personal, and socioeconomic disasters that are beyond our individual control. The individual cannot be held fully accountable for his or her health or illness, for example. This is an issue of social responsibility. We need more comprehensive public health and worker health measures than we have at present. We need stronger occupational safety regulations and better environmental quality control, not only in terms of air and water pollution but also of the depletion of the ozone layer and global warming. Right now, U.S. public policy is a confusion of mixed signals. On the one hand, the Surgeon General's office seeks to discourage tobacco use while, on the other hand, our government grants federal subsidies to tobacco farmers.

In the United States and Japan, we have not yet transformed our health care enterprises to be in alignment with the realities of population aging. Both nations must undertake a major reorganization in the delivery of health and social services. We must keep in mind that group of frail elders who suffer from multiple, complex, interacting psychological or emotional problems, as well as physical illnesses or disabilities. We must seek to understand why it is that in Japan the average length of stay in a general hospital for persons over 65 is 90 days, while here in the United States, that stay is only 9 days' duration. Some of the difference is a function of the omission of various steps on the continuum of care, while some of it may be understood in terms of important cultural differences. But here again, we have so much to learn from each other.

Our medical education, on the graduate, postgraduate, and continuing education levels, must integrate geriatrics into the mainstream of medical education so that every physician, whatever his or her primary specialization, appreciates the special developmental and health care needs of the older patient. Every physician must know the effects of drug interactions in elderly patients and learn to recognize the early signs of mental confusion. This integration is by no means adequate in either the United States or Japan.

The research agenda is incomplete. It is not at all in keeping with the reality of the "age of aging" in the 20th century, nor does it prepare us for the projected realities of the 21st century. The development of disease is due to (1) genetic factors, (2) environmental factors (which we may broadly define to include air and water quality and our health habits), and (3) the effects of aging processes. We have devoted very few of our considerable resources to studying the aging processes. We have made some excellent beginnings, however, both at the Tokyo Metropolitan Institute of Gerontology and at the National Institute on Aging in the United States. There has been some very good work done recently on multi-infarct dementia (also known as repeated small-stroke dementia, which is common in Japan), and on Alzheimer's disease, which is more common in the United States. Nevertheless, our health care enterprises, our education, our services, and our research are still principally oriented to acute-care, high-technology medicine.

What is the responsibility of the family and the community for society's elders? In the United States, we have witnessed some extraordinary changes in the family in this century. We often speak of "blended families," families formed of members of other families broken by divorce, death, or abandonment. There are families created out of economic necessity, families of unrelated adults and children, multigenerational families—I could go on and on. In Japan there has also been dramatic change in family structure. Fifty-five percent of all married women in Japan now work outside the home at least part-time. Changes in family structure, labor force participation, and mobility are forcing people in both countries to find substitutes for blood kin. In both the United States and Japan, women bear an inordinate share of the burden of caregiving for children, the disabled, and the elderly. And because women outlive men by an average of seven years, their burden only increases as they enter their seventies and eighties. Elder care in the United States is daughter care; in Japan, daughters-in-law are the primary caregivers. Spousal care, usually wives caring for husbands, occurs in both societies. This unpaid domestic labor is not factored into the gross national product; when we speak of the productivity of our citizens, this labor remains invisible. Much of the challenge of old age is the challenge of confronting, in a humane and sensitive manner, the very profound impact of population aging on women.

We have seen the emergence of self-help groups, such as stroke clubs and Alzheimer's disease associations, in both countries. There have also been efforts by religious, educational, philanthropic, and political institutions to deal with aging and the burden of care. But all these efforts are still imperfect, still incomplete.

Our job has also been to consider the role of the economic enterprise. By this we mean not only wealth and capital formation, but also labor and management together in all three sectors: Agriculture, manufacturing, and the growing service sector. Here we see some interesting comparisons between the United States and Japan. In Japan, the lifetime employment concept is rapidly giving way, while in the United States there is movement away from increased wages toward increased job security. It's almost as if the two countries were converging in their conceptions of employment. There has been a lot of discussion recently about "fringe benefits," such as pension funds, life insurance, and health insurance. Business is up to its ears in the business of aging, and the health care liabilities are enormous. In the United States, former Health and Human Services Secretary Joseph Califano has estimated that there is $2 trillion in underfunded and unfunded health care liability in the Fortune 500 companies alone.

Sadly, we do not have national health insurance in the United States. Part of the great debate over free trade taking place between the United States and Canada turns on the issue of national health insurance. Canada has such a plan in place, and some in the United States feel that this gives Canada an unfair trade advantage. Of course, we could balance things by deciding to develop a national health care program of our own, but, alas, that does not seem imminent.

In the global economy, the industries that are most at risk are the so-called mature industries. In the United States, there are the "smokestack," or heavy manufacturing, industries, which have high retiree/employee ratios. We should also note, to provide some balance, that the pension funds of these at-risk industries constitute the single largest source of capital formation in the United States. Pension funds own one quarter of the shares in the United States' stock markets.

Clearly, the business of business, and of their unions, is to work together to create a better environment for workers, especially in terms of safety and health care. It's also the business of management and labor to create opportunities for older workers so that they may continue to contribute to their communities and to society at large. In the United States, we have legislated the end of age discrimination in employment and seen a virtual end to mandatory retirement. Japan has also moved its retirement age up from 55 to 60. We are the only two nations in the industrialized world moving in that direction. In the United States in the 1990s we are experiencing a worker shortage, so the possibility of bringing older workers back into the fold increases.

But while there may be a shortage of workers, there is certainly no shortage of work to be done. There *is* a shortage of vision, a shortage of wisdom and the ability to effectively coordinate needs and skills. Recently, American businesses have discovered the "aging market": it has begun to dawn on them (though very slowly) that 70% of all discretionary money is in the hands of people 50 years of age and older. We all know that capitalism and free enterprise require a mesh of producers and consumers. It's not enough to produce all kinds of goods and services. You have to have consumers—individuals who have the financial wherewithal to purchase those goods and services. This balance of producers and consumers is vital to continued economic growth. Unless the economic enterprise acknowledges and nurtures the great buying power of older Americans, it may have trouble sustaining desirable levels of growth.

Science is also vital to maintaining that growth. Here we see a very sharp contrast. Japan is beginning to spend much more of its gross national product on science and technology and on research and development. So is Germany. So, even, is the former Soviet Union, despite its economic problems. But the United States is beginning to decline in its investment in research and development even though the American Nobelist

in Economic Science, Robert Solow, won his prize for demon-
strating the critical role that science plays in economic
growth. If we are to sustain the remarkable longevity that
we've achieved in this century, we must continue to grow economically. We don't have to engage in vicious economic competition in order to grow. One of the benefits of the universal-
ity and internationalization of science is the possibility for
real cooperation. Imagine Japan and the United States working together on the human genome project, engaged in decod-
ing the sequencing of human genetic material. Together, we
might be able to eradicate from the earth the over 3,000 genetic diseases that assault human capacity and dignity.

How can we build effective working relationships and partnerships between Japan and the United States and, within our
respective societies, among individuals, families, businesses,
and government? That is the essential question we are attempting to address in this book. We cannot rely exclusively
on any one of these institutions, nor should we. We can't always rely on a particular individual, or even ourselves. At any
moment any one of us might be struck down by a debilitating
disease beyond our individual control. We can't rely exclusively on governments, which change constantly in terms of
their commitment to a particular segment of the population
or to a particular age or interest group. Yet, to a certain extent, we must be able to count on government. We need it because there is so much external reality that we cannot control. We need a safety net, an umbrella, a threshold, that will
help protect us from those problems that extend far beyond
our individual control of responsibility. This is part of the
great social contract which exists between governments and
citizens.

In our attempt to confront the question, "Who is responsible for my old age?," we should not look at old age in isolation. We must view it as part of the whole life cycle. Today's
elders were yesterday's children; today's children are tomorrow's elders. We must not forget the unity and continuity of
all life on earth. We must be particularly sensitive to the
needs of the baby boomers in both societies, who constitute

such great proportions of their populations. They will reach their "golden years" soon enough, starting in the year 2011. We can't wait until then to start creating effective alternatives to nursing home care, or begin then to integrate our knowledge about the aging process into mainstream medical education. We must create a research agenda that will forever end the scourge of senility, and we must create it now, *today*.

The parent of the longevity revolution was the industrial revolution. This same source that brought us added years of life has also contributed to the destruction of our environment. As early as 1898, the Swedish chemist Svante Arrhenius recognized the threat of global warming, a product of the 19th century's industrialization. To these warnings about global warming we must add the depletion of the ozone layer and the environmental causes of various kinds of cancer. Breast cancer in women, for instance, may be linked to increased lifetime exposure to estrogen, due to earlier onset of menses and later menopause brought about by improved nutrition. We have also, in our technology-mad society, discouraged breast-feeding, which may help to lessen a woman's chances of developing breast cancer. Heart disease, as we've learned from the great Framingham Study, is partly a function of sedentary life-styles and other aspects of our lives that contribute to the so-called diseases of civilization. Science, which has contributed to the new longevity, has also brought about some very unfortunate changes in life-style and in environmental risk. For example, the rapid transportation that has spurred global economic growth has helped to spread diseases like influenza and AIDS (acquired immune deficiency syndrome) around the planet more rapidly and efficiently. Finally, this extraordinary industrial–scientific revolution has brought with it the threat of instantaneous thermonuclear extinction. It is ironic that this century of extended life may also be the century in which we annihilate all life, human, plant, and animal, from the globe.

So here we are in the final decade of the 20th century, faced with moral, political, and economic choices, trying to deal with the important task of the husbandry of life itself. We must constantly evaluate and reevaluate, often far in advance, the kinds of things we do and propose to do and the types of technologies we introduce. We must go far beyond the usual "environmental impact" statements and do extensive moral, ethical, and economic studies. Think of what we could accomplish through the creation of international agreements on wages, health, and safety, We could help make a level playing field for all the world's workers, not only in terms of international competition but also in terms of protecting the hardwon safety net of the industrialized nations in this global economy.

When I was young, I was much taken with a book by Wendell Willkie, titled *One World*. I've since been struck by the contribution of Jean Monnet in France and with the creation of the 12-member European Economic Community, which may help us all lessen our emphasis on national sovereignty and move toward global political expression. We have a great opportunity ahead of us. We are not going to provide a clear answer to the question "Who is responsible for my old age?" any more than we can provide solutions to all the problems of our global village. What will come out of this is a beginning, a set of provocative questions and proposals that will set us thinking.

We will hear from all generations and face the challenges of today and tomorrow. We are indebted to Dr. Jack Rowe, a self-described "card-carrying geriatrician," for his support in bringing this conference to fruition, and to the late Dr. Harold Proshansky, president of the Graduate School and University Center of the City University of New York, where the conference was held. I'm especially grateful to Mr. Ryoichi Sasakawa, the Japan Shipbuilding Industry Foundation, and the Sasakawa Memorial Health Foundation for their sponsorship and support. Speakers at the conference, whose papers are presented in this book, included Dr. Yoshio Gyoten, Toshiyuki Kato, and Ms. Mariko Sugahara Bando, who addressed the issue of individual, corporate, and government responsibility. Professor Takako Sodei addressed responsibility for old age as a woman's issue. Ms. Betty Friedan looked at the changing family and the "mystique of old age," while Dr. James Birren provided us with a model for responsible aging. Mr. Alan Pifer presented a historical overview of attitudes toward aging, and Mr. John Steffens of Merrill Lynch gave us the view from the business world. Dr. Lauren Goldberg, then a medical student at Mount Sinai Medical Center, and Mr. Eugene Lang of the "I Have a Dream" Foundation addressed the issues of intergenerational responsibility, and Ms. Keiko Higuchi and the late Representative Claude Pepper delivered challenges to all the generations. I'd like to add to their challenges my own: May we meet *their* challenges soon and well.

Individual Responsibility: My Good Old Age

I

Introduction to Part I

As Ryoichi Sasakawa did in the foreword to this book, Rosalynn Carter, former First Lady of the United States, and James Birren, an internationally recognized researcher in gerontology, offer the reader their recipes for successful aging. Both Mrs. Carter and Dr. Birren focus on the issue of retirement in the age of the new longevity. Given the fact that every American and every Japanese can now expect to live approximately 25 years—a full generation—longer than their grandparents did, what can be done to ensure that those "new years of life" will be productive and satisfying?

A few key facts are in order here. In 1986, in the United States, over 12% of the population had reached or exceeded the standard retirement age of 65. Nearly a third of all men 55 and older no longer participate in the work force. Many are entirely dependent on Social Security and pensions for their income (Social Security accounts for 38% of the aggregate income of older people in this country. Only 17% of the income of older people comes from their continued employment [Butler, Lewis, & Sunderland, 1992]. The 1986 amendment to the Age Discrimination in Employment Act legislated the end of mandatory retirement, but many other factors act to keep older men and women out of the work force. Early retirement incentives, Social Security restrictions on earned in-

3

come, de facto age discrimination, and our society's emphasis on youth, competition, and individual achievement are just some of the obstacles that prevent people from working as long as they might like or need to (Butler et al., 1991). It is imperative that we create opportunities, not just for continued employment for elders but for a satisfying retirement for those who, by choice or necessity, end their first careers.

Mrs. Carter and Dr. Birren write not only from their professional experience (Mrs. Carter has long been active in mental health issues and engages in extensive research on social issues at the Carter Center at Emory University in Atlanta, Georgia), they also each write from lived experience, from the unique perspective of social researchers who have also attained the status of research subject. Even the most dedicated and rigorous scholars in gerontology are likely to have an incomplete understanding of the issues, problems, and joys of old age because, as Mildred Seltzer (1989) has said, they are not usually "personally involved in growing older" (P. 1). "Growing older" is an action statement, as much as "doing field research" or "operating a computer" (or running a corporation, managing a household, writing a poem), and taking action implies taking control. Responsible action also implies a close examination of all sides of an action and all its possible consequences in one's own life and in the lives of others. It is this kind of responsible action-taking that provides the central ingredient linking the two very different recipes for successful retirement that follow.

The aging process is one of being and becoming, and it is marked by transition, negotiation, and transformation. We receive clues from the outside world that it is time to take a particular and appropriate course of action (Seltzer, 1989). For a man or woman over the age of 60, that course of action might involve taking on the role of mentor or sponsor to a younger person. Or it might be suggested that it is time to step aside, to make room for a new generation of workers. One's children and one's children's children might expect one to take on the character of grandparent. These external clues, and one's internal response to these clues, force one to reevaluate and redefine one's "self-concept" (Seltzer, 1989). If the change required is radical, it can be both disheartening and disorienting. Rosalynn Carter's own experience provides a good illustration of the kind of abrupt transition that leads some elderly people to adopt what some sociologists have called the "roleless role of the aged," where it becomes difficult to tell what one is or should be and what one can or should be doing (Gubrium & Lynott, 1987). Forced to leave public life after losing a presidential election, the Carters found themselves alone in their old house with no real work for them to do. They experienced real "mandatory retirement" and, with that, the realization that they had indeed joined the ranks of the elderly and "useless," despite their relative chronological youth. "You might recognize my name," Mrs. Carter writes in her introduction. It is a bit of good-natured humor directed at her status as *former* First Lady. But behind the gentle joke lurks the very real fear of marginality and invisibility, the feeling that one has, in the obsolete sense of "retired," actually disappeared from view.

For the Carters, the "cure" for retirement and the answer to the question Mrs. Carter poses, "What do we do with these new years of life?," is action. Volunteer, she recommends, find part-time work, care for your grandchildren, write a book (as the Carters did, chronicling their postelection experience in *Everything to Gain: Making the Most of the Rest of Your Life*). The Carters took their own advice and triumphed over their forced retirement. Both President and Mrs. Carter teach at colleges in Georgia; they established the prestigious Carter Center at Emory University and are involved in Habitat for Humanity, a nonprofit organization that builds and refurbishes housing for the needy. They have continued their work in mental health and human rights issues. By every measure, the Carters have made an enviably successful transition into old age.

James Birren's essay embodies another definition of retirement, that of "drawing back," as a painter (or a person looking at a painting) might, to get a better and more comprehensive view of things. According to Dr. Birren, the responsibility of the individual in old age is to all the generations to come. This entails nurturing the growth of all children, working to preserve the earth so that future generations can enjoy its fruits, and writing one's autobiography. Autobiography, to many readers, may seem like a supreme act of self-absorption. After all, who cares to read the life of every single individual who happened to reach retirement age? But Birren stresses that autobiography is not simply a recounting of the events of one's own life; rather, it offers the individual the chance to look back at his or her own life and put it in historical context. After living many years, people tend to take a more holistic view of life. Butler, Lewis, and Sunderland (1991) note that

> [o]ld age does involve unique developmental work. Childhood might be defined as a period of gathering and enlarging strength and experience, whereas a major developmental task in old age is to clarify, deepen, and find use for what one has already attained in a lifetime of learning and adapting. (p. 66)

Dr. Birren illustrates this developmental view of aging with a story about an elderly doctor, an obstetrician, in Chicago, whose nephew thinks that it is time for him to give up delivering babies. Dr. Birren suggests that the young man encourage his uncle to take time off from his practice to write a history of obstetrics in Chicago, based on his experience and research. Such an enterprise would be satisfying for the old doctor and would make room for a younger doctor to practice, but it would also leave an important legacy to the generations in the form of a distillation of the man's knowledge and experience—a textbook, perhaps, to train future generations of obstetricians.

Both Dr. Birren and Mrs. Carter demonstrate for us that old age can be a time of beginnings as well as a time of endings. There are advantages to be gained from the "rolelessness" of old age. For Mrs. Carter, the dropping away of one's old roles gives one the freedom to explore new roles, to find a second career, or simply to explore all the options and adventures that one never had time or mental energy for while engaged in one's so-called life's work. For Dr. Birren, rolelessness may be appropriate to old age, freeing one from the need to perform and allowing one to look over one's own life and one's times in order to discover the larger meaning behind our existence. If old people have a role, he tells us, it is to perform the work of making sense of things, of sifting out the unimportant chaff from the all-important grain. This is their legacy to the young, who are too "green" and too busy to do it for themselves. And there is no reason to think of this work as mere idle thumb-twiddling. Old age, as we have said, can be a time of beginning. One might find that this new role—of mentor, author, sponsor, nurturer—is more satisfying than one's former "career." There are appropriate beginnings and appropriate endings; in Japan, it is the habit of old men to write poetry, often for the first time in their lives. This is how they give voice to their discovery of the larger meanings in life (Butler et al., 1992).

While Japan is not represented in this chapter by an essay, both Mrs. Carter and Dr. Birren stress the importance of crosscultural exchange of ideas on the issues of old age and retirement. Mrs. Carter's research for the Carter Center brings her into contact with scholars from all over the world, and she has had the opportunity to work with Ryoichi Sasakawa in the past. Dr. Birren presents the reader with a delightful synthesis of Western and Eastern philosophies of life and old age. While recognizing the Western need for new experiences and continued "usefulness," he tempers this propensity with an Eastern appreciation of stillness, of beauty in adaptation, and an acceptance of old age and death as natural parts of the life cycle. His essay is an object lesson in cultural crossfertilization.

In his search for historical representations of responsible aging, Dr. Birren decided upon the Ten Commandments of the Judeo-Christian Bible as the appropriate template for his own "Fifteen Commandments for Responsible Old Age," several of which are discussed in his essay. Dr. Birren has also generously furnished us with all fifteen commandments in their original form, though not on two tablets. They provide a fitting opening for this chapter. Dr. Birren begins with a new version of the biblical injunction to "honor thy father and thy mother" and from there provides his model for responsibility toward oneself, the earth, and all the generations, living and to come.

Mrs. Carter and Dr. Birren both stress a kind of reciprocal responsibility among the generations that extends far beyond the so-called intergenerational contract that has been a code word lately for Social Security. Too often, when people speak of intergenerational responsibility, they mean the responsibility of one particular generation to another. "It is the responsibility of our elders to see to it that they are financially independent of their children and grandchildren, and that they don't rob future generations," some, usually younger, people say; while others, very often their parents, cite the debt incurred by the younger generation to the generation that raised them and educated them to the standard of living they now enjoy. This narrow view of intergenerational responsibility is rejected by all the contributors to this chapter.

In our final essay, Mr. Eugene Lang, the entrepreneur who established the "I Have a Dream" Foundation after making a commencement speech to sixth-graders at his old grammar school, puts Dr. Birren's prescription for true intergenerational responsibility into tangible action. Mr. Lang offered to send that entire class of sixth-graders to college at his expense, provided they kept up their grades. "And I kept my promise," he says frequently and with understandable pride. His promise to those kids at Harlem's P.S. 121 offered them a real shot at a better—and more productive—future. It was a promise that offers hope for future generations as well.

REFERENCES

Butler, Robert N., Lewis, M. I. & Sunderland, T. (1991). *Aging and mental health: Positive psychosocial and biomedical approaches* (4th ed.). New York: Macmillan.
Gubrium, Jaber F. & Lynott, R. J., (1987). Rethinking life satisfac-

tion." in B. B. Hess & E. W. Markson (Editors.), *Growing old in America: New perspectives on old age* (3rd ed., p. 228) Transition Books.

Seltzer, Mildred N. (1989). Random and not so random thoughts on becoming and being a statistic: Professional and personal musings *International Journal of Aging and Human Development*, *28*(1), p. 1.

Fifteen Commandments for Responsible Old Age 1

James E. Birren

Recognizing the need for guidance for deciding what my responsibilities are and will be as I grow old, I have devised 15 commandments for a responsible old age.

1. I should honor my children and all children and foster their growth. May I remain close to my children without hovering over them or stunting their maturity.
2. I should leave the land and its people better than I found them.
3. I should avoid becoming bitter if overlooked by the passing young and the events of time. May my spirit not be eroded by the acids of life.
4. I should seek information and learning and avoid dogmatic positions and postures. May I be a source of information for solving or moderating the problems of life.
5. I should not avoid risking "face" in attempting new learning. May I cooperate with scientists and scholars and volunteer to be a subject for their research.
6. I should foster my physical and mental health and avoid excesses that deplete my body and mind and make me prey to illnesses requiring treatment and care, which drain the resources of others.
7. Should I have poor health, I should cushion its impact so that it does not weigh unduly upon others. May I refrain

from seeking an unreasonable share of resources and care that would deprive others and place a disproportionate load upon them.

8. I should manage prudently and with affection my relationships with others. May I manage the passage of possessions with fairness and avoid manipulating them to gain attention or to cause others to vie for material gain.
9. I should initiate the expression of caring and love for others and not blame or rage against others for their inability to control the impossible.
10. I should use the experience of my years for attaining fairness and justice for others.
11. I should promote the beauty and appreciation of nature and of human arts.
12. I should continue to tend the garden of my life, remove yesterday's faded flowers and dead branches, and foster new growth.
13. I should anticipate my death with provisions for the use by others of my body parts.
14. I should prepare myself and others for my death. May I greet my passing with poise, dignity, and peace.
15. May I have planted seeds that will bloom for others in springs that I will never see.

Life after the White House: Making the Most of Your Second Career

2

Rosalynn Carter

You might recognize my name. For four years, I was the First Lady of the United States, "serving" in that office under the administration of President Jimmy Carter. A lot has happened since 1980, when Jimmy left office, so I'd like to bring you up to date on what Jimmy, I, and the rest of our family have been up to.

Jimmy is now a Distinguished Professor teaching political science at Emory University in Atlanta, Georgia. He'd been saying for most of his life that he thought he'd enjoy teaching college students, and thanks to Ronald Reagan, he was able to realize that dream a lot earlier than he expected.

I myself am a distinguished lecturer at Agnes Scott College in Atlanta. I can honestly say that never in *my* wildest dreams did I expect to become a college professor!

Together we've established the Carter Presidential Center in Atlanta, which includes a presidential library, the Carter Center at Emory University, and an Action Center, where we study how to put into practice the results of our scholarly research at the Carter Center. We don't want to simply study an issue like homelessness or hunger, publish papers, and then have the results sit forgotten on a shelf in some library. We try to follow up all our scholarly work with action that yields tangible results. Habitat for Humanity is one of our projects that tries to help solve the problem of homelessness and inadequate housing by actually building and restoring homes for people in economically distressed areas. The Carter Center has fellowships in Mideast peace studies, U.S.–Soviet relations, arms control, democracy in Latin America, human rights, conflict resolution, African Studies, and health issues. We have two or three major conferences a year for discussion of these issues.

Our third grandson, Joshua, was born on May 8, 1984. On the day that he was born, he had a life expectancy of 71 years. When his great-grandfather Earl Carter was born, his life expectancy was only 45 years. The average life span of Americans has been increasing in this century by seven hours each day, or two days every week.

We have seen our workday and work week shrink greatly in this century. Retirement comes a lot earlier for most people. While Jimmy and I were conducting a study called "Closing the Gap" at the Carter Center, we came across a few figures that were thought-provoking, to say the least. According to one report, a third of all American men over the age of 55 no longer work. Only about a generation ago, people labored through a lifetime to an exhausted old age, while we are blessed with the possibility of a full and robust second life in our later years. It is even possible today for a "retiree" to enter into an entirely different second career after the first one has ended.

We also learned that by following a few fairly simple rules—don't smoke, don't drink to excess, fasten your seatbelt, maintain a desirable and healthy body weight, exercise, and eat properly—you can add up to eleven years to your life expectancy.

Now, what do you *do* with all those years?

Recently, Jimmy and I wrote a book entitled *Everything to Gain: Making the Most of the Rest of Your Life*. While writing it, we took a long, hard look at how we can make the most of the rest of our lives. There were the obvious recommendations, of course: stay busy, volunteer, learn something new, travel, write your memoirs. But first we decided to look at the problems faced by those who experience a crisis in their lives, such as the loss of a loved one, a serious illness or physical disability, or unwanted retirement.

We were writing from our own experience of involuntary retirement and the end of a career. We had to leave the White House after a discouraging defeat at the polls and return to our home in Plains. But even home was not the same anymore. The children had grown up and gone, and suddenly Jimmy and I found ourselves alone together in the same house, all day, every day. All our energies had gone into the presidential campaign. It had never occurred to us to prepare for this new kind of life. It was necessary for us to make the difficult transition to a private and, perhaps, even a lonely existence.

Most people have to deal with the very same kinds of changes in their lives as they grow older. I remember how devastated my own mother was when she was forced to retire from the post office where she had worked since my father died, when I was in high school. I had been off campaigning for Jimmy's reelection. When I came home for a weekend visit, my brother said to me, "Mother's been crying all week." I went to her and told her that I thought she would be absolutely tickled at not having to get up early every day to be at the post office for work by seven o'clock.

"It's not that," she said. "It's just that nobody thinks I can do good work anymore."

Well, Mother Allie's story has a happy ending. At age 85, she is still active. She baby-sits for her great-grandchildren. She works a few hours a week at a local florist shop, delivering flowers to the sick and shut-ins in our community. She travels. She's a terrific mother, grandmother, and great-grandmother. She does volunteer work in the Plains Welcome Center, meeting new people who involve her in new experiences. She's really enjoying this second part of her life.

My mother, Jimmy, and I are among the lucky ones. But there are so many others for whom these "golden years" are not so very golden. Despite the fact that recent advances in medicine and public health have made it possible for millions of people to reach a healthy old age, these golden years of life are very often a time of despair and depression, poverty, loneliness, and isolation. And that just should not be in a country as rich and technologically progressive as ours.

After a life of hard work and painful sacrifice, every single person in America should have the chance to live their old age with dignity. No one should go without adequate health care, food, housing, a few comforts, and the simple assurance that America appreciates a lifetime of work and cares about the well-being of her older citizens. We must never waver in our commitment to insure the basic support that Social Security provides in the face of some of the disasters that can befall one in life. However, in these uncertain times, with government facing ever-mounting expenditures for programs and services, it is the responsibility of the individual to make plans to support his or her old age with nongovernment sources of retirement funds.

Recently, I came across an article in our Atlanta newspaper entitled "Enterprising Employers Face Reality." The reality they are facing (finally!) is that we are running out of young people to supply the demands of labor. That's partly due to our declining national birth rate. But it is also unfortunately true that many of our young people today lack very basic social and work skills. One-fourth of the students who enter high school these days drop out before they graduate.

So, the article says, employers "looked around for new blood and found it in older veins." America's employers rediscovered older workers. They learned that these older workers, many of whom had already retired from one career, are good dollar investments. Older men and women tend to value work as a privilege rather than as a right. They see being productive in a job as a social obligation, a personal fulfillment, a service, and an opportunity to become useful. It restores social roles to them, giving them a chance to interact with and relate to new people. Most of these older workers believe in giving a good day's work for a day's dollar. Discovering and hiring older workers makes excellent bottom-line business.

Well, it's about time, wouldn't you agree?

How can we assure that America taps the tremendous store of talent, creativity, and experience of her older citizens? We must first create opportunities for salaried employment, selfemployment, and volunteer work for older people. But how can we do this? Just whose responsibility is it to create these opportunities?

As a nation, we need to dispel the myths and misconceptions surrounding old age, and learn the lesson that the enterprising employers of Georgia learned when they "rediscovered" older workers. We must explore these myths and misconceptions, be aware of them, and question them at every turn.

While waiting for employers to rediscover our talents, individuals can look into opportunities to volunteer their time and talent. When we were writing our book, Jimmy and I found an almost unlimited number of ways that people can expand their lives through volunteerism. Go to your local library, or mental health center, or college, or hospital. They all need volunteers. The great thing about volunteer work is that it is an option available to just about everyone.

You can go outside your community to find people who need your time and effort. Jimmy's mother, "Miss Lillian" Carter, joined the Peace Corps when she was 68 years old and spent two years working in India.

Jimmy and I have learned that volunteering is the best way to invigorate a life and make it rich and fulfilling. Each one of us approaches our late years from a different starting point and with different needs and aspirations. I would like to see every American, every Japanese, every human being in this world have the chance to age with dignity and to continue to grow in mind and spirit. I would like to see America recognize the invaluable fund of wisdom and experience that older people are and provide them with every opportunity to remain an integral part of our nation's life.

As for our own individual responsibility for our old age, Jimmy and I have learned from our experience as retired people—an experience that has so many parallels in the lives of so many others—that we have a lot more leeway to choose our own path and establish our own priorities than we ever had before. We have a lifetime of knowledge and experience on which to base our decisions. And we are most fortunate in that our financial resources are adequate to our needs. Fortunate *and* grateful.

We have had to weather a difficult passage. We had to overcome the crisis of involuntary retirement together with all the strains it placed on us. It took a long time. We had to find our way through all the various stages of self-pity, anger, discouragement, and anxiety. But after this often painful period of readjustment, we finally have come to accept and even love our circumstances.

We have made the very exciting discovery that our lives do not have to be limited to our past, to our first career. The future can be just as challenging and fulfilling—perhaps even more so.

Allan Fromme said in his book *Life After Work,* "It's not what you did. It's what you're doing." That's what really counts.

I can tell you from my own experience and from my heart:

There is life after work.
There is life after old age.
There is even life after the White House.

Understanding Life Backwards: Reminiscing for a Better Old Age

3

James E. Birren

The question "Who is responsible for my old age?" sounds as though it were a catch question. And in fact, it *is* a catch question—one that is timely and designed to get us to think about responsibilities for and of older people and for and to ourselves.

In the process of thinking about my answers to this question, I found myself casting about for a mooring on which to anchor my thoughts. I thought of the Bible and the Ten Commandments, one of which commands us to respect our parents. That commandment carries within it the promise of long life in exchange for obedience. "Honor thy father and thy mother," it reads, "so that you may live long in the land the Lord your God is giving you."

A question I have regarding this commandment is whether the old cannot overfill their spiritual cups with this honor exacted from the young. While we may honor the memories of our mothers and fathers, isn't something more required of us as we live long in the land? I am beginning here to probe for the something more that I must ask of myself as I grow older. Since I am not a Bible scholar, I tend to seek clues for my responsibilities in those times and places where people have lived long lives. I leave it to others to explore the Bible in search of references to the aging process.*

Had the people in those times reached great ages, had they truly lived long in the land the Lord gave them, perhaps another commandment might have been added to the 10 we have today. It would have been addressed to those who became old, who lived longer than their own parents did, and who may have lived to see four generations following them.

But the Ten Commandments were recorded in times when people were not long-lived because of the harshness of daily existence and the many threats to human health. One might observe that even in the New Testament, Jesus and his apostles were young men burning with the fire to reform society and purify the morals of their day. We can find a great deal about how to live morally in the New Testament, but we can discern very little guidance specific to one's responsibilities in one's later years.

We can look, instead, to the cycle of nature. Each of the four seasons of the year brings with it unique responsibilities for us as we move from the promise of spring, through the high growth of summer, to the harvesttime of autumn and the inward gathering of late winter. We speak metaphorically, not only of the seasons of life but of the diurnal cycle: the morning, afternoon, and evening times of our lives. These, like the seasons, come with their own preoccupations and inner weather. If we are not as active as we were in the earlier part of our life's day, afternoon and evening can still be productive periods. These late hours offer us the opportunity to sort out the grain and chaff of the day, allowing us to discard the hulls of our experience to get at the kernel of deeper meaning. The evening of life calls out, I think, for an eleventh commandment, a charge to use these hours in a way different from the busy rush of the morning hours. Our afternoons and evenings should be spent in calm reflection, in the search for meaning.

Before I describe what I believe to be my obligations in old age, I want to take a brief look at autobiography as one tool in

*See especially J. G. Harris, *Biblical Perspectives on Aging* (Philadelphia: Fortress Press, 1987).

the search for the meaning in our lives. Robert Butler has aroused great interest with his discussion of the phenomenon of emergent reminiscence in the later years. He characterized reminiscence as a normal process experienced by a great many people as they aged. After living a long productive life, one often has the leisure time in old age to sort out its contents, to great benefit. In the past 12 years, I have worked with people from many walks of life, encouraging them to write their autobiographies. The purpose of this activity is to help integrate their past and present life experiences and to assist in the search for meaning in one's life.

Increasingly, our lives are lived in the so-called fast lane. Electronic devices constantly remind us of our obligations and monitor our performance. Car telephones, answering machines, fax machines, computerized agendas, beepers—I expect that soon we'll have beepers to warn us that we're taking too much time for lunch, and watches that will remind us to go to bed 15 minutes later to make up for the time lost in that afternoon's traffic jam. The need to do, to produce, to act *now* focuses all our attention on the present moment. When do we ever have the chance to sit back for a moment or an hour, to think back on where we've been and where we're going? When do we ever have that opportunity, if not in the afternoon and evening of our lives?

The Danish philosopher Soren Kierkegaard said, you live your life forward but understand it backwards. If we are running from moment to moment and from place to place, we do not have the opportunity of understanding why our lives flow the way they do, where they are going, and how we can make meaning of them. We can only understand today through tomorrow's look backwards, but we have to take the time to do the looking.

Life review is not merely a perfunctory reliving of the past. It has to have a purpose, and that purpose must be the discovery of meaning and the achievement of integrity. We might also call it "cohesiveness," or "getting it all together." We have a responsibility to get it all together before we exit this life. Otherwise, it's like getting up from the dinner table after a wonderful meal and leaving all the scraps of uneaten food and all the dirty dishes lying about.

One of the most distinguished American psychologists and educators of the first part of this century was the president of Clark University, Granville Stanley Hall. After a career writing about child development, he chose to write a book about old age, entitled *Senescence*. In the book, he noted that in his later years he experienced a great sense of relief, even of catharsis, while sorting through his papers. He had quite a collection of books, some given to him by friends, others accumulated along the way. He realized that, at his age, he was never going to get to read all of these books, so he set aside a small stack of books that he really planned to read sometime soon and gave the rest to the university library or to friends. He also went through his manuscripts, keeping some, setting some aside to give to the library. Many he simply tossed into the fireplace. He was shuffling off the obligation to read these books and manuscripts.

I can think of no more warm and friendly scene than of sitting in front of a fireplace on a winter evening in a long life, burning the chaff and culling the grain. Haunted as we are by the ringing of the telephone, the appointment book, the blaring horn of the automobile behind us, not only do we not smell the flowers along the way, but we can't even perceive any meaning to our lives as we are living them.

Therefore, one of my responsibilities in my old age is to write my autobiography. An autobiography can offer those who come after me some insight into the way I perceived my life and times. Knowing this may give me some hints as to what I should weed out and what I should leave in. An autobiography can also offer *me* a clearer picture of how my life flowed, why it flowed in one direction rather than in another, and what the great and small events were that shaped my life.

I was once asked by a distant relative for some advice regarding his uncle, a doctor in Chicago who, at over 80 years of age, was still delivering babies. His nephew thought that the uncle was stubbornly hanging onto his career while new techniques and information were passing him by. I suggested to him that he ought to try to get his uncle to write a history of obstetrics in Chicago. This would give the aging man the freedom to contribute something to our knowledge, instead of merely continuing his pursuit of the ego gratifications of a demanding career. This is not to say that old people ought to give up their work to write history but only to suggest that there comes a time in life when it may be appropriate to release oneself from past obligations and reinvest one's energies.

David Guttmann is a psychologist who has studied aging in a variety of cultures, including the United States. He makes some very provocative points. "We do not have elders because we have a human gift and a modern capacity for keeping the weak alive," he writes, "Rather, we are human because we have elders." Dr. Guttmann believes, as I do, that elders have roles in society that emerge from what he calls the "parental imperative," which he defines as a transcendent concern people have with seeing others prosper and with seeing their own children, *all* children, grow. Obviously, we can display parenting behavior whether or not we have children. We sense, as we get older, that we should take care of other people, the land, and, perhaps most important, the life we were given.

The parental imperative means that, no matter what my age, I must and shall attend to the growth of those generations that follow me. No matter what my condition, no matter how enfeebled I might become, I should preserve and encourage the growth of others, look out for their well-being, and nourish their futures. For me that means staying out of the way as well as being there for the younger generation. I should not like to die thinking that I was *extorting* my share of honor from my children.

All my effort should be devoted to managing my life and my death in such a way that they leave those who follow me stronger, with enlarged capacities for fulfillment. If the young light their candles at my bedside, I in turn should light candles and put them in their hands. When the petals of the wilting poppy have dried, let them drop gently in the natural progression of life's seasons.

One thing that I must understand as I grow older is that there will always be things—events, circumstances—that are bigger than I am. The challenges of old age can often lead one to reexamine one's fundamental assumptions. We are invited, as E. C. Bianchi wrote in *Aging as a Spiritual Journey*, to take "a spiritual journey among the major facets of our lives."

That spiritual journey can take the form of the cultivation of one's inner garden, the sorting out of memories and moods. We expect young people to write vibrant, dramatic poetry about life, and indeed, the poetry we find written in the morning and midday of life is often appropriately vigorous. But what of the poetry of life's evening? And what if I am not poetically gifted? How then might I express my deepest feelings about my relationships with others? I want to be close to all my children, natural and spiritual, but never so close that I suffocate them and become a living burden that may stunt their growth rather than nurture it. Writing poetry in the evening of my life may be an agreeable outlet for thoughts that would otherwise be difficult to express.

If I had more time and talent, I would write a poem about old age, perhaps one about an ancient dog coming out on a sunny day to watch the puppies playing and allowing them to romp and tumble around and over him. The dog's bones may be arthritic, his gait halting, and he might not be able to run anymore. But if a predator threatens the young, he lifts up his head and barks a warning to them to run, though he himself is not able to escape from danger.

Since I am not particularly gifted lyrically, let's hear from some of those who *were*; first, Dylan Thomas:

> Do not go gentle into that good night,
> Old age should burn and rave at close of day;
> Rage, rage against the dying of the light.
>
> Though wise men at their end know dark is right,
> Because their words had forked no lightning they
> Do not go gentle into that good night.

That's one view of old age. I do not really identify with the old man raging, because I feel that my rage would cause pain to others. It seems to me that Dylan Thomas wrote these words for the young, who are likely to believe that old age will steal "future" from them and that they are bound to rage against that loss.

Let's turn now to William Cullen Bryant's *Thanatopsis*:

> So live, that when thy summons comes to join
> The innumerable caravan, which moves
> To that mysterious realm, where each shall take
> His chamber in the silent halls of death
> Thou go not, like the quarry-slave at night,
> Scourged to his dungeon, but, sustained and soothed
> By an unfaltering trust, approach thy grave,
> Like one that wraps the drapery of his couch
> About him, and lies down to pleasant dreams.

That's a very different strategy for dealing with old age. But I have here in my notes yet another poem, a more recent work by Ray Bradbury, better known perhaps for his visions of the distant future in his science fiction novels and stories. He writes

> What would I say of me if I were epitaph?
> That there were silly bones in him?
> The gnome that made him laugh
> The jolly made him serious
> The glum made him delirious
> The lawyers talked him sleepy and made snooze at noon . . .

The poem continues in that vein, and then ends with

> The empty stars and I speak upon creation
> And with God occupy the time that's left
> For burning a billion years to sup
> Then open wide God's laughter and let him eat me up.

Each of these poems is representative of a major ideological shift tied to a particular time in Western society. William Cullen Bryant wrote in the 19th century, Dylan Thomas wrote just before World War II, and Ray Bradbury wrote much of his work in the 1950s and 1960s. So our attitudes toward old age shift with the times.

Much has been said, and indeed needs to be said, about taking care of the increasing numbers of dependent aged. From an extreme version of this viewpoint, older persons are regarded as absorbers of resources, bottomless sinks into which society pours money, information, energy, and affection. There is an alternative view of age, however, one that does not simply see older persons as limited by poor health and economic and other problems. Rather, we may regard our elderly men and women as sources from which may flow beneficial influences. What should be my responsibilities to manage myself as I grow older? Will I be a *sink* or *source* in the later years of life? The Western, Judeo-Christian tradition admonishes us with the biblical injunction to honor our fathers and mothers. Where is the admonishment to the older person to honor his or her children? Cannot our cups be too full with required honor from children? What, or whom, should seniors honor?

When I was young, I was cared for by my parents, older family members, teachers, and others. When I matured and my body grew stronger, my soul wiser, and my brain more resourceful, I became an active parent caring for my own children. Now it is time for me to be a caregiver to myself. I hope that I will not cling to the role I had as a parent but instead enter a state of detachment from roles. I have a responsibility to myself to achieve the freedom to rest on top of a hill and look out from that perspective upon a view that those who are still climbing cannot see.

As our attitudes toward old age develop, we find ourselves in the midst of an old age information explosion, from the proliferation of research and surveys involving the aged. One survey that impressed me most attempted to measure life satisfaction in over 13,000 people in 13 nations. In all of the 13 countries, older people expressed, on average, a greater acceptance of interpersonal relationships and of their material circumstances. The survey included data on economically underdeveloped countries, such as India and the Philippines, as well as the more highly developed technological economies of the West. The results of the survey revealed a clear trend among old people to accept life as it is lived and extract from it a sense of mastery and satisfaction. Older people, apparently, do acquire a greater sense of cohesiveness and meaning in life, despite the more negative projections of the young about old age.

Another survey reviewed the perceptions people have about old age. Generally, people—at least young people—tend to stereotype the old, placing them in categories of wise or senile, vigorous or incapacitated and idle. It is most interesting to note that the old people surveyed tended to view old age more subtly, with a greater understanding of its complexities and nuances, than did the young. Old people, you see, *know* more about old age. They're living it, seeing all sides through their own experience and the experience of their cohorts, and so they see the differences among old people. The older one is, too, the more one tends to take the details of one's life and distill from them a larger picture of life, a picture that is not always easy to convey to the young. I only hope that the distillation from my life's vineyard will not yield sour wine. This would indeed be a loss of face for me. If I find some aspect of my life particularly bitter, let me turn up my nose in distaste, but let me do so in private and not disillusion the young.

I hope that I may not be made bitter or angry when I see young people who can run faster, play a better game of basketball, or command a computer with more assurance than I can. Shouldn't I be able to glean plenty of wonder and satisfaction from a life that has seen the transition from gas lighting, coalfired steam engines, and radio to computer chips, space flight, and VCRs? And shouldn't I realize that there is something beyond even all these?

All this may sound as if I am preoccupied with taking leave of my life. We might debate the appropriate emphasis to be placed on one's leavetaking, but I think we will all agree that it is an important issue. We should leave the land better than we found it and leave the young stronger than they would have been without us. Now, I don't mean to suggest that I should take it into my own hands to hasten my departure. I *do* mean that I have an obligation to care for my body so that I don't become an unusual burden of responsibility upon others. If I smoke, overeat, and fail to exercise, I am much more likely to need a great deal of care in my later years. If, on top of these, I drink to excess or use illegal drugs without any thought to their effect on my health, I am very likely to require inordinate medical treatment, at great expense to others. I will have failed in my "parental imperative."

The psychologist Klaus Riegel once spoke of dialectical psychology as the final period in our cognitive development. In the process of reasoning about things, a mature person assigns probabilities and avoids extremes of behavior and opinion. Things rarely appear black or white to the mature thinker, who sees the subtle gradations in between the two. Hatred and prejudice are bred of extreme points of view. I hope that as I grow old I can avoid the kind of "categorical imperatives" that can warp my thoughts and impair my reasoning. Many years ago, the Berkeley studies on retirement indicated that different types of individuals tend to have different levels of life satisfaction in their later years. One group, labeled the "mature type," applied the principles of dialectical psychology, assigning probabilities of events and reasoning between polar opposites. These mature types showed a high level of life satisfaction in old age. Two types of people that did not do well in late life were the "self-blamers"—those who felt responsible for negative outcomes—and "passive-hostiles," who projected all blame onto others. It is to my own benefit to reason dialectically and to avoid destructive extremes of passion and prejudice. It violates our sense of proportion, not to mention our sense of aesthetics, to see an old person bitter and chronically angry. My responsibility to myself, here, is to change myself.

In living up to my responsibilities as I grow old, it seems to me that I should learn from those who live in cultures other than my own and look at their experience of later life. I like to consider the example of Japan, an island nation that for many hundreds of years carried on free of the disturbances or influ-ences of the world beyond its shores. During the years of American "manifest destiny," while Americans were conquer-ing nature and the land, the Japanese were living with and re-vering the land. The difference between the American and the Japanese concepts of living on and using the land corres-ponds pretty well with our different aesthetics. In America, the emphasis has been on speed and innovation: we like "the fast track," TV dinners, and brand-new goods fresh from the factory. An object is most beautiful to American eyes when it is brand new. Once the plastic wrap has been removed, once the book or chair or house has been read or sat upon or lived in, it loses its aesthetic appeal. We rarely take the antithetical view and look at the adaptations that people and things make as they age, or regard the marks left by time and experience as revealing subtle truths about our world. On the west coast of the United States, in California, stand great Monterrey pines, constantly buffeted by the high westerly winds. Over the years, the limbs of the trees acquire a characteristic sweeping shape as they are shaped by the wind's currents. An aesthetic that requires that "fresh from the factory" look would also require that these trees be pruned and propped upright, if not actually chopped down and replaced by nice straight artificial trees. The beauty and miracle of their adap-tation to their environment would be invisible to us.

Twenty-five years ago, I had a visit from a Japanese psy-chologist, Dr. Tachibana. He was, in addition to being a psy-chologist, a Buddhist priest. He told me about the Japanese philosophies of *Sabi* and *Wabi* that express the appreciation of long-standing patterns. For instance, if a man owns a wooden house that stands partly in bright sun and partly in shade, he should appreciate the beauty of the different shades of color in the wood, caused by the bleaching action of the sun, and not rush to paint it over. Even the rust spots on an old iron kettle have their own beauty against the black iron background. A Westerner might take one look at that kettle and sandblast it and coat it with rustproof paint so that it looks uniformly new. In *Sabi* and *Wabi*, the coarseness, unevenness, and roughness of the rust spots are appreciated as part of the natural process of change. It is the same with friends one has known for a long time. One accepts and appreciates the weathering of time and experience in one's friends. Dr. Tachibana also told me that, with a friend of long standing, one can allude to things in the heart without ever directly speaking of them. One can cultivate this sort of shorthand of companionship and emotion only with an old and good friend.

When I grow old, I hope that others will not want to prune away the meaningful adaptations I have made to the environment in which I grew up and grew old. Perhaps the shock of my roughened complexion and bent back will be softened by my lively eyes and subtlety of speech. If I cultivate these, they may be worthy of the term *Sabi*.

In my old age, I believe I must learn from others as well as from myself, from the differences as well as the similarities, from congruencies and incongruencies, as I climb my mountain. Armed with my knowledge, I will fit well in my niche on the mountain top, survey the land around me, and welcome those behind me who are still climbing my mountain.

BIBLIOGRAPHY

Bianchi, E. C. (1984) *Aging as a spiritual journey*. New York: Crossroads Press.

Birren, J. E., & Hedklund, B. (1987). Contributions of autobiography to developmental psychology. In N. Eisenberg (Ed.), *Contemporary topics in developmental psychology* (pp. 394–415). New York: John Wiley & Sons, 1987).

Butler, R. N. (1963). The life review: An interpretation of reminiscence in the Aged. *Psychiatry, 26*, 65–76.

Butt, D. S. and Beiser, M. (1987). Successful aging: A theme for international psychology. *Psychology and Aging,1,*87–94.

Hall, G. S. (1922). *Senescence*. New York: Appleton Century.

Riegel, K. F. (1973). Dialectical operations: The final period of cognitive development. *Human Development, 16*, 345–370.

Introduction to Chapter 4

Among James Birren's 15 commandments we find the directives to "leave the land and its people better than I found them" and to "foster new growth." Before Dr. Birren codified these commandments for us, entrepreneur Eugene Lang was already putting them into action for 61 young people from his native New York. Since 1981, when Lang promised to send every student in that year's sixth-grade class at East Harlem's P.S. 121 to college, his impetuous words have borne results. The "I Have a Dream" Foundation, established by Lang in 1986, now has 145 projects making scholarships available for over 10,000 students in 43 cities nationwide. Each patron in the program must pledge at least $300,000 for a single class, money that pays the salary of a full-time project coordinator and guarantees each student $2,000 for each year spent in college.

But Lang insists that money, while it pays the tuition for these students, is never enough. Among Lang's 61 sixth-graders, most came from single-parents homes, and many families relied solely on welfare for income. Their homes and neighborhoods were poor, neglected, and violent.

Of these 61 students, 33 entered college, 20 of whom enrolled in four-year institutions. Two students have already earned their bachelor's degrees, one from Swarthmore and the other from Bard College. But nine students dropped out before finishing high school, and three of the students who enrolled in community or two-year colleges eventually dropped out. Six girls became pregnant, and at least four boys fathered children out of wedlock. But Lang has not abandoned those who "failed" the program. He has found jobs for many students, even given some of them jobs with his own company. He has provided counseling and tutoring, pulled strings, and given fresh chances to those willing to try again. In 1981, Eugene Lang's goal was to send every student to college. His new goal, in 1991, is to provide them with whatever is necessary to help them change their lives and have pride in themselves.

Others have followed Eugene Lang's example, and some have even taken it further. In Louisiana in 1988, a wealthy oilman, Patrick Taylor, made a speech similar to Lang's to 183 seventh- and eighth-graders in New Orleans. Most of these students were several grades behind in reading and math, and many were at risk of dropping out of high school. But even faced with their own apparent failure to achieve, these students held onto their dreams of a better life. When Taylor asked how many wanted to go to college, every hand went up. Taylor promised to send them if they kept up their grades.

As Eugene Lang did, Patrick Taylor devoted time and money to his students. But he took his support a step further and petitioned the Louisiana legislature to do something for at-risk students. In 1989, the Taylor Plan, guaranteeing every qualified student a free college education, became law. Since then, five other states have enacted similar laws.

Both Eugene Lang and Patrick Taylor, and others like them across the United States, have taken the intergenerational contract seriously. They are helping kids succeed, and in return they gain something as well. As one of the benefactors in the "I Have a Dream" program has said, "This program gives me a tremendous sense of purpose and a feeling that I've done something with my life." But the effects of helping disadvantaged youngsters go to college are broad, going far beyond the two generations involved. As Taylor has said, only

14% of America's young people are going to college. If the United States wishes to remain competitive in the global marketplace, that percentage must be doubled by the year 2000. To assure a better future and a higher standard of living for coming generations of Americans, we must work to improve the chances of many more children today. Or, as Dr. Birren put it in his commandments, we must plant seeds that will bloom in springs we will never see.

We Have a Dream: The Generations Working Together Toward the Future

4

Eugene M. Lang

I guess one might say I take a view of old age very different from that of most people. When I was a kid, it always seemed that I was trying to get as old as I could as quickly as I could. I started my first successful manufacturing venture when I was only eight years old, making little toys known as "street checkers" and selling them for a nickel apiece to the kids at school. I went away to college when I was only 14. All my life, I've been somewhat out of step with my generation. My professional peers, the men with whom I spent most of my time, were always much older than I. I couldn't wait to grow a mustache. Unwisely, I also took up smoking to impress upon my peers that I had indeed come of age.

In 1950, when I was 30 years old, I took my first trip to Japan. When I met my Japanese colleagues, men who were presidents of corporations, I was shocked to see that not a single one among them was less than 2 1/2 times as old as I. *They* seemed to find it pretty unbelievable, too, to think that a kid like me could approach them as a business representative and an equal. I'm sure they thought that I couldn't be mature enough or responsible enough to compete successfully in the business world—and I *know* I wasn't dignified enough to satisfy them. I had to continually prove myself to be acceptable to my economic and social peers.

33

I'm not really sure when it was that I crossed the line into maturity, when I stopped being the youngest person in every conference room. My experiences as *Wunderkind* shaped my attitudes toward life and maturity. Now I'm a septuagenarian, and I can honestly say that I have never been busier in my life. I start work at seven o'clock each morning and just keep going. My whole life has been a parade of new ventures and new ideas, and all my time has been spent in developing and carrying through these ideas and ventures. Nearly 10 years ago, I stumbled quite unintentionally into a brand-new entrepreneurial venture. It seems that the best ideas are always the ones you *don't* come up with—they seem to come up with you in mind. If you plan things, they often stubbornly refuse to turn out the way you want them to. But if you wait expectantly and just let things happen, and then weigh them and apply your experience and know-how, well, one opportunity just seems to open up so many more.

This time, I was speaking to a group of 61 sixth-grade graduates at P.S. 121 in Harlem, the very school I attended in my own youth. I was groping for something fresh to say, some new variation on Dr. Martin Luther King's famous "I have a dream" speech. Suddenly I found myself telling these kids that graduation was a time for them to dream. Having a dream, I told them, means that *you've* got to decide just what it is you want to be, and that you've got to believe in it and work toward it. "You have to stay in school," I told them, "and continue to learn because *that* is what makes dreams happen."

"Today," I said, "you're starting on your most important journey in life, your journey through your education into life. That journey will take you from here into junior high or intermediate school, and from there into high school, and then on to college." And as soon as I said that, I realized with a jolt that, for many of these kids, "college" was just a word in their English vocabulary books. "College" had very little real significance for them in terms of their expectations. The same thing went for their parents, sitting right there in the auditorium watching their kids graduate, knowing that, for most of them, college was not even a question. Three-quarters of minority children, African-American and Hispanic, who live in our nation's inner cities drop out before they finish high school. With statistics like that in front of us, how dare we even talk to them about realizing their dreams through higher education?

I'm an impulsive sort of fellow. Right there and then I said to them, "But you *can* go to college. If you graduate from high school and are admitted into a college or university, I will give you the scholarship support that will enable you to go." I promised each of these kids $500 a year for four years of college, as long as they kept up their grades and stayed in school. And I kept my promise.

Well, this sure was a great idea that up and grabbed me. And, unbelievably, it caught on with others. Education was a really hot issue in this country at the time, as it continues to be even now. The statistics are grimmer than we could ever imagine, but sometimes we are so distracted by the statistics that we forget to look at the reality they are meant to represent. I like to use statistics myself, especially when I can speak to groups all over the country and say, "Here are my kids in East Harlem. Three-quarters of them would have dropped out before they finished high school. Their own principal told me that *none* of them would ever go on to college. And here, nine-plus years later, ninety percent of them have or will soon have their high-school diplomas, and already more than half are in college. Two-thirds of them will eventually go on to college." That's an extraordinary set of statistics. But it's not the numbers that are so incredibly satisfying to me; it's the individual relationships that I have formed with each of these children. When I have a child sitting in front of me, presenting me with an urgent problem or a moment of triumph—well, *that* is what the program is all about.

I had formed a relationship with an entire class of sixthgraders. I *adopted* the whole class. You see, I recognized that it was not enough simply to promise kids scholarships. There are a lot of scholarships out there that go unclaimed, a lot of money going unused. You still have to get the kids through to the point where offering them a scholarship has some real meaning for them. Having offered them scholarships for college, I then became responsible for making sure that my kids had the inner "stuff" necessary for them to take advantage of my impulsive offer.

That's how the "I Have a Dream" program was born. Since its genesis, the program has developed into a model support program for disadvantaged youngsters. Our program has forced a national recognition of the fact that we can't solve the educational problems of our children generically. By that I mean that we can only help educationally disadvantaged children by dealing with them as we would deal with our very own children. Each child is an individual, with his or her own constellation of problems. For kids in the inner cities, the problems are a hell of a lot more brutal. We can't possibly understand just how harsh their lives are by reading the paper or seeing the images on TV. We have to get out to them, *talk* to them, see how they live and the pain and horror that they accept as a normal part of their lives. What's all the more terrifying to us is that these kids are hardened to the horror in their lives. They can open their apartment doors to see someone being stabbed in the hall. When we meet a child who is growing up in that environment, how can we turn our backs when he or she goes off the deep end?

The real problem we have in dealing with our dropout rate is motivation—we have to give these children reasons to want to stay in school. You can't tell me that the *only* thing standing between many of these kids and daily life out on the streets is a truant officer—believe me, most kids can run a lot faster than a truant officer. The kids who stay in school stay because they still have some hope and ambition left. We have to capitalize on that hope and ambition and figure out a way to spread it around to all kids.

Obviously, I'm not an educator. What I do happen to be is a parent. When I met my sixth-graders, I found that I really cared about them as if they were my own. And the more I cared about them, the more they began to care about themselves. Suddenly, at my advanced age, I'm discovering a new

life, a life of caring for *all* children and of trying to deal with
them individually, getting to know each one of them the way I
got to know and love my own children. All the children in my
program have a lot more to cope with than my own kids ever
did. My children always expected to be able to go all the way
with whatever they wanted to do or be. The kids in the "I
Have a Dream" program don't have those same expectations.
Born with the same natural abilities that my own kids had,
they have a hell of a lot more to get past in order to get to the
same place.

For four years I kept my idea quiet and just worked along
with the kids. I got no support from the school system and
very little from anybody else. This forced me to develop a
structure that made it possible for me to get to know the children and work with them and help them deal with their problems. I set up the basic support structure of what is now the
"I Have a Dream" program. I make it a point to get to know
every one of my kids. I get to know their family backgrounds
and situations, the conditions in which they live, and what
they think and want. If they don't seem to want anything (and
you'd be surprised how many kids don't seem to want anything), I asked them the same question I asked my own kids,
which is the same question my parents asked me and your
parents asked you: "What do you want to be?" Forty percent
of the children living in the United States today are never
once asked that very simple question. "What do you want to
be?" They grow up with a sense of purposelessness bred of
their environment. And if the figure is 40% today, you can bet
that in 10 years it will be 50% or 60% because the problem of
hopelessness and purposelessness is growing a lot faster than
we can deal with. You don't solve the problem by getting a
thousand kids together and putting them in a room and talking *at* them. You deal with it by dealing with a single child.
The problem we're talking about is nothing more than a huge
agglomeration of individual problems, no two of which are
alike.

The problem of poor education is nationwide. In response
to this problem, the "I Have a Dream" program has grown

into a national undertaking with programs in 24 cities across the United States. And it continues to grow. But even though I am an entrepreneur, I know that growth is not the most important thing. What is most important is that I have discovered something wonderful and that a lot of people are joining with me in that discovery. We have a very special role in our society. While the program has helped to create new programs all around the country, it has also generated new legislation. The president of the United States, the education secretaries, governors, and legislators all over the nation have consulted me about the institutionalization of the "I Have a Dream" program. How can we make what we're doing available to kids everywhere? Governor Mario Cuomo of New York went all the way with the idea and created the Liberty Scholarship Program. The Liberty program will guarantee every high school graduate in New York State an opportunity to go to college. Any family with an annual income of $18,000 or less will qualify for the program. At that income level, most at-risk families will be covered. A child in a qualifying family will not only get full tuition at a state or city college but also full support for four years of college.

Under the Liberty Scholarship Program any qualifying child in New York State who graduates from high school and is admitted to a college in New York State will be assured of getting, each year, over $6,000 to cover tuition and the cost of living at college. The Liberty Scholarship Program will also offer every child the kind of personal support that will help the child succeed all the way. Lack of parental support is the second-greatest reason our kids drop out of school. Many parents just don't understand or believe in the need for higher education. They believe that it's much more important that their child get out into the job market as quickly as possible. The kind of job—or whether the kid can read and write adequately—doesn't seem to matter. The Liberty program will make it possible for kids in the state to have the kind of emotional support they need to choose college and to succeed.

It's not just the children who benefit from these kinds of programs. Programs like "I Have a Dream" and "Liberty" create new opportunities for people of all ages to get involved in making a difference in the lives of the next generation. Every one of us is a part of a vast social ecology. Everything I do has an impact on my neighbor, and my neighbor's neighbor, ad infinitum. One way for older people to feel good about themselves and forget so-called intergenerational conflict is to get involved with others, especially with young people. If we are looking for occupation, for activity, or for fulfillment, we can find it by trying to provide for some of the needs of all these children who are growing up needing our experience, guidance, and caring. This is something new. It creates new opportunities for accomplishment and contentment. It doesn't matter what you did for a living, whether you were a laboratory worker, president of a corporation, a secretary, a housewife. Life has trained you, as it has trained me, and supplied us with all the qualifications we need for this new job, this new life. I urge this upon all of you, all of us. If we work together, young and old, to see that the next generation can follow their hopes and dreams through, so much the better will our lives be. So much the better will this country be.

Afterword for Part I

Rosalynn Carter and James Birren have given us two very different views of successful adaptation to the loss of societal roles that often accompanies retirement. For Mrs. Carter, the transition from active public life to unwanted retirement was distressing at first. Then, no longer constrained by the need to perform the duties expected of a First Lady of the United States, she discovered a great range of activities that would engage and challenge her physically and intellectually. She and her husband, Jimmy Carter, are, if anything, *more* active in public life now than they were during their years in the White House.

For Dr. Birren, retirement offers exactly the right opportunity to reduce the frenzied activity of earlier years, and instead spend time in more leisurely meditation and action on the larger issues: the care of the environment, the nurturing of future generations, the enduring and beautiful mutability of the life cycle. What is common to these two different people and their approaches to aging and retirement is the element of *choice*, the capacity to choose, among many alternatives, how one will spend one's later years.

Whether a person achieves a successful adaptation to old age and retirement is contingent upon a number of interrelated factors. Personality traits; past lived experience; the

40

ability to adequately meet human needs for shelter, food, personal comforts, and medical care; and a reliable system of social supports all play an important role in helping a person to live a satisfying, productive later life (Butler, Lewis & Sunderland, 1991). It has been wryly noted that being rich and healthy certainly goes a long way toward enabling one to have a good old age (Seltzer, 1989). Having sufficient income to meet basic needs, with some left over for additional comforts, certainly increases one's choices; being healthy—free from disease and disability and having the capacity to perform the work one wishes to—also expands one's options when thinking about the course of later life.

For many elderly Americans, choices are severely limited. Many suffer from physical, emotional, or mental disabilities and disorders that restrict their activity or freedom to make choices that will have a beneficial effect on their lives. It must be stressed that these disabilities are often interrelated; mental confusion may result from the interaction of drugs prescribed to treat somatic illness, and hearing loss may have a detrimental impact on personality, causing an elderly person to withdraw or to be suspicious of others' intentions (Butler et al., 1991). External factors and events can further complicate physical or mental problems and can hinder the ability of even healthy elders to adapt and thrive. The loss of a spouse, the reduction in income that accompanies retirement, children's moving far away, negative societal attitudes toward old age and the elderly, associations of old age with decline and approaching death—any of these can have a damaging impact on one's ability to make for oneself a good old age.

Elderly people in general suffer from our society's bias toward youth, individual achievement, and autonomy. But many of our nation's elders are even further victimized by society. African-American elders are disproportionately represented among the very poor; they have lower lifetime incomes and poorer health, and often they receive no retirement benefits at all. Many older African-Americans rely solely on Supplementary Security Income and Medicaid (Butler et al., 1991). Hispanic and Native American elders have been less studied, but their situations are likely to be comparable to that of elderly blacks.

Women also comprise a group whose choices are likely to be limited by social attitudes; their situation in this nation and in Japan is made worse by entrenched sexism. Older women labor under the twin burdens of sexism and ageism. Female retirement in the United States (and in Japan) is a neglected issue, rarely addressed in the few existing studies of adaptation to retirement (Szinovacz, 1987). Women generally have lower lifetime incomes because of job discrimination, pay inequities, segregation into part-time or low-wage jobs, and discontinuous work histories due to childcare or eldercare. As a result, their Social Security income is usually far lower than that of men in the same age group. And the loss of a job through retirement is often followed by the loss of a husband, adding to an older women's "rolelessness."

In our next chapter, two American women, Betty Friedan and Maggie Kuhn, and two Japanese women, Takako Sodei and Keiko Higuchi, will address the issues of old age as they affect women. To the clear vision of a social critic and tireless researcher, Mrs. Friedan, as a woman past the age of 60, adds the personal viewpoint of the "research subject." With wicked wit and shrewd intelligence she "unpacks" what she calls the "mystique of old age," to expose our most secret fears about aging. It is these fears, she says, that prevent us from seeing the elderly as they really are and should be, vital, contributing members of human communities. Takako Sodei and Keiko Higuchi explode the myth that issues of old age affect only the elderly, or only the elderly and their primary care givers. The responsibility for caring for the frail elderly falls upon all of us, and failure to provide for the present and future generations of elders threatens the welfare of all— men, women, children, American and Japanese. Maggie Kuhn echoes Dr. Birren's concern for the generations to come with her dismissal of "senior power" in favor of an activism that crosses boundaries of age, sex, class, and nationality.

While Rosalynn Carter and James Birren wrote about the responsibility of the individual for a good old age, their approaches were not individualistic. Mrs. Carter, while stressing the responsibility of the individual to create non-government sources of income for retirement, also warned us that government and the economic enterprise must ensure that all citizens of the world are provided for. Elderly people living in poverty and loneliness, she writes, "simply must not be" in a wealthy nation. Dr. Birren's approach is based on his 15 commandments, all of which underscore the responsibility of the individual to the entire human community and to the living planet. Finally, Eugene Lang has demonstrated how an individual can apply the commandments dictating responsibility to one's own generation and those that follow. In the next chapter, the contributors, while focusing on women's issues, will also present ideas for shared responsibility, and will raise many questions that, if left unanswered, will be faced again by future generations of young and old.

REFERENCES

Butler, R. N., Lewis, M., & Sunderland, T. (1991). *Aging and mental health: Positive psychological and biomedical approaches* (4th ed.). New York: Macmillan.

Seltzer, M. N. (1989). Random and not so random thoughts on becoming and being a statistic: Professional and personal musings. *International Journal of Aging and Human Development, 28*(1), p. 2.

Szinovacz, M. E. (1987). Beyond the hearth: older women and retirement. In B. B. Hess and E. W. Markson (Ed.) *Growing Old in America: New Perspectives on Old Age* (3rd ed., p. 327). New Brunswick, NJ: Transition Books.

Family Responsibility: It's a Women's Issue

Introduction to Part II

More than a decade ago, Robert Butler (1979) said that the problems of the elderly are largely the problems of women. Women experience "a greater rate of poverty and social unacceptability than do men, combined ironically with a longer life span." (Butler, Lewis & Sunderland, 1991, p. 196). Even a cursory glance at the figures will confirm this. Of the over 27 million people over the age of 65 in the United States, more than 60% are women. Two-thirds of Americans aged 100 years or more are women; 75% of the poor elderly are women. And because women live longer than men, tend to marry men older than themselves, and are less likely than older men to remarry, women are many times more likely than men to end their lives alone (Hess, 1987). And the older women get, the more likely it is that they are alone (some even outlive their children). The majority of the one million Japanese over 65 who are living alone are women, and women constitute two-thirds of those over 65 who receive public assistance (Sodei, 1986).

Women are also at a disadvantage when it comes to healthcare. In both Japan and the United States, the state-funded healthcare systems (Medicare and Medicaid, in the United States) are better suited to the health problems of men than of women. Men have more serious, life-threatening diseases re-

47

quiring hospitalization, while women tend to have more chronic ailments requiring outpatient treatment.

Actually, the physiology of women's normal aging is not really that well understood by the medical establishment. Takako Sodei (1986) has said that in Japan, older women are "invisible" to gerontologists. Nearly every gynecologist accepts the menopausal "hot flash" as a fact of women's lives, but there is not one who can explain its physiology (Butler et al, 1991).

It is an unhappy truth that older women have been an invisible presence even to the feminist movement, at least in the United States. The women's movement in this country has concentrated its efforts largely on issues of pay parity and freedom to enter male-dominated professions. These issues do have an impact on older women's lives: if women can receive equal pay for equal work and have a chance to work in highpaying fields, they will receive higher Social Security benefits when they retire, along with better company pensions. However, those women who are now over 65 have, with a few notable exceptions like Maggie Kuhn and Betty Friedan, found themselves largely ignored by the feminist agenda.

Betty Friedan, in her contribution to this book, attacks what she calls "the mystique of age," which she defines as our tendency to see old age only in terms of mental and physical decline. Because we see old people as useless in a society that values achievement and youth above all else, we ignore the vitality of the majority of people over 60 and create structures, such as mandatory retirement and segregated living, that deny the aged the possibility of participating fully in the human community. The aging process is transformative. Instead of being a time when, as Goethe put it, we "gradually disappear from view," aging can be a time of becoming more and more fully ourselves, by "owning" our experience and our change.

Writing for the *International Journal of Aging and Human Development*, gerontologist and self-declared older woman Mildred Seltzer echoes some of Betty Friedan's concerns about the imagery we have of aging, doing so from the point of view of the "research subject." Personal experience should tell one, she writes, that "the closer you get to the forest, the more the individual trees differ from one another; the same is true of people" (Seltzer, 1989, p. 2). Stereotypes are dangerous because they tend to obscure the very real differences among individuals; by lumping all older people into a single, heterogeneous category, we deny their personhood and thus miss real opportunities to tailor our policies to help people cope with the many and varied problems of aging. Even positive, or so-called compassionate stereotypes of aging can be damaging, especially when older people themselves start to believe them.

> To be wise, patient, kind, giving because one is old is a burden which may be equally onerous. Why must one suffer fools gladly because one has achieved a given chronological age? Why be giving because one is closer to death than to birth? (Seltzer, 1989, p. 3)

While the stereotype of the older woman as an evil-tempered, depressed, sickly, manipulative hag is damaging, the casting of older women in the role of benevolent matriarch can also lead to neglect and/or exploitation. (It is interesting, perhaps, to note that the "positive" stereotypes of old age are curiously like the roles that have been assigned to women in both American and Japanese society.)

But the problems of old age are not just the problems of older women. As Takako Sodei points out in this book, worldwide, the care of the elderly is a women's issue (or *fujin mondai* in Japanese). In both American and Japanese society, the overwhelming majority of caregivers are female. In Japan, for example, 90% of all those who look after frail elders in the home are women, usually daughters or daughters-in-law. In the United States, Harper and Lund (1990), in their 1989 study of caregiver burden, found that women, whether daughters or wives (the primary caregivers in this country), had the highest "burden scores" regardless of income or presence of others in the household. Women, they wrote, reported far lower levels of life satisfaction than did men and also received far less support from community and family.

Despite their governments' claims that Japan and the United States are rapidly becoming welfare states for the elderly and the popular public myth of selfish children "dumping" elderly parents in nursing homes, the vast majority of old people needing full-time care are already being cared for at home by their families, usually at great cost and sacrifice. In both the United States and Japan, at least 80% of such elders are cared for at home (Hess, 1987). And in the United States at least, the majority of nursing home residents (or their children) pay the full costs of their care, averaging about $20,000 per year (Hess, 1987).

In both the United States and Japan, efforts to get people to take care of their elders at home are premised on nostalgic visions of the family that, whatever basis in reality they may have had, are increasingly difficult to reconcile with most people's experience. In the United States, what Betty Friedan calls the "Family of Western Nostalgia"—consisting of a breadwinning father, a homemaking mother, and two children—is also the family model upon which our Social Security and private pension plan benefits are calculated. In Japan, it is the extended patrilineal stem family of the pre–World War II agricultural countryside that informs many people's ideas about the ideal family. (It is interesting to note, however, that on American TV, the "traditional" nuclear family is hardly to be found. Instead, extended families, blended families, and households consisting of unrelated adults and children are the "situations" in many of our most popular situation comedies. It is also interesting that one of the most popular nuclear families on network television is the African-American TV family of Bill Cosby.) Yet both Japan and the United States have seen a rapid rise in the paid labor force participation of married women with school-age children, along with increased rates of divorce, increased mobility, and increased reliance on social services for child care, health care, and care for the elderly. And the governments of both nations, eager to reduce federal expenditures for these services, are calling upon their citizens to take more responsibility for home and community care of children and the aged, to reduce their reliance on government-provided agencies, to increase volunteerism, and to reduce their medical costs by watching their health.

Linda Martin (1991) has noted:

> Emphasis on family care . . . may be on a collision course with increased female labor force participation, a concomitant of economic development that may be beyond government's control and potentially a partial solution to labor shortages due to population aging and slowing population growth. As women are generally the caretakers of the young, they are also the caretakers of the old. (p. 529)

Women are caught in a three-way squeeze by the demands of child care, elder care, and career. In Japan, Daisaku Maeda (1983) has noted that, even while many working women report that they feel overburdened and overfatigued by their responsibilities for caring for their parents (he also notes that half of all women in Japan caring for bedridden old people are themselves over 60 years of age), they nevertheless consistently fail to turn to outside services to relieve their burden. The social system in Japan prior to World War II regarded the dependence of elders on their children as a legal right and even as a moral virtue. And while that is not the case in the United States, with its emphasis on self-reliance and individualism, many middle-aged women find themselves leaving jobs or cutting work hours to take care of their parents or parents-in-law, jeopardizing their own retirements by giving up their paychecks and their continued contribution to Social Security.

Women are the link between the generations, and increasingly they are all that ties the family together. In the United States, the rising divorce rate, the increased acceptability of the unmarried state, and the increase in single-parenting (and the single parent is usually the mother) have resulted in the disengagement of American men from the family and from family issues (Rossi, 1986). With fewer men seeing themselves as having a stake in the welfare of children and women, these issues are unlikely to have a prominent place in our national discourse unless women—and sympathetic men—raise them to that place. Women might begin by asking such "disengaged" men just who will take care of them in their own old age should the entire responsibility for care be shifted to the family.

In Japan, feminists are saying that modern Japanese women are already single mothers, albeit single mothers with living, breathing husbands. The average Japanese husband and father, feminists charge, has already disengaged from the family, spending most of his time at work, taking few vacations, and contributing little or nothing beyond his paycheck to home and children. The popular humorous stereotype of a married woman in Japan is one who takes advantage of her husband's absence to do whatever she wants and raise her children as she pleases. But increasing numbers of Japanese women are growing disenchanted with this model for marriage, and divorce initiated by women is on the rise. A divorced woman is at a great disadvantage in Japan, however. She may become a social pariah, shunned by family and friends, and often has difficulty finding work if she is not already working. Add to this the fact that in Japan only 10% of divorced women with minor children receive any child support (Sodei, 1985). The comparable figures in the United States are 59% awarded support by the courts and 23% receiving the full award from their ex-husbands (Ozaway, 1986), a figure we need not be proud of.

Both the United States and Japan are also seeing a greater tendency among women to delay marriage and childbearing and to limit the number of children per family to one. The Japanese government, alarmed at this trend and warning of a shrinking pool of workers to pay taxes and contribute to the retirement of their aging parents and grandparents, has undertaken a campaign to persuade women to have more children. They are offering "baby bonuses," creating special ceremonies to honor large families, and increasing subsidies for daycare and prenatal care ("In Crowded Japan," 1991). Many Japanese women are alarmed, fearing that the plan may backfire and, by reducing women's participation in the work force, reduce their contribution to their own social security, thus increasing the chances that they will be dependent on the government for their support when they retire. The Japanese government probably hopes that these "extra" children will take over the task of supporting their parents, but as Western individualism becomes more pervasive in Japan, that is a risky wager.)

The "feminization of poverty" we are experiencing in the United States (something that Japan may also experience in the near future as a result of its rising divorce rate) means increased poverty for children as well. Children living in poverty suffer from inadequate food, shelter, and parental attention and, as a result, often do poorly in school. This has profound implications for the future, since these children are less likely to be productive workers when they grow up and will be unable to sustain the high level of economic growth needed to support an aging population. They can also look forward themselves to an impoverished old age, since the majority of those who are poor throughout their lives will remain poor in old age (Butler et al., 1991). All of us, old and young, must take responsibility for our children, if only in our own self-interest. Older people can no longer ignore the problems that plague "other people's kids." With Social Security as a "pay as you go" system, old people need not only their own children; they need *all* our children.

There are other questions and issues. What will the old age experience be for the children of the baby boomers in Japan and the United States? Many of these children were born to mothers who delayed childbearing until their late thirties or early forties, and many of them have no siblings. Many are children of divorce (this is increasingly the case in Japan, despite their far lower divorce rate) or live in blended families, and the societies into which they have been born and are being born are increasingly racially, ethnically, and economically diverse (Japan's celebrated homogeneity is rapidly joining the extended patrilineal family as a nostalgic myth, with the increased immigration of foreign workers from China and Korea, as well as the influx of Westerners representing multinational corporations). The fact that we have few answers to the questions regarding the next generation tells us that we have a long way to go and a lot to learn.

As we noted before, there is also a great deal left to learn about the physical lives of older women and about how the body's wellbeing affects, and is affected by, social, emotional, and mental well-being. Lauren Goldberg, who was a medical student at the time of this symposium, writing about the deficiencies of much of the current gynecological and geriatric training in American medical schools, says:

> It's important, but not sufficient, to know the interrelationship between estrogen levels, menopause, and osteoporosis; it's important, but not sufficient . . . to know that drug dosage for an 80-year-old may not be the same as the dosage for a 50-year-old. . . . It becomes more and more clear that our extensive training in accurate diagnosis and effective treatment of specific diseases and disorders is not enough to help us satisfy the complex social, emotional, and medical needs of our elderly patients.

Lauren (now *Doctor*) Goldberg, like Mildred Seltzer, is aware of the complex demands of her dual role as physician and woman. As a product of the baby boom, her life expectancy is 77 years. Even as she herself ages, she can expect to treat many older women—and men—as part of her regular practice. The same holds true for her colleagues in the medical profession, regardless of specialty—urology, dermatology, ob-gyn, cardiology, or internal medicine. The new longevity will afford Dr. Goldberg and her colleagues with nearly limitless opportunities to observe and study the progress and variety of normal human aging and the effects of disease and environmental factors at every stage of human life, perhaps leading to new discoveries in preventive medicine as well as new technologies for maintaining life.

Dr. Goldberg is also aware of her status as an aging woman,

a member of a generation that often has to choose between career and childbearing. Who will take care of the women who opt *not* to have children? Her experience shows us that there are no simple answers to the questions of responsibility. As professionals, as parents, as children, as men and women, our responsibilities to ourselves and others cannot easily be disentangled.

What can women in Japan and the United States teach each other? How can they help each other cope with the aging of our two societies? Perhaps one of the more heartening features of the "graying" of our populations is their concomitant "feminization." Most experts agree that the gender gap in longevity has stabilized and that women will continue to outlive men even as longevity increases for everyone. This means that as the median ages of our populations grow older, women will constitute a large majority of voters. Perhaps they will be a force for sweeping social, political, and economic change, addressing such issues as pay parity; comprehensive national health insurance that truly addresses the health needs of women and children; a more realistic formula for calculating Social Security and pension benefits for working women, full-time homemakers, divorced women, and widows; and a system of direct cash payments to enable every member of our societies to achieve an established minimum standard of living.

The women of Japan and the United States, as they press for these measures, can share strategies for long-term reform and can comfort each other when the road seems too hard and too long. Women in the United States, living in a society that places great value on individual achievement and self-reliance, have seen the damage that such an ethos can engender. By privileging individual rights over community needs, we have allowed too many of our people to live in poverty, to live without adequate health care, and to languish alone in our cities. Japanese women, however, have until recently lived, for the most part, only through and for others. The *Ie* family system kept women subservient to their husbands and their children, and allowed them little time or freedom for discovery of what Betty Friedan calls their "personhood." Perhaps the women of our two nations, with their strong and clear voices, can teach not only each other but the world how to live fully, until the end of all our days.

REFERENCES

Butler, R. N. (1979). *The older woman: Continuities and discontinuities.* (Washington, DC: Government Printing Office.

Butler, R. N., Lewis, M. & Sunderland, T. (1991) *Aging and mental health: Positive psychological and biomedical approaches* (4th ed.) New York: Macmillan.

Harper, S. & Lund, D. A. (1990). Wives, husbands, and daughters caring for institutionalized and noninstitutionalized dementia patients: Toward a Model of caregiver burden *International Journal of Aging and Human Development, 30*(4), 250, 258.

Hess, B. B. (1987). America's elderly: A demographic overview. In *Growing old in America: New perspectives on old age* (p. 7). B. B. Hess & E. W. Markson (Eds.) (New Brunswick, NJ: Transaction Books.

In crowded Japan, a bonus for babies angers women. (1991, February 17). *New York Times*, pp. 1, 14.

Maeda, D. (1983). Family care of impaired elderly in Japan. *The Gerontologist*, Vol. 23, 579–583.

Martin, L. G. (1991). Population aging policies in East Asia and the United States. *Science, 251*, 529.

Ozawa, M. N. (1986, February). Women and children in aging society. Paper at Conference on the Societal Impact of Population Aging in the United States and Japan, Oiso, Japan.

Rossi, A. S. (1986). Sex and gender in the aging society. In *Our aging society: Paradox and promise*, A. Pifer & L. Bronte (Eds.), New York: W. W. Norton (p. 127).

Seltzer, M. N., (1989). Random and not so random thoughts on becoming and being a statistic: Professional and personal musings. *International Journal of Aging and Human Development, 28*(1).

Sodei, T. (1985). The fatherless family. *Japan Quarterly, 32*(1), 78.

Sodei, T. (1986, September). Older women in japan. Paper presented at International Conference of Social Welfare, Tokyo, Japan.

Beyond the Mystique of Old Age

Betty Friedan

5

Twenty-five years ago, I wrote a book called *The Feminine Mystique*, which questioned the only image of women that we had in American society in the years following World War II. Woman was defined only in terms of her sexual relation to Man. She was man's wife, his mother, sex object, housewife, minister of the physical needs of husband, children, and home. Never, never was Woman regarded as a person defining herself existentially by her own actions, her own agency in society. This image, which I called "the feminine mystique," permeated the mass media, the television commercials, the magazines—especially the "women's magazines"—and even the textbooks. The "feminine mystique" was perpetuated in the postwar years by the popularizers of psychoanalysis. Using the new psychoanalytic and sociological language, they revived traditional images of women, which had their genesis in ancient history—and in our own, more recent early American history—when to define women solely in terms of their childbearing roles had, perhaps, some basis in actual experience. Childbearing *did* define a woman's life in times past. At the turn of this century, life expectancy was a mere 45 years. Two hundred years ago—even only *one* hundred years ago— women had no control over their reproductive lives. Many children had to be born in order for a few to survive. Much of

57

the important work of society required great muscular strength, and women could not compete in that work. Child-bearing, a woman's main function in life, marked the boundaries of her life.

This is no longer the case in the 20th century. But when I wrote *The Feminine Mystique*, I saw our society clinging to this very *limited* and *limiting* image of women, an image that kept women *and* our society from reaching their full potential. This image blinded us to what the problem really was. Twenty-five years ago, everyone was discussing "the woman problem"—or "the problem that has no name," as I called it in my book—in terms of the frustrations of housewives. What was wrong with these women?, we asked. Male experts, psychoanalysts, sociologists, intellectuals—all went around lecturing us on "the woman problem" and its possible solutions. Perhaps the source of feminine frustration was education. That must be it: women were overeducated for their "natural" roles as wife and mother. Society, in the person of the psychoanalyst, must help women to readjust, and to find their satisfaction in the role allotted them by biology. These were the great days of biology as destiny: a woman was identified by and with her body.

The personhood of woman was obscured by the feminine mystique. In the past 10 years, I've come to realize that we've also developed a "mystique of age," which obscures the personhood of people over 60. I'd like to share some thoughts that might help us break through this age mystique. I've taken all that I learned in my 25 years of conceptualizing and theorizing the feminine mystique and have begun applying it to the question of age.

This "mystique of age," as I've called it, defines age solely in terms of a drastic decline from youth, deterioration into senility, and, ultimately, a custodial burden on society. The mystique of age denies the personhood of people over 65. It denies their unique *emergent* personhood and all the unknown potential of that extra 25 years of life, made possible for all of us by the new longevity. But this mystique is even more insidious than the feminine mystique because it keeps us from seeing what that potential is, what our possibilities are, and even from being able to distinguish *real* problems from mere chimeras, from spurious problems and fraudulent terrors.

The mystique of age permeates our mass media, and it also permeates our medical and scientific treatment of age. It permeates our public policies. It is manifest in the United States in our national obsession with youth and our obsessive personal fear and denial of our own aging. By asking the question "Who is responsible for my old age?" we are trying to break through some of that denial. At the same time, it is apparent that by asking this question we risk slipping back into the fallacy of viewing old age only as a custodial problem for society. There is a tremendous body of research now in the United States, in Japan, in Sweden, and in other countries that indicates that what had been perceived as the normal aging process is now known to be *pathological* aging. There is tremendous variety in the ways people develop, or decline, or change in the years after 65, but what emerges from this research is the very narrow range of pathological decline— much of it reversible—that has been used to represent "normal" aging. "Normal" aging, we know now, is healthy aging, and the words "normal" and "healthy" can no longer be perceived as synonymous with "young."

In fact, most of the deterioration and decline that we associate with the "normal" aging process occurs in the two years before a person's death. Without denying the problems of custodial care and without denying the very real problems of the most deteriorated, ill, and infirm members of our society, we should remember that, in the United States, only 5% of people over 65 are in nursing homes or other kinds of custodial care. And only 5% suffer from that terrible mental and physical deterioration that has been the focus of so much research in the United States today: Alzheimer's disease. And yet these are the images we carry with us when we talk about aging.

Our culture has *no imagery* for healthy aging. At conference after conference, the scientific and medical communities get together solely to deal with the problem of custodial care of *them*, the *elderly them*. What emerges from so many of these conferences is a vision of the aged person as *other*, someone we must not, cannot, dare not identify with ourselves. We can never become *them*, those dreary, decrepit, isolated, lonely, incompetent, childlike—even *smelly*—old folks. Oh no! Not us! We deny even the possibility of our own bodies' aging—bodies that age even as we deny the process.

It's as if one day you're fine, and the next you have a disease called "old age." I don't think that Betty Friedan functions any less well than she did 20 or 30 years ago. I'm working at a new career, at Hunter College. My *son* is retired, after having put in his "20 years." Now, I'm certainly not opposed to government support for those who are frail or handicapped, no matter what their age. What I *do* resent is the implication that, after a certain age, we are somehow incapacitated and need to be, deserve to be, supported by others, whether the government or our children. I don't object to Social Security or half-fare cards for public transportation. I *do* object to all the baggage that the term "old age" carries with it—the baggage of sickness, decrepitude, death. Instead of asking, "Who is responsible for my old age?" I'd like the question to be "Who is responsible for my *good* old age?" Let's break away from the euphemisms of "senior citizen" or "goldenager." We are aging, and our language attempts to deny that reality.

My biggest problem in writing about old age has its genesis in this denial. Friends ask me about the book I'm writing. They ask, "Betty, is it true that you're writing a book about aging?" And I'm quick to answer, "Oh, no, no, no! I'm not writing a book *about* aging. Of course not! I'm writing about men and women, changing sex roles, new kinds of families, and [always in a whisper] the aging process." Talk about writer's block! I couldn't figure out why I was having such a hard time writing— much harder than usual. Then it struck me: I was writing about *THEM*. Now why was I so interested in age when I wasn't *really* interested in age? I was interested in discovering why women live so much longer than men, in finding out why men seemed to be dying before they really had to die. But instead I found myself sitting on panels at conferences on policy for the aging, discussing nursing homes, home care for the elderly, and so on. I would find myself facing all these "young turks" in the fields of gerontology and social policy for the aging—and if they had any gray hairs at all, they kept them well hidden—and they were talking about *them*. What do we do about *them*? When do we pull the plug on the life-support machine? In the meantime, I'd begun talking to some very vital women and men, women and men who were moving and evolving and changing. Were we really talking about these people at our conferences? What was going on?

As I thought about these things, I looked around me at all the young turks of the aging business, and was suddenly overcome by a sense of déjà vu. I realized that *I had been here before*. Twenty-five years ago, at conferences on "the woman problem," male experts would be discussing frustrated housewives and proposing ways to deal with that frustration that didn't deviate from "biology as destiny"—things like continuing education, arts and crafts classes, volunteer work, and so forth. No one at that time thought of asking *women* what they wanted. But if we've come such a long way, why aren't there more people talking about aging who are actually talking about themselves, defining their own problems and strengths? And yet if I started to ask questions like that, people might look at me and say, "My God, she must be getting old!"

That was the source of my writer's block: I was going to have my 60th birthday. I knew then that I was going to have to start writing about age the same way I had written *The Feminine Mystique*: from personal truth, coming out of personal experience. I would have to listen to myself and others. I had to use everything I learned from more than 25 years of breaking through the feminine mystique to break through the mystique of age and let age define the terms for discussion. First of all, we must begin to really look at those new years, the 25 years of average life expectancy courtesy of the new longevity, as years of capital-L *Life*. Too often, our culture characterizes these years either by desperate and obsessive attempts to hold on to fleeting youth, or by illness and senility, waiting for death in a nursing home. We have no image, really *no way* of picturing real women and real men, real *emergence*, at this time of life. We have not even begun to study what might emerge in terms of human maturity. None of our institutions—social, political, religious, or educational—has very much to tell us about age. American society especially has been both a male-defined and a *youth*-defined society.

I feel uneasy with the question of who is responsible for my old age. It's true that the possessive personal pronoun "my" might help us to consider the question of personhood in age. Nevertheless, the question implies passivity, that someone besides yourself has to take responsibility for you. Everybody— family, community, government, the individual— is responsible for the well-being of everyone else, of course. Perhaps we need to ask different questions or simply ask the same question differently. But before we can even begin to formulate the right questions, we have to approach the years after 50 or 60, or whatever as a unique stage in life. This time of life is really an undiscovered country. We know it is not simply mourning for lost youth, nor is it only the decline that precedes death. Our job is to explore a new and for the most part unknown part of human development. What an exciting road lies ahead!

We have to set some new objectives for ourselves. If we are to live our old age well, we have an obligation to contribute something different from or simply beyond what we contributed in our youth. In this culture of corporate greed, of buyouts and megabuyouts, I've always been impressed by the young turks at the roundtable, who talk bottom-line and maximizing short-term profits—but it's the older men who are asking the long-term questions: what is this going to do to the future of this company, the industry, the community, the *country*? These men—and women—are concerned with larger, broader questions. Some years ago, CBS-TV brought back one of its "old turks," a former president, to try to apply some of his longterm strategies and revive the network's sagging ratings. This has happened to others. Perhaps we're not really talking about merely giving old age permission to do the things of youth. Perhaps we're also talking about changing values, about generativity and wisdom as more than just sheer competition, mere win-or-lose bottom line.

But to return to the mystique of age and our persistent belief in age as decline: In the United States the gerontological study of aging has traditionally been a study of aging *men*, men who were taken out of the home and the community and placed in institutions for the infirm elderly. In fact, when researchers first began to study aging populations, most of the residents of nursing homes *were* men. Women were cared for at home by the family. So the original gerontological picture of aging as drastic decline was based on studies of populations of institutionalized men. Later studies by James Birren, the National Institute on Aging under the direction of Robert Butler, and others first began to deal with healthy men still living in the community. These studies showed that so-called normal decline had more to do with removal from the community than with the aging process. Loss of testosterone and decline in sexual function, for instance, was in many cases due to the absence of any available sexual partners. But even these ground-breaking original studies on "normal" aging— of healthy individuals still living in the community—were based solely on male populations so that they could be compared with the earlier studies on pathological aging. It was almost as if women over the age of 60 didn't exist. These days, menopause is, or ought to be, something we hardly notice. Women who have finished raising their children move on to the next period of growth in their lives. But only 25 years ago, menopause, the end of a woman's reproductive life, was regarded as the end of her useful life. Mental hospitals were filled with menopausal women diagnosed as suffering from something called "involutional melancholia." Even the term seemed to signal the end of life—"involutional" meaning "degenerative"; melancholia, a sort of mourning. The American Psychiatric Association has since dropped "involutional melancholia" as a diagnostic term; it just doesn't exist anymore. Over the past 25 years, women have been breaking out of the narrow stereotypes that define them in terms of their repro-

ductive capabilities. If we had been studying aging by studying those women who were seeking new growth and identity
after their childbearing and childrearing years, we would be
looking not just at *problems* that have no name but at
strengths that have no name and at new patterns of evolving
personhood. We would have to focus on older women not as
victims but as persons stripping away the final vestiges of the
feminine mystique and defining themselves—ourselves—in
ever new and varied terms.

Women of the generation that fueled the women's movement—women of my generation and the generations to follow—will not go gently into anybody's good night. Women
like Maggie Kuhn, the founder of the Gray Panthers, are in-
sisting that we all confront the mystique of age, this mystique
that only addresses questions about age with endless discussion of passive custodial care. My Japanese sisters, who are
working so hard to improve their own rapidly aging society,
are rightfully saying, "Don't think that daughters and daughters-in-law—the ones you mean when you talk about family
responsibility—are going to continue to be the answer. Not
when we have to work, when our apartments are so small,
when our children demand so much of our time." But what
they are *not* saying is that they absolve themselves of all responsibility and concern for age in an aging society. Women's
concerns and strengths have been bred within the family, and
we will take our strengths and concerns into the community
and into the larger society. If we can break through the mystique of age, that breakthrough will catalyze a new movement
for social change in the final years of this century, a movement comparable to the feminist and civil rights movements
of the past 25 years. But to break through the denial of age
and to see it *not* as merely a decline from some peak of male
youth but in terms of emergent men and women, that breakthrough will require new concepts of family and of intimacy,
bonding, and sexuality. It will require that we change our educational system, our ideas about recreation and leisure. It
will require new economic and social policies, a new ap-

proach to medical care—and a new way to approach our death.

Whenever we discuss age and responsibility, we always seem to mean custodial care, as if all of old age has only to do with illness and infirmity, with the sick days, weeks, or months preceding death; or with those pathologies that have been induced by lack of human bonding, by lack of human work and projects, by lack of social participation, and even by improper or inadequate medical care. We talk about the family's role in aging, and what we really mean is that we don't need any new social policies; our daughters and daughters-in-law will take care of their mothers and fathers. We talk about family responsibility in order to evade our responsibility to put into place new social, educational, and housing policies; new labor and health care policies; policies that will address the needs and strengths of these "new" 25 years of life. We must structure our society so that we all may continue to the end of our days to be a part of the society, which makes us human and keeps us human.

From 1951 to 1986 the number of women working full-time tripled, from 15 million to 46 million. Today over 50% of all American women are in the work force on a full-time basis. And when you add to that women who work part-time or who work part of the year, that figure rises to 90%. Ninety percent of all women are working part- or full-time, at a time when they are being asked to shoulder more of the responsibility for taking care of Mom and Dad. Of the generation of women just coming up, those who are now 20 to 24 years old, 90% expect to become pregnant, raise their children, *and* continue working part- or full-time. These women are naturally—and rightfully—going to resent the implication that they should also assume most of the burden of caring for their parents or grandparents.

Women have traditionally been the caregivers in our society, while men have taken control of business and politics, not always to the benefit of the human race as a whole. Perhaps we need to place a higher value on care while continuing to open up opportunities for women in areas traditionally dominated by men. But in so-called traditional communities with so-called traditional values, there was indeed a joy in caring. It should not be one's burden but one's delight to give care to the young and the old and the sick and the poor. Sometimes people may want to care, and our society is not structured to provide that opportunity.

We are reaching the end of the babyboomers' childbearing years. It will be 20 or 25 more years before *their* children enter the labor market in force. Studies indicate that between now and the year 2000, 85% of the projected 25 million new jobs will be filled by women, immigrants, and minorities because there won't be enough young white males to fill them. Given those demographics, it is not inconceivable that the concept of mandatory retirement at any age—or indeed, the concept of retirement itself—may fall by the wayside. The labor market will be forced to discover the talents and capabilities not only of women and minorities but also of older people. But these older people may not wish to continue in the same jobs or at the same pace. They may want to switch careers, to start a new second life. In more and more fields, employers are beginning to discover things like wisdom and experience, flexibility and responsibility. And they are finding these qualities in older workers. So they call them back to work or ask them to stay on as consultants or in other capacities that can put these "mature" qualities to good use in the market.

We need new kinds of employment policies. Abolishing forced retirement is only a very small part of that policy. We still have our age mystique blinders on when we expect people to want to continue working just as they worked when they were 20 or 30. There's a whole range of possibilities for more flexible working arrangements that will enable people to continue to participate productively in society without demanding that they maintain a rigid work pattern over their lives. It would seem to me that these policies would even be bottom-line beneficial, since they would supply a whole new resource at a time when the labor market is facing a serious worker shortage.

Let's go back to the question that is the title of this book and rephrase it. Who is responsible for my *good* old age? In the final analysis, I am responsible. My good old age is dependent upon my ability to keep myself human by continuing to operate within human society. How can I do this in my new adventurous period after 65? Sigmund Freud—who wasn't *always* wrong, however off the mark he may have been concerning what women want—said that the two most important things in life are love and work. Let us consider love in the years after 60. Is it merely an attempt to re-create the sexual romance of our twenties and thirties with ever younger partners? Or do we perhaps find newly emergent values of intimacy and bonding that keep us healthy and human long after our reproductive years have ended?

I began questioning our society's images of aging when seeking to discover why it is that women in advanced industrial societies live so much longer and so much more *vitally* than do men. Perhaps, I thought, we could use that information to work toward a model for affirming the personhood of all women. While looking into the research, especially the studies done by the National Institute on Aging and the National Institute of Mental Health, I began to find explanations for the sexual differences in longevity. Aside from tobacco use, the only thing that makes a real difference in the quality of one's later years is the number of social bonds one forms and maintains during life. Women seem to have a better capacity than men not only for sustaining the bonds formed in the past but for forming new bonds, new intimacies, to replace those lost in the course of a lifetime. Research shows that if a man's wife dies, he is more likely to die within two years of her death than other men of his age—*unless* he remarries. If he does remarry, his life expectancy returns to normal for his age. However, when a woman's husband dies, even though she is far less likely to remarry than is a man, her life expectancy is not reduced. Women are somehow able to form new intimate bonds, new friendships, and these sustain their life and health. By forming bonds of friendship and love outside those of the traditional family, a woman retains the capacity to operate humanly in human society long after sixty.

Every few months, we receive a new bulletin from the United States Census Bureau telling us that the percentage of American households in which the persons who live together are related by blood or marriage has declined by 20% in the past 40 years. Families now make up only about 70% of all households, down from ninety percent in 1948. And if we want to consider the *conventional* Western Nostalgia notion of the family, these families make up only seven percent of American households today. The largest increase is in the number of single-parent families, but there has also been a very large increase in the number of people—mostly women over 60—living alone. Many Americans live together without marriage; many others live in what are called *blended* families—her kids, his kids, their kids. We are only beginning to discover how those bonds are configured, what those families *look* like. There is a very interesting study being done at the University of Southern California on multigenerational vertical families of three, four, or even five generations. I recently had the privilege of talking with a young couple, not married, whose household consists of the woman, the man, and the man's grandmother.

But multigenerational living may not be the most satisfactory arrangement for a woman; living with one's children or one's grandchildren may simply reinforce the stereotypical image of a woman's life being defined by childrearing. The women I know don't suffer terrible pangs of despair when they turn around and find the old nest empty. They move on to the next big thing in their lives. Many of them do this by moving into roles, professions, and occupations that had once seemed to be exclusively the province of men. But *unlike* men, women in those professions are not dying young. They are saved by some other attunement to life that rises from their socialization within the family and the strength required of them within that family.

One area that has not been studied and that will have enormous importance in the decades ahead is the changing perception of the family, from one of blood and marital ties to one of choice. The bonds of intimacy and friendship, those very precious bonds that we make by *choice*, become as sustaining in our later years as our blood relationships or even more so. These bonds of choice must be nourished with the kind of care and commitment we had expected to give only to our children or parents. This nourishing of the bonds of choice is the kind of generativity that is characteristic of vital old age.

About 20 years ago, I found myself divorced, with two sons moved out and one little one at home. About this time, I formed a sort of commune arrangement with some friends, women and men, who were themselves in various states of nonmarriage. We ate together, fought together, and shared housework, Thanksgiving, Christmas, and Passover together. And we sustained each other. Some of us made new marriages and moved out; others moved on to other things. But despite the fact that we no longer share the same house, we remain close. Our experience, our *commitment* to each other, knit us together into a true family—a family of choice. Even today, my apartment in New York is known as the Friedan Hilton, open to those members of my now far-flung family of choice who need a place to stay. These bonds are what can provide the life-giving, life-sustaining support necessary for a vital old age.

The American Home Economics Association defines a family as two or more people who make a commitment to each other. They might not share the same living quarters, but they share a past and a future. They commit themselves to sharing resources and support, joys and sorrows. Your family means the people you come home to, even if you don't come home to them at five o'clock every day. They are your true community, that which sustains your humanity.

So the real challenge to us all, for the future, is to come up with economic, social, and political policies that will enable people to remain active and contributing members of a community at every age of their lives. These policies don't necessarily involve huge expenditures. Certainly they can't be as expensive as maintaining huge numbers of people in nursing homes. Simple measures, such as rezoning the suburbs so that the woman living alone in her big World War II–era single-family house can ask friends and family of whatever generation to share her home with her. These are creative measures, not expensive ones, measures that will make possible whole new kinds of family constellations beyond legal and blood ties. Not all of us will be as adventurous as some—I'm thinking especially of Maggie Kuhn of the Gray Panthers, with her huge multigenerational commune. But all of us need to break through our old metaphors, our old ways of conceiving family. Perhaps we can even erase the stigma of age segregation, as heretical as that may sound. Many of the people, women and men, who move into the so-called leisure worlds, the retirement communities, manage to forge incredibly strong peer-group connections. You'd be amazed at how many of them have found some work, some project that keeps them vital. I'm not attempting to vindicate old Sigmund when I repeat that he was not wrong in that respect: love and work are the two essentials of life. And work that you love, work that challenges you, that plumbs the very depths of your talents—that is what keeps you tuned in *productively* with all of society.

That view of old age—as a productive period in our lives—is a view that we resist in this society. Some years ago, I was working with James Birren and Robert Butler on a project called "Health, Productivity, and Aging," in Salzburg, Austria. Most of our colleagues on that project were drawn from government and the medical establishment, from many different countries. We were not meeting to discuss custodial care or nursing home policy or Alzheimer's disease. Instead, we wanted the focus of the project to be change—changes in the community, in labor and housing, in the nature and structure of the family—changes that would redefine productivity and enable people to continue as part of their communities long after age 65. But we found ourselves constantly being redirected to questions about nursing home policy and the social and financial burden of elder care. Why were we resisting the image of old age as a real period in the human life course? The answer was, or should have been, obvious.

We live in fear of our own old age. The only image we have of old age is one of sickness, of deterioration and decline, of loss of control, of physical and mental *decay*, and, ultimately, of death. That's the only "old age" we have in our youth-mad culture, where the greatest compliment anyone can get is "Oh, you certainly don't *look* forty or fifty or sixty or whatever!" Everywhere, we see the pretense that youth can last forever, that age can be, must be, denied for as long as possible. We see this in our advertising, where the only sign of age in the models is gray hair over an unlined face and trim, toned body. Age, we tell ourselves, is really youth. And that is part of the mystique of age. Because age is *not* youth, nor should it be. The people I've met who are most vital, who are moving and developing and growing and *doing* in the years after 60, are the people who *own* their age. They are interested in the fact of their aging and in the changes that accompany aging. These people don't deny that very real physical, social, and psychological changes are taking place—they *affirm* those changes. What others might see as short-term memory loss, they see as a shift from attention to detail to more holistic patterns of thinking, in which larger meanings take precedence over particulars. Suddenly, they are concerned, not with the chronological *fact* of old age but with the *personhood* of age.

Once we begin with that personhood of age, we ask many of the same questions, but we ask them differently. Questions about sexuality become not questions of loss or diminishment but of new possibilities for real intimacy, for the kind of sharing and caring that comes with maturity. Questions about work become questions about creativity and satisfaction. Even questions about health care are transformed when we think about old age in terms of personhood. The kind of health care we have now, that treats age as if it were in itself a pathology, is in danger of underdiagnosing the real ills of old age and also of underestimating its real strengths. We have to study our old age and find out what it really *is* and who we

really are in this wonderful period of our lives. We have to begin with the person and bring new standards of human interaction into our health care institutions. We have to see to it
that our health care policies foster purpose, and project, and
individuality. At every age, we have to begin to be responsible
for our own old age before we can begin to make policy for
anyone else. That means seeing the adventure that lies ahead
of us in these wonderful new years of life.

Old Age Policy as a Women's Issue

6

Takako Sodei

Care of the elderly has long been exclusively a women's issue. Everywhere in the world, the majority of caregivers, at home and in institutions, are women. In Japan, the normal life course of a woman has been to care for her children, her parents-in-law, and her husband and, finally, to be cared for by her own daughter-in-law. Recently, however, this care cycle, which once seemed so simple and natural to most Japanese, has become problematic. We need to discover why it has become difficult and where and how we might find solutions to this problem.

In advanced industrial societies such as the United States and Japan, women commonly outlive men. In Japan, the average life expectancy at birth in 1985 was 80.46 years for women and 74.84 years for men. The Japanese are the longest-lived people in the world. The Research Institute of Population Problems of the Ministry of Health and Welfare estimated in 1986 that life expectancy in the year 2000 will reach 82.69 years for women and 76.81 years for men. And according to the 1985 National Census, among people 65 years or older, the ratio of females to males was 1.44 to 1; among people 85 years or older, that ratio was 2.07 to 1.

The percentage of the elderly population that is bedridden or senile increases with age: among people 75 years or older it

73

exceeds 10% and the percentage of those who are bedridden *and* female is higher than that of males. Therefore, based on these numbers, it is estimated that there are many more bedridden and/or senile women than men.

In Japan, people 65 years or older now comprise about 11% of the total population. In many Western nations, that ratio is higher than in Japan, but the Japanese population is aging more rapidly than that of any other industrialized nation. The doubling of the proportion of people 65 and older took 115 years in France, 85 years in Sweden, and 75 years in the United States. In Japan, a similar increase took only 25 years! The Research Institute has estimated that by the year 2020, nearly one of four Japanese will be over 65. No other nation in the world will have such a large "gray" population.

It is important that we recognize the age distribution among the elderly themselves. The numbers of the old-old, that is, people over 75, are increasing rapidly. It is estimated that in the year 2025, when the baby boom generation reaches old-old age, there will be more people over 75 than people in the 65- to 74-year (or young-old) range. And women are "graying" faster than men: the numbers of old-old women will exceed the numbers of young-old women by 2020, five years earlier than the general population.

Continued improvements in sanitation, nutrition, and medical treatment are likely to reduce the percentage of elderly who will be bedridden and/or senile. Nevertheless, the *numbers* will increase because the old-old will be represented in such large numbers in the population.

Today it is estimated that there are about 600,000 bedridden elders and 600,000 senile elders in Japan. Unless the percentage of bedridden and/or senile elders decreases, by the turn of the century, over 2 million elderly will be bedridden, senile, or both. And most of these "care recipients" will be women.

Care of the elderly, along with housework and care of children and the sick, has long been women's province. H. Graham (1983), in "Caring: A Labour of Love," noted that the demands of caregiving are shaped by the social relations within the larger society. In societies with clearly defined gender-role divisions, caregiving has a profound impact on the identity and activity of the women in that society.

The 1984 Basic Survey for the Health and Welfare Administration in Japan indicated that the primary caregivers for male bedridden elders at home were wives (74%), daughters-in-law (15%), and daughters (6%). For bedridden elderly women, caregivers consisted of daughters-in-law (59%), daughters (18%), and husbands (10%). In the United States, wives were the primary caregivers for men, with daughters the next largest group. For women, daughters were the primary caregivers, followed by husbands. Daughters-in-law made up an insignificant proportion of the caregivers for either men or women in the United States (Stone, Caferate, & Sangl, 1987).

Both care of children and care of elders constitute unpaid work situated within the small world of the family circle. But, at least in Japan, care of children and care of elders are not perceived in the same way. A mother's care for her children is, ideally, based on love and affection. But a daughter or daughter-in-law caring for an elderly parent or parent-in-law in the home is bound not only by ties of love but also by filial and social obligation. And unlike childcare, which is oriented toward the future, eldercare is marked by the care-recipient's increasing frailty and dependence and ultimately by his or her death. A woman who wants a career outside the home may feel constrained by her child-rearing responsibilities, but at least she can look forward to the day when her children no longer need her constant presence. However, caring for an elder has no predictable end, especially given the new longevity. Compared with childrearing, care of the elderly carries a heavier physical and psychological burden for a woman.

Why do women—why *should* women—comprise the overwhelming majority of caregivers in Japan? Even today, 90% of those caring for bedridden elderly are women, most of them middle-aged housewives. What is it about the perceived social role of women that forces them into that role in such numbers? We often talk about "traditional sex role differentiation": men earn the money; women manage the household. But women's alienation from productive work is a rather recent phenomenon. In preindustrial Japan, both production and consumption occurred mainly in the home. The family was the basic economic unit, with husbands, wives, and children working together in order to survive.

It was only after the industrial revolution, when production was transferred from the home to the factory, that men and women began to work in separate, gender-bound spheres. In the Edo period, from the 17th to the 19th century, common wisdom held that "the husband is responsible for things outside the home, and the wife is responsible for things inside the home." This was regarded as the ideal division of labor in the upper-class samurai family, though such rigid sex-related role differentiation was not usually found among the lower classes. Poor rural men and women worked side by side to achieve a subsistence living.

After World War I, the rise of capitalism removed production from the home for all classes. Men were transformed into wage earners, while their wives stayed at home as full-time homemakers. Women were once again chiefly responsible for caring for children and old people. This work, however important it might seem, was not highly valued, since it took place privately, without being evaluated by others. And, of course, women earned no money for such labor. In a capitalist society, nonremunerative work has no value.

Beyond traditional sex roles (which, as we have seen, have a very short "tradition"), the ideology of the patrilineal stem family system, which grants the status of family head to men and utter dependence to women, persists even in many highly industrialized societies. In Japan this system continues to be the ideal for many people even though it was legally abolished after World War II.

The idea that a woman's proper role is that of a homemaker dependent on the male head of the household has profound consequences for all our lives. Our wage, promotion, tax, and social security systems are all still based on the "ideal" household headed by a wage-earning male. The status of women in the work force has always been affected by the perception that a woman's "normal and proper" position is that of dependency. Thus, women are expected to stop working whenever a family member becomes sick or physically impaired.

In Japan, the patrilineal family system, known as _Ie_, stresses the subjugation of women to men, young to old, and daughter-in-law to mother-in-law. It is the force behind the pressures on women to take on the role of caregivers. Those men and women who have internalized the ideologies of sex-role division and _Ie_ expect women to "naturally" accept this role. Relatives, friends, neighbors, employers, colleagues at work, doctors, and even social workers, all expect a woman to quit working and stay at home if someone in her family needs care. Daughters-in-law especially are subject to these pressures, given the special obligation they have toward parents-in-law.

Feminine identity has been largely shaped by the interaction of sex-role differentiation, _Ie_, and the expectations of society. Even women who are under no pressure from friends or family may "voluntarily" take on caregiving. It is natural for a woman to do so, they will say; they would feel guilty if they were to be so selfish and uncaring as to neglect their duties. Better to give up one's career than to be such an unnatural, undutiful woman. The role of caring is "given" to women (Graham, 1983). It defines their lives and their work. At the same time, caring is taken away from men; _not_ caring constitutes part of the definition of manhood.

Recently, however, there has been a radical change in the attitudes of many women toward caring for frail elders. A recent study by the Center for Development of Welfare for the Aged (1987) indicates that if a bedridden elder has a living spouse, then a daughter-in-law, even one living in the same house, is _not_ likely to be the primary caregiver. And those daughters or daughters-in-law who _are_ primary caregivers now often express the fatalistic attitude of _Shikataganai_: "There is no other way, even though I would like to escape from the present situation." Some women, the study suggests, simply cannot see themselves solely in the role of caregivers. Such attitudes present a serious challenge to the government's recent campaign to promote home family care for the elderly. So, in many societies, including Japan, people would prefer to be cared for at home when they become old and frail. Families may also wish to keep their elders at home for as long as possible. However, "aging at home" has become increasingly problematic because of drastic changes at the societal and family level.

There is a perception in Japanese society that all frail elders are receiving their basic care at home from family members. Based on a survey of patients and social welfare institutions conducted by the Ministry of Health and Welfare, Hideo Koyama (1986) estimated that, in 1983, 6% of those over 65 were in hospitals, nursing homes, or other institutions. The percentage of elders living with their children has been steadily, if slowly, decreasing. The percentage of those over 80 living with their children or with other relatives has, on the other hand, been declining much more rapidly, from 94% in 1973 to 88% in 1983.

What might account for this decline in home care? Several factors in recent Japanese history would seem to present serious challenges to caring for frail elders at home. The first factor is demographic change. After World War II, Japan experienced a high birthrate and a high death rate. Between 1933 and 1937, the average birthrate was 30.8 per thousand, while the average death rate was 17.4 per thousand. Just after the war, a steep rise in the birthrate, the so-called baby boom, was matched by a correspondingly precipitous *drop* in the death rate. Between 1947 and 1949, the average birthrate was 33.6 per thousand, while the death rate dropped to 12.7 per thousand. The resultant increase in the population was followed by sharp decreases in *both* the birth and death rates. In 1985, the birthrate was 11.9 per thousand, and the death rate was only 6.3 per thousand. Naturally, such a steep fall in both birth and death rates dramatically affects the proportion of potential caregivers to those in potential need of care. Before World War II, the average couple had five children. Under *Ie*, the responsibility for the care of the parents in their old age usually fell to the wife of the first son. Today, the average couple has two children, and more and more couples are opting to have only one child. If an only child should marry, he or she may wind up caring for *four* elderly adults. And if those adults also have parents still living (which will become even more likely as life expectancy and the number of old-old persons increase), an only child could wind up with the responsibility for caring for *eight* grandparents as well.

According to the Survey on Care for Frail Elders (Management and Coordination Agency, 1987), among those 60 years or older, 44% of male respondents and 66.5% of female respondents had some experience in caring for frail elders. Men usually took care of their own parents, while women usually took care of their husband's parents as well as their own. Recently, it seems that women, at least, have reached a new stage of increased responsibility for care of elderly parents. Until about 1950, average life expectancy in Japan was only about 50 years. Only a few people ever had to face the possibility of a lifetime of care for elderly parents. The new demographics have made elder care a potential reality for everyone, male and female.

Because of improvements in nutrition and housing and advances in medical treatment, even the frailest elders can expect to live long lives. In 1984, the Health and Welfare Administration estimated that one quarter of all bedridden elderly have been in that condition for more than five years; some reported having been bedridden for more than ten years! It is no longer uncommon for an elderly person to live for twenty years after the onset of serious chronic illness. It is certainly reasonable to expect, then, that the numbers of very old bedridden and/or senile elders will continue to increase.

This increased longevity of frail elders makes it very difficult for the family to continue to keep them at home, especially as the caregivers themselves age and become subject to the same illnesses and limitations of old age that plague their parents. About one-fourth of all caretakers of bedridden elderly are themselves over 60. And a National Association of

Democratic Doctors (1983) survey estimated that in 1982–1983, among all caregivers of bedridden elders, more than a quarter were suffering from chronic illness, while an additional 10% reported that they "did not feel well" but had no time to see a doctor. Occasionally, care recipients were predeceased by their caregivers.

CHANGES IN THE FAMILY

One of the biggest cultural, social, and demographic upheavals in Japan is taking place within the family itself. The declining birthrate, with a corresponding reduction in the size of families, has been accompanied by an increase in geographical mobility—especially movement out of rural areas and into the cities—and a resulting shortage of housing in urban areas. Taken together, these changes have led to a decrease in the percentage of those over 65 who are still living with their children or grandchildren. In 1960, nearly 90% of all elders lived at home with children or grandchildren. By 1985, less than 66% were in such shared living arrangements, and it is estimated that by the year 2000, only half of all elders will live with children or grandchildren. The percentage of elders living only with a spouse (who may or may not be elderly) has increased markedly, from 7% in 1960 to over 20% in 1985. And the percentage of elderly persons living *alone* has risen from less than 6% in 1960 to nearly 14% in 1985. By the year 2000, one-fifth of all elders will be living alone, with an additional 30% living only with his or her spouse.

Rapid industrialization, urbanization, and economic growth have contributed to the shift away from traditional living arrangements and traditional home and family care for elderly persons. Japan's booming economy led to an increased number of jobs in the manufacturing, service, and information sectors, which absorbed much of the labor from the so-called primary industries like fishing and agriculture. Young people began to move out of rural areas and into the cities, following the secondary and tertiary industries of manufacturing, service, and information. Even only sons left the family home to live and work in the cities. Many old people found themselves alone, "abandoned" in remote rural areas.

Industrialization, modernization, and urbanization seem to have had an impact on attitudes toward both family and living arrangements. In urban areas, since there is no longer a family farm or property to keep together, sons feel little obligation to live with their parents. Both young and old people living in the cities express a preference for privacy and for the opportunity to enjoy their own lives, free from the demands of the other generation. However, many older persons also say that, when they become ill or are widowed, they would like to be able to move in with their children. Their vision of their final years is colored by the ideology of *Ie* and a desire to maintain the tradition of multigenerational living. But because the generations are no longer living and working together, parents often discover that their children no longer share their cultural values. Modern capitalist society values achievement, independence, and privacy; people living under this system tend to become more self-oriented and less family-oriented.

The severe shortage of adequate housing in urban areas has also contributed to the recent decline in multigenerational living arrangements. The high cost of land makes it difficult for young couples even to think of owning their own houses, and low-cost public housing tends to be situated away from the cities. Recently, the Japanese housing industry has begun to sell what are known as "two-family houses," which allow two families to live under the same roof, but with separate facilities. The Japanese Housing Loan Corporation also offers a special "two-generation loan," with an extended term of payments to be passed on from father to son. Such measures may encourage multigenerational living, but in the metropolitan areas, land for the construction of new housing is very scarce. Usually, only those who already own land will be able to build two-family houses or remodel existing housing to accommodate two families or several generations of one family.

Industrialization also moved many functions out of the home, transferring production to the factory, education to the schools, security to the police, and so on. As more and more women began to work outside the home after the 1960s, even more of those chores that had been the province of the home were moved out into the world of work. Much of what had been considered "housework" has been shifted to the service industry. People eat in restaurants and fast-food places, buy ready-made clothing, send out their clothes to be laundered or dry-cleaned, hire housecleaning services, and leave their children in "baby hotels." Women, having loosened their dominion over housework and childrearing, are sometimes perceived as having given up their only power in the home. Some older women complain that this has weakened their own power over their daughters-in-law. Conflicts between daughters-in-law (*yome*) and their mothers-in-law (*shutome*) are common and are, in fact, a popular theme of Japanese TV soap operas.

One of the most important functions of the traditional family was the support of elderly parents. Before World War II, older people were respected by their families, not only because their knowledge and skills were valuable but also because the Confucian idea of filial piety shaped the attitudes and behavior of Japanese people. Filial piety and responsibility* were continually stressed, and children internalized the concept in the course of their moral education, in the home and at school. The patrilineal stem family system of *Ie*, which originated in the *Edo* period among the upper-class samurai, was characterized by a powerful male family head, low status for women, respect for elders, and ancestor worship. Perpetuation of the family lineage, the task of the family head and his

Editor's note: Sodei has defined filial responsibility as "adult offsprings' obligations to meet the need of their aging parents." This usually involves shared living arrangements as well as physical, emotional, and financial support (T. Sodei, *The Effect of Industrialization and Modernization on Filial Responsibility Toward Aging Parents: A Comparative Study*, Paper presented at the 5th Asian Regional Conference of Sociology, Seoul, Korea, Dec. 3–4, 1987).

heir, had priority over all concerns about individual happiness and fulfillment.

The family heir, usually the first son, inherited the entire property. In turn, *Ie* obliged the heir to live with his parents, to support them financially, and to care for them in their infirmity. The family heir learned his future responsibility in his earliest childhood and was usually treated differently from the other children. He knew his obligations, and his parents were secure in the knowledge that they could depend on him for full support in their old age.

The Meiji Civil Code of 1898 mandated priorities for support within the family: the first priority was support of the male head-of-household's parents, followed by support of his children, and, lastly, support of his wife. After World War II, the American Occupation Forces, and some Japanese, felt that *Ie* helped to create the social and psychological conditions for Japanese militarism and emperor worship. Ultimately, the system was legally abolished.

In 1946 and 1947, the new Japanese Constitution and the amended Civil Code changed the legal definition of the family. From the patrilineal family of the *Ie* system, the ideal type of family was changed to that of the conjugal family, based on the legal equality of husband and wife. The provision for marriage in the 1947 constitution states: "Marriage shall be based only on mutual consent of both sexes and shall be maintained through mutual cooperation with the equal rights of both husband and wife as a basis."

Family property was to be divided equally among all children, regardless of sex or birth order. Therefore, the obligation to support parents in their old age fell on all children equally. The Meiji code of priorities of support within the family was also restructured. The family head's first obligation now was to his spouse and minor children, followed, in descending order of obligation, by other close kin, such as parents, siblings, uncles and aunts, and nieces and nephews. Even if his financial resources are very limited, a man is legally obligated, at the very least, to support his wife and minor children. In other words, every man is obliged to support his nuclear family, even if that means that he must lower his own standard of living and give up his own pleasures. However, he is *not* obligated to impoverish himself or even to lower his living standard in order to support his parents. Elderly parents can demand financial support from their children only if those children have money to spare. Some experts have recently advised amending the present Civil Code so that elderly parents will have the same legally mandated priority as minor children.

Although the *Ie* system was legally abolished, many people maintained the traditional structure within their homes. Until the 1960s, the first son still succeeded his father in the family business, inherited most of the property, and, usually, lived with his parents. The idea that the first son was morally obliged to live with his parents and perpetuate the family lineage persisted until the recent period of rapid economic growth raised the per capita income, permitting a level of financial independence for the majority of Japanese.

Until 1960, more than half of Japan's labor force was composed of self-employed workers, most of them in the primary industries, such as farming. As the decade advanced, it became more and more difficult to support a family in an agricultural community, and many first sons joined the emigration to the cities. Public education campaigns and the mass media stressed the rights and obligation of all children, not just first sons, to inherit property and care for elderly parents. As the pressures to be sole support for their parents were diminished, many more men were willing to leave their parents behind in the villages. Men became more concerned with their obligations within the nuclear family, and the *Ie* tradition of filial piety seemed to erode. Few Japanese today are willing to sacrifice themselves in order to meet the needs of their parents.

In addition to legal changes and the pressures of industrialization, modernization, and urbanization, Western ideas, especially American concepts of democracy and individualism, have shaped modern Japanese attitudes toward the family. Young people especially have internalized a "me first" attitude through exposure to Westernized education and images of Western society in the mass media, and they tend to express mostly negative feelings toward any suggestions of self-sacrifice or absolute obedience to parental authority.

The traditional family of *Ie* might be likened to a little, self-contained world in which most of its members' needs were met. Today, there are all sorts of agencies and services available to satisfy these very same needs. Many people still express the sentiment that the family is the center of their lives, while their behavior demonstrates a willingness to sacrifice family relations to the pursuit of their own needs or aspirations. The least powerful members of society, children and the elderly, are most affected by these changes in attitude and behavior.

OLD AGE AS A WOMEN'S ISSUE

Nearly 90% of all caregivers in Japan are women. If the frail elder at home is a male, his wife is most likely to be the primary caregiver; if the elder is female, caregiving usually falls to a daughter or daughter-in-law. At the present time, most caregivers are middle-aged housewives. However, the increased participation of women in the labor force and changes in attitudes toward the family and the elderly combine to make family care at home increasingly burdensome.

Until recently, the average Japanese working woman was a young, single woman. In 1955, 69% of employed women were under 30, and 65% were single. By 1985, however, nearly 38% of all women working outside the home were over 40, and nearly 60% were married, with another 10% divorced or widowed. This "graying" of the female labor pool has its roots in declining birthrates and increased levels of education. During the period of the most rapid economic growth, secondary and tertiary industries solicited the "woman's touch," as well as women's cheaper labor. In addition to this strong "pull" from the labor market, other factors contributed to "push" women out of the home and into the workplace. Needless to say, inflation pushed the hardest. Inflation had made the cost of educating children and of building or buying a house an enormous drag on the household economy. Women who had previously found their work inside the home were forced out of the home and into the wage market.

Another "push" was the increase in women's leisure time. Electrical appliances like refrigerators, washing machines, and vacuum cleaners considerably reduced the amount of time and energy consumed by housework. Women were looking for ways to fill up spare time their mothers had never known. The world outside the domestic arena looked inviting. Economic need supplied the motivation. Now many woman also had the time to work outside the home and receive a paycheck.

A third factor pushing women into the work force was the changing female life cycle. Women born in 1905 married at an average age of 23, had five children by the time they were 40. Most women died before the youngest child had left the home. Women born in 1927, who reached marital age after World War II, also married, on average, at 23 , but finished having their smaller families (average, three children) by the time they were 30. By the time these women were 40, their younger children were in school and no longer required all their time. Women born in 1959, at the end of the baby boom, married, on average, at 25, and had an average of two children by the age of 29 (Ministry of Labor, 1986). Women spent fewer and fewer years engaged in child rearing, and the period of time between the last child's entrance into school and the onset of a woman's menopause has grown much longer. It seems only natural that many married women would begin to seek roles other than those of wife and mother.

As more women reached ever-higher levels of education, their expectations for a fulfilling career began to rise. The mass media also projected many images of smart, glamorous, well-traveled women engaged in exciting, fulfilling careers. Given the new cultural stereotypes, it would be difficult for a modern Japanese woman to be completely satisfied with the role of wife and mother. Today's Japanese woman wants it all, the opportunity to use her mind and talents and the opportunity to earn money she can spend on herself.

While many middle-aged married women hold part-time jobs, at low wages, they seem to enjoy their work and their associations with their colleagues. As long as her annual income does not exceed 900,000 yen, a woman can continue to be claimed as her husband's dependent and will not have to pay any income tax on her earnings. A dependent wife can also be covered by her husband's health insurance and pension plan.

In recent years, many day-care centers for children were built because employers needed women workers and because various women's groups pressured local governments to provide public day care. However, there are not very many day-care centers for the elderly, and those that exist take care of elderly persons only one or two days a week, for about five or six hours each day. A woman who works full-time must find other resources for the rest of the week. The shortage of adequate care facilities for the elderly, combined with strong pressures on women to live up to their "responsibilities," causes many women to quit their jobs or take leaves of absence in order to devote themselves to the full-time care of their parents or in-laws.

Not all women are so willing to give up their careers to spend all their time caring for frail elders. Many women, especially younger and more highly educated ones, resist the pressures to care personally for their parents or in-laws and instead depend on social services for daily care (National Life Center, 1981; Yokohama City, 1984). However, the government has lately begun to increase pressure on housewives to keep elders at home in order to reduce federal and local government expenditures for health care and welfare.

In 1987, the Japanese federal government introduced a special tax deduction for full-time homemakers. Some local governments offer a special allowance to caregivers or hold special ceremonies honoring daughters-in-law who have devoted many years of their lives to caring for bedridden elders at home. However, these measures have not yet achieved the government's desired effect of stemming the movement of women into the labor force and keeping them at home. Other approaches are needed, ones that will recognize women's double burden of work and family *and* their contribution to the nation's continued economic growth. We need laws and policies that will enable family care to coexist with work responsibilities.

In the traditional agricultural community, where the same families lived and worked together for a long time, people knew their neighbors and were willing to go to great lengths to help those in need. Urbanization and geographical mobility have contributed to the weakening of these traditional community ties. In Japan, especially during the 1960s, there was widespread migration to the cities, while many rural areas were urbanized. People began to rely on paid services rather than community relationships to meet their needs. In the traditional community, when someone became ill, neighbors helped out with housework, shopping, and child care. Today, even in rural areas, there are few housewives left to act as "helping hands." So frail elders often have to rely on social services for daily care.

Many of those who were brought up under the *Ie* system continue in the belief that parents have the right to demand that their children take care of them and that daughters-in-law are the only proper caregivers for the elderly. Women in their fifties and sixties often express the fear that they will never be able to depend on their children and that their daughters-in-law are too involved with careers to live up to their "responsibilities," even when they have their mothers-in-law living with them.

In fairness to working daughters-in-law, it must be admitted that many Japanese elders refuse to do even the most basic tasks for themselves, even when they are perfectly capable of doing so. Instead, they demand that their daughters-in-law wait on them. Some women, fearful of the censure of their husbands or neighbors, give in and wait on their parents-in-law. This perception on the part of many Japanese elders—that a state of utter dependence upon their children is right and proper—may help to explain why Japan has such a high percentage of bedridden elders, compared to the United States (U.S. Senate, 1986).

HOUSING CONDITIONS

The average Japanese house is very small, built on multiple levels with many stairs. It is very difficult for those who are wheelchair-bound to live independently in one of these houses. Also, since most Japanese houses traditionally have paper screens instead of plaster walls, it is nearly impossible to equip a house with handrails for those who have difficulty walking. Heating is also generally poor, and many elderly suffer from hypothermia. Specialists in housing point out that poor housing conditions exacerbate many of the chronic illnesses of the elderly and thus add to the numbers of bedridden and hospitalized elders.

The overreliance of many elderly persons on hospitals for basic health care presents an enormous problem, as well as a huge expense, for the Japanese government. The average hospital stay in Japan is 48.7 days (in 1984), compared to a third of that time in France and West Germany. A survey of elderly hospital patients in 1985 revealed that more than half of them had been in the hospital for six months or longer.

Why do so many old people spend so much time in the hospital? There is a very simple explanation for this: hospitalization is cheap. Japan's National Health Insurance covers most of the hospital fees; patients' costs usually consist only of a very small co-payment. Also, while there is a social stigma attached to placing an aging parent in a nursing home, it is considered properly responsible and respectful to send them to hospitals. Hospitals are also seen by many elderly persons as a healthy alternative to poor or overcrowded housing. And, oddly enough, the fiercely competitive Japanese educational system contributes to the increasing reliance of the elderly on hospitals. When one of the children in a family is studying for the very competitive secondary school entrance examinations, parents often send the child's grandparent to the hospital, so that the child can use the grandparent's room as a study area. Parents will even ask the family doctor to keep a grandparent hospitalized until the child has passed the examination.

SOLUTIONS

We have seen, in recent years, a worldwide trend toward the promotion of family home care and community care for elders and away from government-funded institutional care. Japan faces the prospect of unprecedentedly large numbers of very old people in this and the next century. The government of Japan is especially eager to reduce its expenditures for health and welfare for the elderly and is vigorously pursuing its campaign to get families to take care of their elders at home. But "home care" does not *have* to mean "daughter-in-law care." Though many women still feel a strong sense of filial obligation toward their aging parents and/or parents-in-law, they no longer wish to sacrifice their lives and careers to them—nor should they. Most women would prefer to supplement home care with community services. Home help services, visiting nurses, short-term stays at nursing homes or intermediate care centers, day-care services, and bathing services (unique to Japan!)—all can help to relieve the burden on caregivers. Most of these services are subsidized by local and/or national government.

In order to expand services without increasing expenditures and to strengthen community ties, many local governments have established "paid volunteer" systems. People who need help with basic care and those who wish to offer their labor register with a membership clearinghouse. A full-time staff, whose salaries are paid by the local government, administers the system. User fees vary according to the service rendered. Housekeeping may cost 600–700 yen per hour, while bathing an infirm elder costs 1,000 yen per hour. Part of the fee goes to the organization, to cover administrative costs. A "volunteer" may also turn the entire fee over to the organization, in order to build up "credit" against the time he or she needs care.

"Paid volunteering" is not full-time work, and it operates outside the ordinary labor market. The volunteers, mostly middle-aged housewives, receive no pension or health insurance, though they are insured against work-related accidents. However, like part-time working wives, they may retain their status as their husbands' dependents. Most of the women who work as "paid volunteers" don't do it for the money. Volunteers' pay is often well below the local minimum wage. Instead, volunteer work is promoted as a way for middle-aged housewives to find personal fulfillment in their "empty nest" years. There is even some debate as to whether volunteers should be paid at all. Needless to say, it is dangerous to women to create a pool of cheap female labor. It reduces the average income of women, and it might be used to justify lower wages for women generally. But housewives don't always find it easy to get permission from their husbands or mothers-in-law to devote their time to helping others without a paycheck to show for their labors. Volunteerism in Japan is still at a very primitive stage, and volunteer work is not valued socially.

Volunteerism is a difficult concept to "sell" in Japan. Family and kinship ties were traditionally very strong, and problems were usually dealt with within the family or kin group. It was (and still is) considered very shameful to discuss family problems outside the kin group. The stigma attached to exposing one's family's affairs to public scrutiny makes it difficult for Japanese to create support networks beyond the boundaries of blood relationships.

MEN'S ISSUES

All over the world, caring is woman's work. But as societies age, the numbers of available caregivers will not keep pace with the numbers of those needing care. In the next century, when one out of every four Japanese will be 65 or older, it will be increasingly common for couples to find themselves caring for four parents, and some may find themselves responsible for eight grandparents. It is physically impossible for one woman to take care of all these elders at home. Necessarily, even inevitably, Japanese men will have to take up their fair share of the burden and participate in caregiving.

One barrier to men's participation in caregiving is the structure of the workplace. Japanese men work long, hard hours to earn their salaries and rarely take full weekends off. Many even feel guilty taking their scheduled paid vacations. Japanese men for the most part do not share housework or involve themselves in domestic matters. They are often alienated from other family members, spending very little time with them. Japanese husbands are often derisively (or perhaps pityingly) called "boarders" or "salary-carrying robots." In order to encourage men to participate in family affairs and caregiving, the workplace will have to be restructured to give men more time away from their jobs to spend at home.

However, shorter hours will not automatically increase men's participation in caregiving unless their attitudes toward the sexual division of labor undergo a radical shift. Some men will not help their wives with any kind of "women's work" because they see it as degrading. Changes in attitudes are always more difficult to effect than changes in institutions. It will take a long time and a great deal of work before we can achieve a society in which men and women share family responsibilities equally.

At this historical point, many women continue to give up careers in order to care for elders. Responding to a government survey, many said that such policies as flex time and paid care-taking leaves would ease some of the burden on women who needed to care for elderly parents but wished to continue working. Only a very small number of companies and local governments offer any kind of special leave for employees who must take care of sick family members. These leaves usually range from three days to six months—without pay. The Ministry of Labor is trying to encourage companies to offer such leave, but it will be difficult. Even when the ministry subsidized special maternity leaves for up to one year after birth, such policies were not popular with business, and many companies still don't offer such leave.

The government is also seeking to reduce its role in providing social services. Until the oil crisis of 1973, the Japanese government seemed to be heading toward the establishment of a welfare state. But as the economy began to weaken, the government sought to shift the burden of social services from the public sector to the private sector. Without higher taxes, the government cannot continue to provide adequate services to the ever-increasing numbers of frail elders living in Japan.

Today, many companies have begun to provide home help services, visiting nurses, bathing services, or wheelchair rentals to their employees. At first, most of these were smaller companies, but even some large corporations and American subsidiaries are participating in this "silver market." It seems inevitable that we will have to rely more and more on the private sector for the provision of many social services. In this case, we will have to demand regulations to control the quality and cost of these services. In 1987, the Ministry of Health and Welfare authorized a special office that deals exclusively with commercialized services for the elderly. Under this office's guidance, the Association of Private Sectors to Control and Promote Services for the Elderly was instituted that same year.

Japan is also gradually coming to realize the importance of caring for our caregivers. Caregivers are often isolated from the rest of the community. They have no time of their own to socialize with friends and neighbors, and studies indicate that friends, neighbors, and even relatives rarely visit homes where frail elders live. Caregivers' welfare has long been neglected or ignored because so many people, women as well as men, still believe that caregiving is woman's lot. We are only now beginning to appreciate the need for respite care and care for caregivers. Bathing and day-care services, or even short-term stays in nursing homes for the frail elderly, go a long way toward relieving some of the physical, psychological, and emotional burden on caregivers. Informal support groups, such as the Association of Families of Senile Elders and the Association of Families of Bedridden Elders, have branches in many cities. These self-help networks, a new concept for the Japanese, seem to be quite effective in providing needed information and emotional support for caregivers and their families.

According to all projections, there will be enormous numbers of bedridden and senile elders at the beginning of the next century. It will be impossible—and unfair—to expect that Japanese housewives will be able to provide adequate care for all of our frail elders. It is likely that there will be increasing numbers of households with two or more bedridden or senile elders cared for by an only child and his/her spouse. So who *will* be responsible for my old age, for *everyone*'s old age? Shouldn't the responsibility be shared, not only within the family but within the community and the larger society? Right now, government, business, and individuals share the financial support of the elderly in the form of public pensions. It is time to put new systems of support into place that will enable us to distribute fairly the responsibility for caring for all our elderly. We must establish a "care-sharing" society, and in order to do so, we will have to change our systems of education and employment and, most of all, our system of values. In the 20th century, caregiving is truly a women's issue. Our plan for the 21st century must be to make it *everybody*'s issue.

REFERENCES

Brody, E. M. (1981). Women in the middle and family help to older people. *Gerontologist, 21*(5), 471–480.

Center for Development of Welfare for the Aged. (1987). Study on care and household economy of the seriously impaired elderly at home. The Center for Development of Welfare for the Aged, Tokyo.

Graham, H. (1983). "Caring: A labour of love," in J. Finah & D. Groves (Eds.), *A labour of love: Women, work and caring.* London: Routledge and Kegan Paul.

Koyama, H. (1986). *Trends of intermediate care facilities.* Chuohoki-shuppan.

Management and Coordination Agency. (1987). *Survey on care for frail elders.* Government Printing Office, Tokyo.

Ministry of Labor. (1986). The present status on working women. Government Printing Office, Tokyo.

National Association of Democratic Doctors. (1983). Report of the survey on old people living alone and bedridden. National Association of Democratic Doctors, Tokyo.

National Life Center. (1981). Survey of housewives attitude toward their old age. National Life Center, Tokyo.

Stone, R., Caferate, G. L., & Sangl, J. (1987). Caregivers of the frail elderly: A national profile. *Gerontologist, 27*(5), 616–626.

U.S. Senate Special Committee on Aging. (1986). *Development in aging* (Vol. 51), Government Printing Office, Washington, D.C.

Yokohama City. (1984). Survey on work and life of women in Yokohama City. Yokahama City, Japan.

From Curing to Caring to Sharing: Competing for a Better Old Age

7

Keiko Higuchi

There is a bright side as well as a dark side to the graying of a nation's population. Our goal must be to further brighten the bright side and to illuminate our darkness, to gain insight into those shadowy areas of old age. We must create a healthy environment in which to expand opportunities for a healthy and independent later life, for what I call a "double-crop life." We must abandon our obsession with and orientation toward youth and move toward a more diversified and mature society, in which each person is an active, contributing member and is appreciated for his or her unique qualities. American senior citizens have given the world a shining example of civic and political activitism. In Japan, we have not yet reached that same level of involvement, but many older people are expanding the scope of their activities beyond mere hobbies to occupy idle time and are moving into various community service activities, such as visiting those who are bedridden at home or in hospitals.

One of the key concepts in this topic is the movement of our societies from curing to caring to sharing. Curing—that is, effective medical treatment for the illnesses and disabilities that can accompany old age—is, of course, indispensable, but many older persons' illnesses are impossible to cure completely. Therefore, the elderly appreciate heartfelt caring beyond the simple promise of cure. After curing and caring, the next stage in our evolution is *sharing*. By that I mean that everyone in a society shares the responsibility of caring for the frail elderly. There are many kinds of sharing and cooperation. There is the collaboration between the public sector and the private sector, between the family and the community, between central government and local government, and between the sexes. At a recent OECD Social Welfare Summit Meeting, the Japanese delegation stressed the importance of successful social welfare policy. While it is true that the Japanese put a large percentage of their income into savings and that we value self-sufficiency, we realize that it is crucial that government provide us with a basic structure for dealing with a rapidly aging population. The Japanese National Women's Group for the Improvement of the Aging Society (Koreika Shakai wo Yokusuru Josei no Kai) has made the following recommendations to the government:

1. The Japanese government must establish a Ministry of Aging. We also recommend that the minister should be a qualified *woman*. Women have for so long been the primary caregivers for the elderly that it would be a shame to let this enormous fund of practical experience and expertise go untapped.

2. The government should draft a Declaration of Basic Human Rights for the Aged. The fact that the elderly are recipients of the government's "largess" must in no way abrogate their rights to full expression and freedom in our society.

3. New kinds of jobs will have to be created for those whose task it will be to serve the needs of the elderly. We will rely on our manpower (and, of course, our *woman*power) to cope with our graying society.

4. The government must establish a *national* health and retirement insurance program that will serve every citizen regardless of his or her employment history.

5. Internship with a social welfare agency should be made a mandatory part of civil service training.

6. To encourage volunteerism, government should work with the private sector to provide community service leave for all employees in all corporations.

7. The government should establish senior home-care centers in each school district. One hundred years ago, the Japanese were able to establish a nationwide primary school system despite the meager resources available at that time. I am optimistic that we can do the same to establish a nationwide network of senior service centers.

8. The Japanese educational system should revise its core curriculum to incorporate community service and education for and about old age. Our students should learn about senior citizens' rights, the pension system, and social welfare benefits in the schools. Above all, they must learn that old age is an integral part of the life course and that responsibility is an intergenerational issue.

I'd like to focus for now on the government's role in fostering shared responsibility for our elders between the sexes. In Japan, women's wages are still far lower than men's, with the average woman earning only 51% of a man's income. A household headed by a single female parent has an income of only 40% to 50% of that of the average Japanese household. Remarriage after divorce is still fairly uncommon in Japan, so a divorced woman is unlikely to be able to improve her economic status through marriage. Add to the already low wages of divorced women the fact that they save less of their income than most Japanese do and rarely own property, and it becomes clear that most of our divorced women are facing the prospect of an impoverished old age. While the divorce rate in Japan is still relatively low, it is slowly but steadily rising. This trend is, unfortunately, likely to continue as women increase their participation in the labor force. And a higher divorce rate means that a greater percentage of women will be alone in their later years, dependent largely on government welfare to meet their needs. If only for this reason, it is important that Japan move toward wage parity for the sexes.

One might think, reading the above, that only women were

at any disadvantage when it comes to aging in Japan and that old *men* living alone enjoyed a blissfully comfortable old age. That's hardly the case! Japanese men, for the most part, are deficient in even the most basic housekeeping skills. Most of them have never cooked a meal, washed a dish, or laundered a shirt in their lives. Such men become truly miserable if their wives die first. The situation is even worse if a wife becomes bedridden and must depend on her husband to be her care-giver. Some older men, unable to cope with the responsibili-ties of caregiving and domestic tasks, have murdered disabled wives and then committed suicide. So, for a Japanese woman, her husband's ability to cope with housekeeping and health care may truly be a matter of life and death.

But the situation is far from hopeless. There are signs of slow but very real change in the sexual division of labor in Ja-pan. For example, the Kanaga Prefecture government has printed and disseminated a poster for staff training that reads: You Are Not a Real Man If You Cannot Take Care of Your Daily Needs!" Some companies even distribute ques-tionnaires to their male employees to determine whether or not they will be able to cope after they retire. These may in-clude questions like "Can you cook rice?" or "Do you know where your underwear is kept?" or "Can you name your child's three best friends?" (How many men, Japanese or American, can answer that last question, I wonder?) Such posters and questionnaires are truly ground-breaking and may even signal a new epoch in the relations between the sexes.

But for most women, one prefectural government's concern with their domestic arrangements is not nearly enough. When there is true cooperation and shared responsibility for human welfare between men and women, the public sector and the private sector, and the younger generation and their elders, only then will our society restore some of the social integra-tion lost in the years of modernization and urbanization. By working together to cope with the realities of our aging soci-ety, we will all be united as brothers and sisters in a common effort.

The United States and Japan have recently been rivals in the quest for economic and technological domination. Perhaps, instead of competing against each other economically, we should compete *together* in the race to build a better society. Let us work hand in hand, sharing ideas and talent, to build a better future for young and old.

Gray Panthers, Red Kimonos: Perspectives on Aging

8

Maggie Kuhn and Takako Sodei, with Peter Troiano

In 1970, the year Maggie Kuhn reached her 65th birthday, she embarked on a project that would change the course of her life. That was the year Ms. Kuhn founded the Gray Panthers, an international organization that works toward eradicating "ageism" (discrimination against the elderly) and bringing about social justice and peace for all.

Ms. Kuhn also serves on the boards of many organizations and has served on President Jimmy Carter's Commission on Mental Health. She is the author of several books and magazine articles; her autobiography, No Stone Unturned: The Life and Times of Maggie Kuhn, was published by Ballantine Books in 1992.

"Old age is a time for freedom and play," she says. "But it is also a time to ask societal questions and to take risks."

Peter Troiano: Could you define the Gray Panthers as an organization?

Maggie Kuhn: I think of myself and my colleagues as the elders of the tribe, and the tribal elders are concerned about

This article first appeared in *Economic World*, February 1989, pp. 58–61. It is reproduced here with their permission.

the tribe's survival—not our own. I'm very turned off by the 'gray power' idea. There's a lot of politics around the gray lobby and the gray power people. That is all very self-serving. The Gray Panthers are not a gray power group. The issues that we've worked on are societal issues. We've lobbied to desegregate the gray power organizations. There ought to be child care in senior centers.

PT: What have the Gray Panthers accomplished since their founding in 1970?

Kuhn: We [the Gray Panthers] have documented the discrimination against age in American society. We raised the issue of ageism in the context of a social malaise at a time when everything in our society was being questioned. As with sexism and racism, there is the issue of stereotyping involved. With ageism, the stereotyping of people is based on age.

PT: Do you think that ageism is as serious a problem as sexism or racism?

Kuhn: I've done a lot of thinking, speaking, and writing on this subject. We believe that there is a new public awareness of the problems that come along with aging, but we *do* discriminate against people because of their age—only now it is beginning earlier.

People who are separated from their jobs at 50 have a very difficult time getting another good job, and at 60, forget it. It is really serious and it is an enormous social loss, and often people are retired with a level of experience that is irreplaceable. With regard to ageism in the workplace, we challenge mandatory retirement. This was one of the issues we brought up with the Japanese at the conference.

PT: There is still mandatory retirement in the United States?

Kuhn: Yes indeed. It has been outlawed for public employees who work in the federal government, and in certain states retirement is optional, but mandatory retirement still exists. Some changes are taking place, though.

For example, Polaroid has been doing some very significant things. They recycle their older workers and use them in a very important training program, where the older workers are the mentors of the young. But the facts are, with the merger mania of the 1980s, we have changed the workplace; also, we have exported so many of the manufacturing jobs. This has changed the economic base of our society to a service economy. The Gray Panthers support Polaroid in its efforts and would like to see more done in this direction. We want to see if new agendas can be given for employees late in their life within the organizational structure of corporations.

PT: What are some other goals of the Gray Panthers for the 1990s and beyond?

Kuhn: Advocating changes in the health care system, patient advocacy in nursing homes, and generally being social critics because we have nothing to lose. We are also setting up a series of forums called "Housing America for the 21st Century." These will deal with the issues of homelessness and our vision of what housing should be.

PT: Could you talk a little bit about how the media portrays older people?

Kuhn: We've had a media watch for over a decade and there have been some changes. We did a workshop in connection with the 1981 White House conference on aging, which was very successful. We involved the three commercial networks, and they sent all their top people. We looked at the pervasive feelings of rejection and stereotyping of old people that are presented through television. These images still prevail to some extent, although there have been some changes. Johnny Carson doesn't dye his hair, Phil Donahue has a shock of white hair, and there are many older people, though mostly men, in the industry.

PT: You have traveled throughout the world. Are there any countries whose policy toward the aging you especially approve of?

Kuhn: We've been very interested in what's happening in Scandinavia and in Canada. Of course, they each have a public health care system. We're working for that, and ultimately we're going to get it. In 1988, we had a number of health hearings in different parts of the United States and we asked people to bring their medical bills in and to detail their experiences with and complaints about the system. All of this evidence was videotaped. We've appointed a commission to evaluate the testimony and to build it into legislation and then into a series of hearings that we will call across America.

We have excellent press, and such organizations as the American Medical Students Association, the American Nurses Association, and the American Public Health Association are with us. There are many people in the health professions who endorse a national health service.

PT: When do you think we are going to see a national health service happen in the United States?

Kuhn: I think we are going to see it by the turn of the century; maybe before. About 38 million Americans have no health coverage at all. There are many public hospitals that are closing and in many parts of the countryside there is no health care—it's all tied up in urban areas.

PT: Have you ever been in Japan?

Kuhn: Yes, I've been to Tokyo, and I learned that the graying of Japan is a very big problem. I hear that the islands are very crowded. In late 1988, one of our members who is involved in housing was approached by two Japanese businessmen who are searching for land in America, Canada, and Australia for the purpose of resettling elderly Japanese.

PT: You mean the Japanese are considering building housing communities for their old people in other countries?

Kuhn: Yes. We were shocked. We asked, "What happened to the family connection and the status of the red kimono people in Japanese society?" [Starting at age 60, Japan's elderly often wear red hats and red vests over their kimonos on special occasions, as a mark of respect for their advanced years.]

PT: Getting back to the United States, could you put your finger on the greatest problem old people are facing?

Kuhn: Trying to find a useful role. The displacement and alienation . . . people look forward to retirement, but what do you do with the rest of your life? There is loneliness, and often the men die first. Women have a longer life span, by 8 to 15 years.

There is poverty because we don't have a good pension system. Many women don't know that their husbands' pensions do not include survivor benefits; when their husbands die, they lose that pension. Pensions are not portable in this country, meaning you cannot take them from one job to the next, even within some corporations and some unions.

PT: Are you against placing older people together in planned communities?

Kuhn: It's not good for old people, and it deprives society of a historical perspective. Places like Sun City or Leisure World— these are violations of the essential wholeness. They make old age pretty lonely. I helped to organize a shared housing resource center. For over 25 years I have shared my house. I never married, but I have a family that I enjoy through a wonderful group of young people with whom I have shared my house. In my late life it has been a godsend. The shared housing idea has grown, and now we have a network of house sharers in some 400 communities in different parts of the United States.

PT: What message would the Gray Panthers like to get across to the corporate world?

Kuhn: That corporate America and the corporate world face an enormous challenge and can help make the way for a changing society by utilizing the historical perspective and understanding of life that older workers possess that should not be wasted.

Takako Sodei, professor in the Department of Home Economics at Ochanomizu University in Tokyo, is on the editorial staff of the journal of the Japan Social Gerontological Society and has written extensively on the topics of aging, the status of women, and family relations. In 1980 and 1981, Dr. Sodei was a visiting scholar at the National Council on the Aging as a senior researcher of the Japan-U.S. Educational Commission.

Peter Troiano: From what you have seen in both countries, do the problems of the elderly in Japan differ from those in the United States?

Takako Sodei: Some problems are the same, but others are different. In Japan, two-thirds of all old people are still living with their children or grandchildren. There aren't that many old people living alone in Japan, but there are many old people living alone in the United States. We are a more family-oriented society.

Another difference is that, in Japan, many old people are working, even after 65; 40% of men and a little less than 20% of women are working. Most of them are working in agriculture or small shops or business. Our retirement age in big companies is 60. After 60, many people go to middle-size companies and work until 70.

PT: So then many small and midsize companies have people working for them that have many years' experience?

Sodei: Yes, our economy is broken into two economies. At the top are the big companies, and at the bottom are the small companies. The big companies are nationally or even internationally famous and profit from high technology. Many small-size companies are still using traditional skills, so after workers retire from a big company and even if their skills and knowledge are out of date, they can still make use of what they know.

PT: Is there forced retirement in Japan, or can people stay on if they choose?

Sodei: There is forced retirement for most companies at 60, and there are some companies that retire their employees at 58.

PT: Do Japanese people look forward to retirement?

Sodei: No, they don't! The Japanese people like to stay on their jobs. They are workaholics.

PT: Does Japan have special retirement and old age communities as the United States has?

Sodei: We have a few, but not so many. Just recently, they started building some, but they are very, very expensive, and most old people like living with their children. Often these retirement communities are located outside or far away from cities and towns, near the seaside or in the mountains; usually far away from children and other relatives, so most Japanese don't want to live in these places.

PT: Will the concept of forced retirement ever change in Japan?

Sodei: I don't think so. It's a way to keep the economy moving. Also, it gives young people a chance to get promoted.

PT: I think the American perception of the Asian family is that the old person is revered, highly respected, and may be the most important person in the family. Is this the way it is in Japan?

Sodei: Yes, I think young people still respect old people but not as much as a long time ago. But we still keep the seniority system; that means that age is still a good thing. [In Japan, a male worker's wages are directly linked to his age, no matter how long he has worked for a particular company.]

PT: Do you ever hear of old people getting attacked or any other kind of violence directed at the old people in Japan?

Sodei: Sometimes but very seldom. But it does happen that children who grow up in the city and live in a nuclear family (just mother and father without grandparents nearby) don't ever get to know how old people can be. They don't know how to deal with them, and there have been stories, though very, very rare, of violence toward the elderly.

PT: Does Japan's media have negative stereotypes of old people?

Sodei: The media always shows a nice old person, very kind and always respected. TV programs like to show the big extended family, even though we are losing it in Japan. In TV programs, many dramas are about the big family, and the grandfather or grandmother is the dominant figure, the wise person who gives good advice. This is not the way it really is today—it's a kind of nostalgia, I suppose.

PT: Does a woman's status increase as she gets older?

Sodei: I think so, but compared with a man her status is low; but I think an old woman can enjoy a high status.

PT: How does health care differ between Japan and the United States?

Sodei: There's a big difference! We have national health insurance; you don't. Up until four or five years ago, all medical treatment for persons over 70 was free. This has changed slightly. A new law was passed that old people have to pay a small fee, but it is still cheap. Only 800 yen (approximately $7) a month covers treatment and medicine. Hospital care is about $3 a day.

Before that law was passed, sometimes people would stay in hospitals for two or three years at a time. Of course, such a system was a major headache for the government.

PT: Do a lot of Japanese people revere the old traditional medicines and healing practices, or do they prefer modern medicine?

Sodei: They are interested in modern medicine, but for old people, the traditional medicines are covered by the government. For example, acupuncture is covered but only for the elderly.

The bad thing about the system is that medical fees are higher for dispensing medicine. Old people go to clinics and accumulate lots of medicines, and the doctors make more money. Treatment is cheap, but medicine is expensive. It can be a waste of money, and the pharmaceutical companies are the ones making large profits.

PT: Does one's experience of aging differ according to one's social background as is so often the case in the United States?

Sodei: Not really. We are a homogeneous society, so there is no real racial problem. In terms of income, most people are middle class.

I saw an interesting statistic recently. The difference between what the president of a corporation makes and what the lowest worker earns is only about five times in Japan. In the United States, corporation presidents make 20 or more times as much as their lowest-paid employees. Also, our tax system ensures that those with higher incomes pay higher taxes.

A funny thing is happening, though, with the financial status of older people. Recently, an economist calculated that in Japan, old people are much richer than young people, especially with the cost of land skyrocketing. Ninety percent of old people own their own houses, and more old people have amassed assets. For young people, it is almost impossible to buy land. Older people's pensions are improving, but when the baby-boom generation reaches retirement, they don't know if there will be enough money left for pensions. Young people in Japan also despair of ever owning a house.

PT: Are young people left property and amassed fortunes through wills in Japan?

Sodei: The will does not have the same power in Japan as it does in the United States. As a rule, property must be divided equally among children, so no one can be favored. At most, a will can deed one-half of the property to any one person.

PT: Is Japan becoming a youth-worshipping culture as so many Westernized countries in the world are? Are people afraid of growing old?

Sodei: No, I don't think so. Not like in the United States. In Japan, age means something important. We appreciate youth, but old age is special. Of course, much music and art is geared toward the young, but old people still have a lot of power to control these media. In Japan, people want to look dignified. Old people don't have plastic surgery. Some people *try* to look old, especially managers and people in administrative positions. It sometimes happens that if you look *young*, you are not respected.

A Gerontology for the 21st Century

9

Lauren Goldberg

Who's responsible for my old age? That is a question that my peers and I don't really think about often or hard enough. As a future physician, I will need to be prepared for a large number of patients being older men and women, regardless of the specialty I choose for my practice (with the obvious exception of pediatrics). Currently, only about 700 of the 400,000 members of the American Medical Association (AMA) devote most of their time to geriatrics. But current demographic studies indicate that 8 to 10 thousand geriatricians are needed in 1991. As a female baby boomer, I can expect to live until the age of 77, approximately seven years longer than my male peers. I am therefore part of the fastest-growing segment of the population, a group that will number some 40 million by the year 2050. So I will attempt to respond to the question of who will be responsible for my old age as a physician-in-training and as a woman. I will also expand my remarks to consider why this question is such a difficult one to answer or even to confront.

Throughout much of my medical school training, doing my clinical rotations, I faced questions like "What is the differential diagnosis for third trimester bleeding in a pregnant woman?" Or "What is the drug treatment of choice for hemophilus meningitis in a two-year-old child?" I wasn't ex-

110

pected or trained to consider anything more far-reaching or more holistic than that. Unfortunately, due to this kind of training, most medical students end up as highly skilled experts within narrowly defined specialties. And despite the fact that, regardless of specialty, we are likely to see many older people as patients; in most medical schools, students are not really taught to understand older people's special needs. It's important, but not sufficient, to know the interrelationship between estrogen levels, menopause, and osteoporosis; it's important, but not sufficient in our treatment of older patients, to know that the drug dosage for an 80-year-old may not be the same as the dosage for a 50-year-old. American society and the medical profession within that society seem to have difficulty understanding or even addressing matters that can't be easily changed.

A recent report in *The New England Journal of Medicine* points out that, in Japan, the elderly are using an increasingly large portion of medical care resources, in part because of the comprehensive insurance that's available there, but also in part as a response to changing cultural trends. Respect for the aged appears to be diminishing in Japan. It's burdensome to care for an elderly family member at home, and more and more Japanese women are working outside the home and can't take on the added role of primary caretaker. So what do those elderly Japanese men and women do? Where can they go? Well, they visit doctors more frequently and don't complain about long waits. Time spent waiting to see a doctor affords them an opportunity to socialize with their peers. Many elderly Japanese even prefer unnecessary admission into hospitals to outpatient or home care and will strenuously resist being discharged. Believe it or not, we are witnessing a very similar phenomenon among America's elderly. Perhaps elderly people living in fast-paced, high-tech societies like the United States and Japan often feel lonely and left out. Visiting a doctor and going to the hospital are ways of getting some of the attention they need. It becomes more and more clear that our extensive training in accurate diagnosis and effective treatment of specific diseases and disorders is not enough to help us satisfy the complex social, emotional, and medical needs of our elderly patients.

Even when our training includes specific instruction in geriatric medicine, we must ask ourselves whether we are willing to apply it. The attitude of many medical professionals toward older people is a major stumbling block. When my peers and I discuss career plans, I hear them say things like "Well, I thought I would end up in internal medicine when I started medical school, but that turned out to be nothing but geriatrics. Old people with four different chronic diseases, none of them curable, half of them induced by smoking, drinking, or overeating. Who needs that?" When they do a rotation in the geriatrics ward, many say that it's nothing but another four weeks in internal medicine. In addition, many older patients are labeled OMS—organic mental syndrome—which in practical terms means "demented and unable to communicate." These patients receive little serious attention. Thus, many of my peers make career choices that reflect their negative attitudes toward the elderly and their problems. Nearly one-third of graduating medical students apply for residencies in either anesthesiology or radiology, both of which are specialties with relatively low patient contact.

As a society, we have invested a tremendous amount of time, energy, and money in developing high-tech responses to most medical problems. We focus on curing specific diseases rather than on prevention or more holistic treatments. Now, curing diseases is very important; it's what helped us to increase longevity. But many people aren't being cured, and life is prolonged for many who are in a permanently disabled state. Many physicians don't really know how to respond to the needs of patients in chronically morbid states. This makes them feel ineffectual, and the average doctor's ego doesn't handle that feeling well.

It is as a physician that I would like to consider my responsibility for my patients who are facing old age. I would expand my job description to include serving as an advocate for my elderly patients. If I had to choose between having limited contact with many patients or the extensive ability to effect change for just a few patients, you can be sure that, all other things, including compensation, being equal, I would choose the latter. If I could prescribe a drug for a patient's over-stressed heart and arrange for nutritious meals to be deliv-ered to her home, my job would be that much more satisfying. The patient would benefit from improved health care and a sense of well-being, and the health care system would benefit from increased efficiency.

The physician may not always be the best person to serve as the patient's advocate. An advocate might better be a fam-ily member, if one can be found who is willing and able, or a social worker or clergyman. Ideally, it would be the elderly person herself. Whoever it may be, we all need *someone* to act as our advocate when our mental or physical health is even slightly impaired. An advocate can identify problems as they arise, or even anticipate them, investigate possible solutions, help choose a reasonable course of action, oversee its imple-mentation, and follow up on it, making sure the service was delivered as expected and yielded the desired benefits.

To put it simply, the key word in the question of who will care for each one of us as we become less able is "who." It may sound cynical of me, but I don't think it will matter very much which new insurance package becomes available or which newly coordinated care program is established. While there is always room for improvement in individual services, each highly touted initiative is merely a new or repositioned piece of a complex puzzle that is and continues to be user-*un*-friendly. If I can at all assist my patients in resolving any problems that diminish their well-being, I would just be do-ing what a doctor is *supposed* to do.

Finally, as a physician, I am well aware of the fact that many of my patients will be elderly and female. It will be vi-tal that I be properly trained to attend to their gynecological needs. Women frequently ignore their reproductive organs as they grow older and experience the end of childbearing and a diminishment of sexual activity. After menopause, many women fail to see an obstetrician/gynecologist on a regular basis. When I treat an elderly female patient, I will need to know enough not to dismiss a common complaint, such as vulvar pruritus (vaginal itching), which for many women can be difficult to describe and embarrassing to talk about. Pruritus is a common nonspecific complaint that may have its cause in any one of a number of different diseases, but it is also a classic symptom of vulvar cancer. All too often, this type of cancer is diagnosed in its most advanced, untreatable stages because the patient's doctor never did a pelvic exam, choosing instead to prescribe a topical steroid to treat the symptoms.

We also tend to ignore the sexual needs of older women. Careful attention to this issue may contribute enormously to the patient's well-being, but it demands great care and sensitivity, as well as interest and skill, for a doctor to elicit a history drawn on a patient's experience with painful intercourse, to use just one example. This specific problem, by the way, commonly occurs in postmenopausal women due to hormonal changes and is very amenable to treatment.

I would also like to consider the issues from the standpoint of a female baby boomer. First, a few cautionary notes. We must be careful when we use the characteristics of the current population of elderly women as a basis for planning for future generations. My generation of women may be a truly different breed from the current generation. Most of us work and have careers. We were brought up to think and act independently. We have more formal education. We marry later, have fewer children, and have those children later. All these factors may make a difference in our ability to remain healthy and independent as we age. Given the generally negative effects of our increasingly stressful life-styles, we may not outlive our male counterparts. Some experts predict that the "gender gap" in longevity may eventually close. If that is indeed the case, should we be planning our policies based on a population of elderly females living alone?

Of course, my generation is also perceived by many as being generally healthier overall. We participate in sports to a far greater extent. We are intellectually stimulated by our careers and educations, and we are active consumers of health care. It is possible that we will not be disabled by as many chronic diseases as early as elderly women are now. One thing we *do* share with the current older generation: we will not be able to depend on family members as primary caretakers. Our own children won't have time. Because we began bearing children later than previous generations of women, our sons and daughters will be beginning their own families and careers just as we reach retirement age.

Why is it so difficult for women to think about who will be responsible for our old age? Other issues seem to demand my attention right now. Like so many other women, I began my second career, medicine, in my thirties. I worry about having children. Will it be difficult for me to conceive? What are the risks of my having a child with Down's syndrome? If and when I decide to have children, how will I manage my residency training? Will I find it impossible to become a surgeon because of my desire to have a family? And once I'm established in my career and have children, will I be able to do it all well?

I also have to worry about my own aging parents, who live thousands of miles away from me. They're in generally good health and they're independent, but I can sometimes see the threads of their lives unraveling at the edges. I've started to worry a lot about their health. My father, for instance, is hard of hearing and refuses to wear a hearing aid. Sometimes this makes Dad a social outcast; he doesn't participate in conversations as he would in the past. This can be embarrassing to my mother. Dad's also overweight, a borderline diabetic, and hypertensive. Occasionally he falls asleep at the dinner table or while talking on the phone. Mom smokes, is overweight, is in a high-risk category for breast cancer, and hasn't seen an internist or a gynecologist in more than 20 years. With all this to worry about, I don't have any time or energy left to spend considering my own old age. I'm sure many women of my generation are in the same boat.

I have come to a few conclusions about who is responsible for my old age. First and foremost, I plan to stay in charge of

my own life, which means being independent and involved
and economically stable for as long as possible.

Everyone ages differently, and I certainly don't want to be
lumped under the category of "just another old person." I'll
always be Lauren Goldberg, I'll just be an older Lauren Goldberg. People need some sense of purpose in their lives. Without it, they deteriorate mentally and physically. I don't want
anybody telling me that I have to stop working at some artifi-
cially determined retirement age. In most cases, we should
abolish forced retirement and encourage employers to provide opportunities for part-time work for older workers who
can't or don't want to work full-time. We must devise ways to
draw older women who have not had experience working outside the home into paid or volunteer activities. We must consider with respect the individuality of old people. I know that
I do not want to be segregated from the rest of society in a
nursing home or retirement center, going from the geriatrician's office to one "senior citizen" activity after another. Diminishing opportunities for communication and contact with
people of all ages leaves everyone in a position to be misun-
derstood and isolated. We need to find different ways to accommodate people with varying abilities (a term I much prefer to "disabilities").

I can't take responsibility for my old age without considering my death. With each new technological advance and each
new medical breakthrough, the line dividing life from death
becomes less distinct. Doctors these days are frequently
asked to play God and decide when that line has been crossed.
I hope that my doctor will be able to inform me of all my options, but I never want a doctor or a hospital ethics committee
to decide for me whether I live, die, or exist in a vegetative
state. We all need to spend more time thinking about our
deaths. We might consider it a good idea to make Living
Wills—a simple statement of one's choice for the end of life—
a standard and legally binding part of the traditional will. A
Living Will could be revised to fit the changing needs and desires of the individual, just as easily as a traditional will is
now. Merely by going through this process of making a Living

Will, an individual can feel more in control of his aging and more at ease with the prospect of his death.

It was great to have this opportunity to step outside my narrow medical training, just for a brief time, and consider all the issues surrounding the question of who is responsible for my old age. An experience like this inspires me to go back and spread the word to all my colleagues and help them see just how much responsibility we all share for the good old age of ourselves and others.

Editor's Note: Fortunately for Lauren Goldberg, she received training in geriatrics during her fourth year of medical school from the only medical school department of geriatrics in the United States.

Afterword for Part II

In Part II, we heard from Betty Friedan, Takako Sodei, Keiko Higuchi, Lauren Goldberg, and Maggie Kuhn as each discussed various kinds of shared effort to cope with the challenges presented by the fact of a rapidly aging society. So-called women's issues, such as child care, health care and health insurance, education, pay parity, and fair and equitable divorce laws, are in fact societal issues, with far-reaching implications for everyone, male or female, young or old, poor, middle-class, or wealthy. They thus require the combined effort of all citizens in a society to create the kind of conditions that will lead to a better life for everyone living in it. Such effort in turn requires shared commitment, which must come from a sense of community, of common interests, common goals, common good.

The feminist historian Elizabeth Fox-Genovese (1991) has warned against embracing an oversentimental view of human community, however. The kind of communities we recall nostalgically—whether the extended family and kinship networks of *Ie* or the small towns made up of nuclear families that evoke so much sentimental emotion among Americans—have in the past created the conditions for women's oppression within the family and society and for the devaluation of their lives and work. Feminism has changed the way we view the family and the larger society, and it offers possibilities for the development of new kinds of human community.

But, as Fox-Genovese (1991) has also pointed out, human community, however motivated by mutual need and desire, does not arise from sheer human will. Communities cannot exist independent of structures and institutions created by legal and social sanctions that recognize communities as real and valid. "Empowerment" is a word much in vogue these days, and while it sounds formidable to most and threatening to some few, it really means nothing beyond the ability to act, free of the fear of oppression or condemnation. Feminists, who have worked to empower women in the United States and Japan, are well aware that there is no such thing as an idea whose time has simply "come." Most people in the United States and increasing numbers in Japan support the idea of equal pay for equal work, but without legislative measures, such as Title VII of the Civil Rights Act of 1968, such general acceptance would have been a longer time coming. As the poet Adrienne Rich (1980) has said, it is our material reality that shapes our psychological reality, not the reverse.

Betty Friedan spoke of the need to create new kinds of families and new bonds of intimacy that would unite the sexes and the generations in pursuit of shared goals and dreams. Such "new families"—blended families, extended families, homosexual families, multigenerational non-related families—already exist in fact, brought together by love and need. What is needed is legislation that will facilitate and encourage the growth of such families. We can move to rezone our towns and cities to accommodate the housing needs of those who, for one reason or another, cannot share living arrangements with blood kin. We can legislate changes in our legal definitions of "family." For example, some states and cities have enacted laws that will recognize gay and lesbian partnerships as constituting true families so that one partner can be covered under the other's health insurance or inherit or transfer property to his or her partner. Without such legal sanctions, however, we may remain entrenched in outdated, narrow notions of what "family" and "community" mean.

An interesting recent trend may offer evidence that *some* communities can develop organically. In many parts of the country, demographers and gerontologists have identified what have been called "naturally occurring retirement communities," or NORCs: places—sometimes a single building, apartment complex, or development, occasionally a small town or resort area—where at least half of the residents are over 60. In some cases, most of the younger residents have simply moved away; but in a few cases, NORCs have resulted when an entire community remains stable and grows old together. The existence of these communities raises new legal and social questions: Should these communities offer special services to their residents, such as communal meals, housekeeping services, or even social workers? And who will pay for such services? Should cities and states make efforts to attract younger residents to these communities or simply allow them to "happen"? Should certain areas be zoned as retirement communities, barring families with children? While these communities of the elderly and retired may have developed naturally, their very presence may make them the focus of much legislative attention in the future (Lewin, 1991).

As Takako Sodei has shown, even so "natural" and "noble" a concept as volunteerism is not necessarily so natural, nor is it always easy to promote among the Japanese, a people who have traditionally seen their obligations within the bounds of the extended family (or, as in the case of the Japanese corporation, high-tech capitalism's modern surrogate for the extended family). Volunteerism is also difficult to promote in times of economic recession, when most people, men and women, spend more of their time and energy trying to meet their own needs and those of their families. And women in every society have good reason to be suspicious of any government push toward volunteerism, which, like "home care," has usually meant the unpaid labor of women. Our governments must legislate the conditions that would permit all of us to help ourselves and others achieve a higher standard of living, in the very best sense of the word. Incorporating community service into the school curriculum and helping companies implement paid leave for community service are just two ways government can promote volunteerism without placing unnecessary burdens on its citizens.

In Part III, the participants will discuss the responsibility of the public sector (i.e., federal, state, and local government) for supporting its citizens and ensuring that everyone, regardless of age, race, sex, or income, achieves a minimum standard of living and has the opportunity of participating fully in all facets of society. Governments, however, are often short on vision, and depend on the creative powers of their citizenries for solutions to problems that seem too large and complex to even approach. In Part III, some of the world's citizens will offer their visions of the role government must play when we ask, "Who is responsible for my old age?"

REFERENCES

Fox-Genovese, E. (1991). *Feminism without illusions: A critique of individualism.* Chapel Hill: University of North Carolina Press.

Lewin, T. (1991, July 21). Communities and their residents age gracefully." *New York Times*, pp. 1, 16.

Rich, Adrienne (1980). Compulsory heterosexuality and lesbian existence," *Signs,*5(4), 632.

The Triangle of Responsibility: The Individual, the Private Sector, and the Public Sector

Introduction to Part III

The title of this book and that of its parent symposium is "Who is Responsible for My Old Age?" The words of that title have defined the terms of the conversation that took place in the auditorium at the City University's Graduate Center, which we have presented on these pages. Every participant has made responsibility the focus of his or her thoughts. In Part I Rosalynn Carter, Dr. James Birren, and Eugene Lang wrote of the responsibility of the aging individual to the self and to others. In Part II, feminists Betty Friedan, Takako Sodei, and Keiko Higuchi examined the issue of responsibility in terms of the burden of care for the elderly that has typically fallen upon women, in both Japan and the United States, and the need for men, governments, and communities to share in that responsibility. Finally, in Part III, Alan Pifer, of the Institute for Policy Analysis; Mariko Bando, Councillor to the Japanese Minster's Secretariat; and John Steffens of Merrill Lynch & Company, Inc., will address the "Triangle of Responsibility"—the relationships of individual and family, private sector (business), and public sector. Most of the current debate about responsibility for old age—for retirement pensions, for health and long-term care, for Social Security, and for job opportunities for older workers—centers on the question of who will pay for these programs; and since the governments of both nations would like to reduce federal expenditures for the elderly, it is appropriate that we begin with Alan Pifer's call for a more active government role in securing a basic standard of living for all Americans—young, old, male, female, white, African-American, poor, and middle-class.

The responsibility of the federal government for the welfare of its citizens and the degree to which the federal government should be a presence in the daily lives of its people are questions that were present at the birth of the American republic. In 1787, in an essay addressed "To the People of the State of New York" on the subject of "The Necessity of the Senate"—a paper better known today as Federalist No. 63—James Madison coined the very word *responsibility*, drawing upon connotations of accountability and responsiveness to the needs of another. Madison was worried that the great heterogeneity of the as-yet-unmolded American nation and its "want of a due sense of national character" might lead to "the want . . . of a due sense of responsibility in the government to the people" (Hamilton, Madison & Jaya, 1961, pp. 413–414). He worried that the "changeable" and varied American people might choose a form of government that would reflect that very changeability and diversity, one that would make decisions based on fleeting popular passions, without regard for long-term impact on the general welfare. Without a responsible, active central government, the new United States would become the world's laughingstock and eventually, for all intents and purposes, disappear from the face of the earth.

PUBLIC VERSUS PRIVATE SECTOR

Alan Pifer threatens no such annihilation for the United States should the current administration, a legacy of the Reagan years, succeed in its attempts to dismantle many of the programs achieved by nearly a century of active federal government. However, by opening with a historical analysis of the American government's role in caring for the elderly, Mr. Pifer does advise caution. The United States, unlike Japan, has no history of legally sanctioned filial piety; nothing in the Constitution or in the American tradition of individualism and independence mandates "stewardship" of the elderly. And as America moved toward a capitalistic, industrialized society, the elderly became even more vulnerable. "Old" and "unproductive" became synonymous; youth, wealth, and individual achievement were what made an American valuable to society. The cult of individualism, while it may indeed help foster self-reliance, self-improvement, and outstanding achievement, may also lead to a sense that the individual bears the sole responsibility for every success or failure—indeed, for every single aspect of his or her life.

Pifer argues instead for a collective of society and government. He agrees with James Madison that government in America, whether federal, state, or local, is nothing more nor less than a reflection of the collective will of the people and exists solely to meet their needs. This is both its strength and its weakness. Whenever the American people take a long-term view of the "greatest good for the greatest number" of its citizens, as they did during the Great Depression, then will the federal government pass the kind of legislation and take the kind of activist role that will ensure that great good. In the meantime, even when the American people seem shortsighted, when they demand (or accede to) lower taxes and increased defense spending, cuts in services and social programs for the poor, the federal government can continue to display the kind of leadership it has evinced in this century. For Alan Pifer and many like him, the government is the best provider of its citizens' needs. Pifer points to programs like AFDC (Aid to Families with Dependent Children, what is commonly meant when the term "welfare" is used) and Medicaid, which, when administered by the states, often result in broad inequities in benefits state to state. And OASI (Old Age Security Income), a federal pension for the elderly, is responsible for lifting millions of the elderly out of poverty. Only the federal government can see that such programs are equitably distributed. It goes without saying, perhaps, that Alan Pifer is a staunch opponent of privatization of social programs, in which privately owned businesses take over some of the functions of the federal government in administering these programs.

Mariko Bando is a Japanese baby boomer, an official in the Japanese government, and therefore a civil servant. Dr. Kenzo Kiikuni of the Japan Shipbuilding Industry Foundation, one of the sponsors of the symposium, mentioned that, in Japan, government officials are civil servants rather than politicians. Since they are less likely than American elected officials to be tossed out of office for their "sins," Japanese officials often have the leisure to take the long view of the impact of social programs and legislation. We might be able to attribute Ms. Bando's balanced view of the triangle of responsibility to her experience in looking at long-term effects.

As Mr. Pifer did, Ms. Bando provides some historical background for the creation of the Japanese welfare state. While she is sympathetic to the Japanese government's desire, in an era of fiscal constraint, to reduce its social security and health care expenditures for the elderly, she points out that the Japanese people have come to expect that the government will bear most of the responsibility and cost of caring for Japan's elderly. Without a carefully planned transitional strategy for shifting at least some of the responsibility for care onto the family and the community, the federal government's attempts to cut spending can boomerang. After all, in times of fiscal austerity, at the same time that government is trying to contain costs, Japanese citizens are also feeling the pinch, and they turn to the government to meet their needs in increasing numbers.

Privatization, while it may help reduce some of the government's burden, is not a final solution. Instead, private enterprise might best be viewed as playing a supplementary role, offering a wide array of services and products to those who have the means to choose, while the government guarantees a basic income and level of benefits for the needy. (Alan Pifer might offer a caveat here regarding the propensity of governments to cut or underfund those programs that are aimed at the very neediest.) While Ms. Bando stops short of calling for *increased* government responsibility, she does remind her colleagues in the Japanese central government that extending pension and health care benefits to *all* constitutes "a very productive investment in Japan" and its future. Above all, she reminds us that the question of "who pays" for social security and health care has no final answer and that government, individuals, and private enterprise need to be flexible as they devise strategies for dealing with uncertain economic and demographic futures.

If we view the triangle of responsibility as a spectrum, we might find Alan Pifer at the far "government" end with Mariko Bando somewhere in the middle, leaning toward government responsibility while acknowledging the role that private enterprise and individuals must play in the future. John Steffens, on the other hand, comes down firmly on the side of the privatization proponents. In the face of the serious problems posed by the aging of populations, Steffens proclaims himself an optimist. He sees challenges ahead, true, but also opportunities. According to Mr. Steffens, the public sector—that is, federal, state, and local government—can no longer contain the costs of social programs; nor can it administer these programs equitably and efficiently. These programs, especially the non-means-based entitlements (such as Social Security), are out of control, he says, and are a drag on the national economy.

Private enterprise has the foresight and creativity, according to Mr. Steffens, to offer everyone the prospect of a good old age and a good retirement. After all, he explains, businesses can survive and prosper only if they listen to clients and consumers and tailor products and services to their needs and desires. The consumer should define the services and then be prepared to understand the cost to the provider of making those services available (including, presumably, the added cost to the consumer of the provider's profit). By expanding into the new "gray market" of insurance plans, pension plans, long-term care plans, and products and services for the elderly and disabled, the private sector will also increase productivity, thereby expanding the economy, providing more jobs, more income, and a higher standard of living for all Americans.

This is not to say that Mr. Steffens sees no role for government. The public sector's job, in the kind of "new partnership" that Mr. Steffens envisions, is to create legislation, the tax structure, and the regulatory climate that will enable private enterprise to create and administer the kinds of programs that will guarantee every American a good old age. Rather than raise taxes to pay for government programs like Medicare and Medicaid, he suggests, the federal government should provide tax incentives that will induce individuals to save for retirement and long-term care and persuade corporations to invest in their employees' futures with pension plans and health insurance.

While Mr. Steffens declares himself on the side of increased private sector responsibility for supporting and caring for the elderly, he clearly expects the individual to bear the greatest share of the costs. Many of his proposals—including tax incentives for individuals and employers and an increase in the type and number of on-the-job savings plans—involve forcing or inducing individual workers to save a higher percentage of income for retirement and long-term health care. The proposal that Merrill Lynch made before Congress was for an on-the-job, interest-bearing, long-term health care savings account, with employer and employee each contributing $500 annually. Such a plan, he says, would require new legislation designed to force the worker to participate in such a plan. Even in a democracy, according to Steffens, there comes a time when "benevolent dictators" (who are also, perhaps, corporate executives?) are needed.

PRIVATIZATION: GOOD AND BAD

Mr. Steffens, and other proponents of privatization, do offer some very good ideas for helping to contain the costs associated with the support of a large elderly population. The average individual savings rate in the United States is abysmally low—estimates vary from 5% to 7%—compared with savings rates in other developed nations (though the high cost of housing and health care in the United States may have an impact on savings). For those who can afford to, diverting income from consumption to savings for retirement income and health care needs may serve all or most of their needs. For some others, "managed competition health insurance plans," in which individuals (or their employers) choose among competing private insurers for the best services at the lowest premiums, may be an attractive alternative to either government-funded health care plans or the private plans presently offered. The government could then devote more of its resources to taking care of the income and health care needs of the very poor.

But troubling questions arise, despite the glowing picture of a nation run, like a sleek well-oiled—and profitable—machine, by the corporate genius of America (or Japan). There are those who point to the often bloated salaries paid even to those corporation managers who are inefficient. (Recent surveys indicate that in some corporations, top executives receive combined salaries and bonuses that are 95 *times* the salaries of the lowest paid employee. Let's read that another way: such an executive brings home, every week, nearly *twice* the annual salary of some of his employees.) Short-term profit-motivated thinking, the antiprivatization forces accuse, is rampant in U.S. business. Corporations may be good at cutting costs, but they do so by "downsizing," retiring or laying off employees or relying on part-time or temporary employees who receive no pensions or health benefits; and by "saving" on benefits, these corporations add to the pool of employees who must rely on the government for retirement income and health care (Greene, 1991).

Others point to the private sector's record on pensions and health insurance. In the 1980s, for example, many corporations invested pension funds in junk bonds and other risky ventures, with the result that several companies dismantled pension plans altogether and many others put their pension funds in jeopardy. Private insurance companies are notorious for canceling the policies of those most in need; for refusing to insure the elderly, persons with cancer or AIDS or other preexisting conditions; and for closing offices in areas with large numbers of high-risk clients, such as inner cities or rural areas. "Managed competition" might prove no better. If employers are constantly switching HMOs in order to get the cheapest rate, the employee will suffer: the doctor-patient relationship will be constantly disrupted, medical records will be in constant transit, quality of care will vary (Woolhandler & Himmelstein, 1991).

Those who would like to see a national health insurance plan guaranteeing universal coverage often point to the Canadian National Health Insurance as a shining example of the "single-payer" model. Instead of relying on a large number of private insurers, each of the Canadian provinces pays virtually all health care bills incurred by residents of that province. Paperwork is at a minimum, administrative costs are low (less than 1% of total premiums, compared to 16% of premiums devoted to administrative costs in the United States), and the quality of care is high. But the Canadian model has its critics, who cite long waits for elective procedures and less motivation for research and development in medical technology, forcing many Canadians to travel to the United States for high-tech tests and treatments.

GOVERNMENT SHORTSIGHTEDNESS

In the United States, Medicare and Medicaid have failed to fully cover the health care needs of the elderly and the poor, respectively. Medicare and Medicaid reimbursement schedules are often so low that some doctors refuse to treat these patients or may order unnecessary or excessive tests and treatments to maximize reimbursement. Many older people have had to "spend down" assets in order to qualify for nursing home care. Often, "cost containment" measures actually backfire on the government because they are a result of shortsighted efforts to keep current costs down while failing to look at the long-term impact of such cuts. Actual long-term costs are higher, for instance, when Medicaid patients fail to get early diagnosis and treatment of diseases or disabilities

and end up in hospitals and emergency rooms, sicker and requiring longer, more intensive—and more expensive—
treatment.

The United States is not the only nation guilty of short-
sightedness. In 1980, Yoshio Gyoten, Japan's leading television commentator on public health issues, produced and
hosted a film with the NHK (Japan Broadcasting Corporation) that generated a great deal of controversy when it was
broadcast nationwide in Japan. In his television film, entitled
"Who Is Responsible for Your Old Age?," Mr. Gyoten presented a sobering picture of the current state of care for the
disabled and bedridden elderly in Japan. As with Medicaid
and Medicare, Japanese national health insurance reimburses
doctors and hospitals on a fee-for-services basis—the more
drugs and tests ordered, the higher the payment from the government. In order to cut their own costs and get the maxi-
mum reimbursement possible, many patients in so-called old-
age hospitals receive all drugs and most nourishment
intravenously. Little effort is made to rehabilitate these patients or reintegrate them into family and community. The
grim image of long rows of bedridden patients, diapered, in-
tubated, and hooked to life support machines, is contrasted
with scenes of elderly men and women cared for at home by
family members with the aid of volunteer home help
workers.

Proponents of privatization in the United States cite the
federal government's lack of imagination and failure to inno-
vate. But there are signs that some in government are at least
as creative and imaginative—and as cost-conscious—as the
captains of industry. In Oregon, recently, the state government managed to secure a waiver of Medicaid rules, allowing
the state to move some elderly Medicaid recipients out of
nursing homes and into "Assisted Living" communities,
which offer communal meals; small, partially subsidized private apartments; and, when needed, day help and nursing
care. Costs went down, and most of the participants reported
a significant increase in the quality of life ("The Best Homes,"
1991).

Both the United States and the Japanese governments have expressed alarm at the high cost of caring for and supporting the elderly and the need to shift more of the responsibility onto states, municipalities, communities, and families. And it is true that the number and proportion of older people, current and projected, can be sobering. Persons over 65 now constitute 12% of the population of the United States and 10% of the population in Japan. By 2030, over 20% of the populations of both nations will be over 65. In 1982, the United States spent $196 billion—28% of total federal outlay—to finance programs for the elderly, such as SSI, veterans' pensions, food stamps, housing subsidies, etc. It is projected that, in 2000, expenditures for the elderly will total 35% of federal outlay; by 2050, 65% (these numbers are reduced significantly, however, if one deducts those programs, such as Social Security and Medicare, that are largely self-funded, financed by payroll taxes and employer contributions). And while people are living longer, they are not necessarily living healthier: the age of onset of chronic illness has not risen along with life expectancy and is not expected to rise appreciably in the next century. And even now, nearly 14% of the nation's elderly live at or below the poverty level; most of these are women, many of them minorities (Hess, 1987).

Many predict that Social Security will be threatened by bankruptcy in the next century, that governments cannot continue to pay the increasing cost of health care for the elderly, and that intergenerational resentment, triggered by inequitable distribution of scarce resources among the generations, will soon reach the breaking point. Both Japan and the United States have begun to investigate ways to ensure the continued viability of their social security systems.

Alan Pifer and John Steffens both point to the fact that there will be a $12 trillion surplus in the Social Security Trust Fund by 2030; both ask if it will be enough to support the legions of elderly who will be collecting Social Security in that year, when the baby boomers will be in their seventies and eighties. Alan Pifer sees that surplus as comforting—the news of Social Security's demise is, he says, very premature.

But John Steffens points out that, even if Congress resists the temptation to use the Trust Fund surplus to reduce the deficit or fund other programs, by 2030, Social Security will be paying out $100 billion per day and will exhaust the surplus by 2050. Both Pifer and Steffens suggest a tripartite model for funding old age, comprising Social Security, private pension, and savings. They differ only in their views of the proper mix of these elements.

The image of the elderly as a "bottomless sink" using up money on health care and nursing home care may be a gross exaggeration. In Japan, few Japanese would like to see their parents totally dependent on welfare programs, and 68% of Japanese elders live with their children (though the rate of institutionalization, while still very low, is increasing), and most bedridden elderly are cared for by family members, at their expense (Sodei, 1987). In the United States, most elderly Americans die at home, among family and friends ("The Best Home," 1991). And most nursing home residents, or their children, pay the full cost of care, averaging $20,000 per year (Hess, 1991). Most Americans and Japanese do not want to see their parents live out their lives in poverty; neither do they wish to bear the full burden of their support.

QUESTIONS AND ANSWERS

There are many problems, with many solutions proposed. There are many questions, but are there any real answers? Both the United States and Japan have similar goals for this last decade of the 20th century and for the 21st century. Both countries would like to maintain a high rate of economic growth, reduce federal expenditures, and support an increasingly aged population in good health and financial security. Every measure proposed for meeting these goals raises more questions than it answers. Both countries would like to reduce the proportion of income paid out in pensions and Social Security. To meet this goal, Japan and the United States have become the only two industrialized nations to raise the age of retirement and pension eligibility. If people work longer, the reasoning goes, they will earn more of the money needed to support them in their old age and collect less as pension or Social Security. They will also make up the gap in the worker-recipient ratio and prevent labor shortages.

But, as we noted before, living longer does not necessarily mean remaining healthy longer. Many older workers would prefer to reduce their work hours. Many workers eagerly anticipate their retirements, feeling that they are well deserved. Many corporations are reluctant to keep older workers and offer early retirement incentives to reduce salary, pension, and health care outlays. Social Security regulations are also a disincentive to continuing employment, reducing benefits for every dollar earned above a set limit. In Japan, workers' wages are linked to age and duration of service, and employers are often very happy to get rid of such "expensive" employees. In both countries, stereotypes about "difficult," "slow," or "untrainable" older workers militate against aggressive recruitment and retention of older workers.

Home care for the bedridden or ailing elderly is promoted as a way to reduce government expenditures on nursing home care while improving the quality of life for elders. But who is going to be at home to care for those elderly patients? In both the United States and Japan, women are entering the paid labor force in unprecedented numbers. Women's increased participation in the work force contributes to productivity, fuels the economy, eases labor shortages, and ensures that they will have higher lifetime earnings so that most of their Social Security benefits later on will be based on earned income. To ask these women to give up their jobs to care for elderly parents will have severe long-term consequences for both governments. "Family-based" policies, appealing though they may be, can be as shortsighted and counterproductive as the policies they are meant to replace.

It has often been suggested that entitlement programs be made "age-neutral," based on need rather than on age, in order to counter the perception that they discriminate against certain age groups. Alan Pifer points out that needs-based programs are by their nature redistributive, and, at least in the United States, redistribution policies are increasingly unpopular. This may be a legacy of the Reagan years, when much of the nation's wealth was redistributed upward to the executive classes, who were expected to invest money in the economy. The middle and working classes paid an increasing percentage of their income in taxes, which funded social programs such as AFDC, food stamps, and public housing. These programs, which the Reagan administration hoped to cut, were maintained by a resistant Congress. But many people who were paying the taxes to fund these programs began to resent the beneficiaries. Unlike Japan, which despite recent increases in immigration is still a very homogeneous society, the United States is racially, culturally, and linguistically diverse. The perception of the (mostly) white middle and working classes is that they are paying for programs for African-American and Hispanic families and that they will never see the benefits of these programs. Because of the current antitax climate, the unpopularity of needs-based programs, and the low level of protest when they are reduced or eliminated, there is always the danger that these programs will be the first to fall in a fiscal crisis. One possible advantage to universal health care and pension plans is that everyone benefits, regardless of income, and those who wish to supplement government plans by purchasing additional services may do so.

As we said earlier, there are many questions but very few permanent answers. The last two entries in Part III offer two models for dealing with the health care and income maintenance needs of retirees. Both models are Japanese. The Silver Plan, presented by Toshiyuki Kato of the Mitsubishi Electric Company, is a private sector model for preparing workers for retirement. The Silver Plan offers life-style counseling, preventive health care, and help with pension planning. The Golden Plan is the Japanese government's 10-year plan for coping with population aging and especially for dealing with the health and social service needs of the elderly. It proposes a shift from long-term institutionalization to home care, intermediate short-term care, preventive health measures, and caregiver support. The plan is designed to be flexible, to meet special regional, income, and generational needs. We offer it in the spirit of cross-cultural cooperation and education.

REFERENCES

The best home for older adults [Editorial]. (1991, August 17). *New York Times*, p. 20.

Greene, L. D. (1991, August 15). [Letter to the Editor]. *New York Times*, p. 20.

Hamilton, A., Madison, J. & Jay, J. (1961). *The Federalist*, (B. E. Wright, Ed.) Cambridge, MA: Belknap/Harvard

Hess, B. B. (1987). America's elderly: A demographic overview. In B. B. Hess & E. V. Markson (Eds.), *Growing old in America: New perspectives on old age* (p. 14). New Brunswick, NJ: Transaction Books.

Sodei, T. (   ). *The effect of industrialization and modernization on filial responsibility toward aging parents: A comparative study*, Paper presented at the 5th Asian Regional Conference of Sociology, Seoul, Korea, Dec. 3rd and 4th.

Woolhandler, S., & Himmelstein, D. (1991, August 13). [Letter to the Editor]. *New York Times*, p. A16.

The Public Sector: "We the People" and Our Government's Role

10

Alan Pifer

Responsibility for old age security is surely one of the most important issues confronting both Japan and the United States. It is an issue that the people of both societies must consider carefully if they have any concern about their future social and economic well-being. Our first realization must be that responsibility for old age must be shared: I am responsible, my family is responsible, my employer, my government, my community are all responsible. The trouble is that this obvious realization doesn't take us very far.

My job is to address the issue of government responsibility for old age security from the American side. Despite the enormity of the subject and the necessary limitations of time and space, I find the assignment an agreeable one. I believe strongly that the government in a complex, modern, industrialized state such as ours bears a major share of the responsibility for its older citizens. The term "government responsibility," I must caution, is merely shorthand for something much more basic: the collective societal responsibility for old age. A government is not a sentient being with an autonomous will. In a democracy, government is no more and no less than the agent of the people, an instrumentality that we, the people, have created to serve our needs and purposes.

This is an important point because it forces us to consider

the nature of that collective responsibility for old age, distinct from the responsibilities we have as individuals, family members, or employees. Recognizing the participatory nature of that entity we call government should prevent us from trying to transfer onto its shoulders a responsibility we ourselves must accept as members of the body politic. In the case of old age, as in many other areas, government simply serves as our watchdog over the political economy, staying alert to social trends as they develop and dealing with the problems that emerge out of these trends.

Looking back over the development of our nation from its earliest days to the present, guided by W. Andrew Achenbaum's illuminating book, *Old Age in the New Land*, one discovers that perceptions of the role of the elderly in our society, and hence public attitudes toward them, have varied widely over the centuries. As a consequence, we have had no consistent, long-term rationale, either philosophical or practical, for the treatment of the elderly, needy or otherwise. That this has been true of public perceptions of, attitudes toward, and treatment of that other major vulnerable group in our population—children—does not make it any less surprising, or less shocking to our sensibilities.

We learn from Achenbaum that in the early days of the American republic, because the achievement of old age was in itself believed to be proof of a virtuous life, the elderly were recognized as having a special social role as exemplars and guides in the moral development of the young nation. Old people possessed knowledge about a wide variety of practical matters, and were looked upon as holding the key to an understanding of life's ultimate meaning. For these reasons, they were entitled to respect, even veneration. Nonetheless, they were, like everyone else in that society, expected to remain economically and socially active as long as they could work. Since most people did not live very long lives back then, they worked until they died. Mandatory retirement was unthinkable because it was impossible.

In the late 19th and early 20th centuries, as the nation became more industrialized and urbanized, attitudes toward the elderly underwent a gradual shift, from almost wholly positive to largely negative. Achenbaum writes:

> Instead of depicting the elderly as stately and healthy, more and more observers described them as ugly and disease-ridden. Instead of extolling the ageds' moral wisdom and practical sagacity, popular and scientific commentators increasingly concluded that old people were incapable of contributing anything to society. By the outbreak of World War I, most Americans were affirming the obsolescence of old age.

This was also the period in which the idea developed that older people no longer had much value as workers. Productivity came to be regarded as the exclusive province of the young. Except on the farm, where their practical knowledge still had value, the elderly were gradually pushed aside. Retirement, voluntary or otherwise, came to be a recognized turning point in one's life. With it often came poverty and dependence. Nevertheless, the elderly were considered to be no more vulnerable than other disadvantaged groups, such as immigrants, and no special provision was made for them beyond the pittance provided to the very poor under state and local relief programs. The elderly at that time were not regarded as meriting special consideration simply because of their age or past service to the country or community. The one exception—and it was a very large one—was the provision of military pensions, first to the Northern veterans of the Civil War and later to the veterans of the Spanish-American War and World War I. By 1929, four-fifths of the beneficiaries of all public or private pension plans were the recipients of war-related survivor and disability pensions.

Gradually, in the period just before World War I, concern about the economic plight of the elderly developed in some quarters. Agitation for old age pensions began. This movement was stimulated in part by the advent in 1908 of social insurance in Europe, particularly in Britain, and by the rise of social scientific research that documented the extent to which environmental forces made individuals vulnerable. Social insurance became part of the Progressive party's plank. It was not until after World War I, however, that public old age pensions began to be established in this country. These first pensions were established principally at the state and municipal levels and were almost exclusively for the benefit of retired public service employees. At the federal level, a compulsory old age and disability insurance program was enacted in 1920 for the half-million civil service employees of the time.

This was the state of affairs when the Great Depression struck in the 1930s. It was then recognized that among the millions made destitute and homeless by that catastrophe was a disproportionate number of old people. The idea gained currency that society had a collective responsibility for the elderly, along with widows and children, the disabled, and the unemployed. Protection for these groups was incorporated into the Social Security Act in 1935. What was most remarkable about that legislation was that it not only provided federal relief for impoverished elderly under Title I but that it also, under Title II, created a permanent contributory pension program for the elderly generally, irrespective of need.

In the years that have passed since the Depression and the enactment of Social Security, a new public attitude toward the elderly has gradually developed. While they are still generally regarded as a "problem" group in our society, they are also, simply by virtue of having achieved the magical age of 65, regarded as having a certain right, or entitlement, to a wide range of benefits, privileges, and protections. The "senior citizen discount" is a fixture of our national life. Publicly provided old-age benefits have acquired a seemingly contractual status between the larger society and the elderly individual, and this in spite of the fact that there is nothing in the Constitution that guarantees these benefits. Moreover, the Supreme Court of the United States, in the case of *Flemming v. Nestor*, decided in 1960 that there is no constitutionally guaranteed contractual right to a Social Security pension.

It is not entirely clear to me what lies behind the recent emergence of the notion that the simple fact of reaching a specified age, 65, automatically confers a special—though not a respected—status on the elderly individual. I wonder sometimes if the concept of veteranship, with its unhappy tradeoff of respect for privilege, rests somehow on a collective feeling of guilt about the plight of the elderly. It's a disturbing thought that the large class of providers of services and products for the elderly that has developed over the past 20 years has a very strong economic interest in preserving the concept of the elderly as a homogeneous group with characteristic disabilities and needs. Historically, there has been no tradition in the United States of collective responsibility or concern for the elderly as such, whether they have been considered an asset or a liability to society. There has been no consistent philosophical, practical, constitutional, or even religious rationale—unless, of course, we consider the biblical injunction to "honor thy father and thy mother."

Because we lack such a tradition, we might suppose that the present system of benefits, privileges, and protections for the elderly, dependent as it is only on legislative mandate, may be in some jeopardy. This is possible despite the system's current popularity, the political and consumer power of the elderly themselves, and society's sense of guilt for the neglect of its parents and grandparents. Fortunately, collective responsibility for old age is just part of a much broader political tradition stemming from the very nature of the American democratic state: the federal government is answerable to the people and exists purely to meet their common needs.

The American state, when it was founded in 1787, rested on two sets of principles. The first, enunciated by the great British and European liberal political philosophers of the 17th and 18th centuries, had to do with the social contract. The ideal government, these thinkers maintained, was one created by social contract. Originally, human beings lived in a state of nature, where they enjoyed natural rights and absolute equality. When human beings became "civilized" and it became necessary to protect these rights from abuse, people came together and created governments, which by their very nature depended for their existence on the consent of those governed. Government was therefore accountable to the people and could be changed or dissolved at their will.

Thomas Jefferson expressed this concept brilliantly in the second paragraph of the Declaration of Independence.

We hold these truths to be self-evident, that all men are created equal, that they are endowed by their Creator with certain unalienable Rights, that among these are Life, Liberty and the pursuit of Happiness. That to secure these rights, Governments are instituted among Men, deriving their just powers from consent of the governed. That whenever any Form of Government becomes destructive to these ends, it is the Right of the People to alter or abolish it, and to institute new Government, laying its foundation on such principles and organizing its powers in such form, as to them shall seem most likely to effect their Safety and Happiness.

A second and very important antecedent of the American state was the 18th-century British doctrine of utilitarianism, which consists partly of the notion that an action is good or right if it results in the greatest happiness of the greatest number, a result, it was argued, only attainable in a democracy.

Out of these two powerful streams of political philosophy, brought over from across the Atlantic, there developed the American Constitution. Enshrined in it, however, was the classic dilemma of liberalism: how are we to have an instrument of national government that will simultaneously enable the elected authorities to act decisively in the national interest, while at the same time preventing these authorities from curtailing the liberties of the people? The final version of the document that was drafted in Philadelphia in 1787 had provisions in it that cut both ways.

On the one hand, we have the General Welfare clause, which appears in the Preamble and again in Article I, Section 8. This clause enumerates the purposes for which Congress can levy taxes and thus grants the federal government great power. This clause ultimately provided the constitutional basis for the American welfare state. The Supreme Court, in confirming the constitutionality of the Social Security Act in *Helvering v. Davis* in 1937, relied heavily on the General Welfare clause. On the other hand, the Bill of Rights and a provision that limited the role of the federal government to specified enumerated powers were designed to protect the liberty of the people. In a book I wrote with Forrest Chisman, entitled *Government for the People* (W. W. Norton, 1988) we traced the subsequent history of that apparently irreconcilable contradiction. It is an important story, because it directly relates to the eventual development of a collective responsibility for old age expressed through the agency of national government.

After George Washington took office as president, two schools of thought quickly developed as to the degree that the newly created national government should play an active role in the lives of its citizens. Each school of thought had its brilliant young proponent serving in Washington's cabinet. Thomas Jefferson favored the concept of limited government. "That government is best," he wrote, "that governs least," and added, "I own I am not a friend of a very energetic government. It is always oppressive." Jefferson was skeptical about the General Welfare clause. In 1791, he complained that relying on it to justify federal action would "reduce the whole instrument to a single phrase, that of instituting a Congress with power to do whatever would be good for the United States."

The second school of thought, led by the Federalist Alexander Hamilton, favored a strong, activist national government. In Hamilton's view, the United States would never be able to protect its newly won independence unless it developed economically, and this would depend on strong government intervention.

As secretary of the treasury, Hamilton used the institutions of government to help develop the new nation's infrastructure, establish a stable currency and a national banking system, and carry out other, similar projects. In doing so, he pushed the scope of government far beyond that specifically outlined by the Constitution, relying on the doctrine of "implied powers." This was the idea that the Constitutional clause authorizing the federal government to take any measures "necessary and proper" to exercise its enumerated powers allowed virtually any form of activism in the public interest.

Ever since those early days of the Republic, the debate has raged about the proper role of national government in the lives of its citizens. There have been activist periods, such as those during the presidencies of John Quincy Adams, Abraham Lincoln, Theodore Roosevelt, Woodrow Wilson, Franklin Roosevelt, Harry S. Truman, John Kennedy, Lyndon Johnson, and Richard Nixon. There have also been periods of revolt against activism: the latter part of the 19th century, the presidencies of Warren Harding, Calvin Coolidge, and Herbert Hoover in the 1920s and 1930s, of Dwight Eisenhower in the 1950s, and most recently of Ronald Reagan in the 1980s.

On balance, however, the activist tradition has prevailed, simply because of the overriding need for pragmatic solutions to pressing national needs. Thus, in the 19th century, activist national government was used to promote economic development when that was a primary need and, under Lincoln, to preserve the Union. By the end of the century, unbridled laissez-faire monopoly capitalism had such a deleterious effect on the national welfare that the powers of the federal government had to be brought into play to regulate it. In the 1930s, when the nation was gripped by the Great Depression, with more than a quarter of the labor force unemployed and misery stalking the streets, there was no choice but a renewed wave of federal activism. In the 1960s, the civil rights movement stirred a vigorous federal response.

With each swing of the pendulum, however, the concept of affirmative government has become more deeply entrenched. Technological change, population growth, and the transformation of a scattered rural society into a modern, integrated, mobile society have made the problems faced by the nation increasingly complex. Many of these problems have a commonality that puts them beyond the scope of state and local government, the private sector, and voluntary organizations.

The growing social role of federal government is embodied not only in federal spending programs but also in loan programs, federal regulations, the enforcement of basic constitutional rights, and tax expenditures (that is, tax preferences to individuals and employers to encourage activities judged to be in the public interest, such as the establishment of private pensions and health insurance).

The federal role has become very much a part of our national life. So integral is it to the welfare and living standard of the great American middle class—that is, most of us—that there is very little chance of ever going all the way back. It is revealing that Ronald Reagan's administration, the most conservative of the past half century, which would have taken the nation back to late-19th-century social Darwinism and uncontrolled laissez-faire capitalism, accomplished so very little toward these ends. Reagan did manage to reduce spending on the poor, but since only 10% of federal spending goes to the poor, a reduction there is negligible in terms of the overall size and durability of the federal social role.

It seems possible to me that we have reached a point in the nation's development where the great debate over the proper role of national government in the political economy has been forever resolved. The *debate* will no doubt continue at a high rhetorical pitch, but for all practical purposes, affirmative government is here to stay. From now on, the issues will not be whether we should have an activist government but what it should include and how we can make it more responsive to the needs of the people.

I have traced for you the history and nature of activist government and the growth of the federal social role in some detail because I can find no other rationale in our national life for our present well-developed sense of collective responsibility for old age. Indeed, no part of the federal social role seems to be more firmly entrenched than the panoply of programs that now exist for the benefit and protection of the elderly. The entrenchment of activist government protects them and, reciprocally, their popularity helps to further entrench activist government.

Nonetheless, I must reiterate the point made earlier that provision for the elderly rests on no firmer base than legislative mandate. The Supreme Court in *Helvering v. Davis* did not say that Congress was obliged to provide old age relief and pensions. It simply said that it *could* do so constitutionally, since the Court was satisfied that old age poverty had become a threat to the general welfare sufficient in scope and severity to justify federal action. As Justice Cardozo said in the majority opinion,

> Nor is the concept of the general welfare static. Needs that were narrow or parochial a century ago may be interwoven in our day with the well-being of the nation. What is critical or urgent changes with the times.

Thus, if some future Congress were to decide that the needs of the elderly were no longer critical or urgent, it could abolish or scale back the programs that serve them. There are, indeed, voices today advocating that very thing.

Estimates of the number of federal government programs that in one way or another benefit the elderly vary widely. A survey by Carole Estes, 10 years ago, reported in her excellent book *The Aging Enterprise*, showed a count of at least 80 programs, and that figure is doubtless still valid today. These programs, which have been put in place incrementally over the past 50 or 60 years and are administered by about a dozen federal departments or independent agencies and cover a wide range of purposes but can be classified broadly under seven headings: income maintenance, employment and volunteer service, housing, health care, social service, transportation, and training and research.

These programs can also be classified by the means used to achieve their ends. This divides programs into five principal groupings. First, there are the insurance-based programs, financed partly by general revenues and partly by a dedicated payroll tax. These programs are available to everyone who qualifies, irrespective of income, and include OASI (Old Age and Survivor Insurance), military and civilian service pensions, and Medicare, the health care program for the elderly. Second, there are the income-tested welfare programs, financed out of general revenues and available to the poor elderly. These include Medicaid for medical and long-term care, and SSI (Supplementary Security Income) for those who don't qualify for Social Security or are so poor that they can't live solely on Social Security.

Third, there are the programs that provide special services to the elderly regardless of income and that are financed out of general revenues. Most of these programs are authorized either under the Older Americans Act of 1965 or Title XX of the Social Security Act.

Fourth, there are the incentive programs that achieve their purposes by means of tax relief. For individuals, there are 401 K plans, IRAs, and the extra deductions for age on the income tax. For employers, there is the deductibility from taxable income of contributions to employee retirement and health care programs.

Finally, there is a wide range of government regulations whose purpose is to benefit and protect the elderly. One example would be the regulatory provisions of the Pension Benefit Guarantee Corporation, designed to safeguard an employee's stake in a private pension plan.

Collectively, these programs enjoy considerable public approval. At the top of the popularity list is OASI, the retirement insurance program. First, because its benefits are regarded as a right derived from an implicit, but by no means formal, intergenerational compact; second, because it helps relieve the young of the burden of supporting their parents; and third, because there is no stigma attached to anyone receiving its benefits, even though they involve a small redistributive element.

Also generally popular is the system of tax preferences for individuals and employers that subsidize private pension plans. In fact, so much do we take these tax advantages for granted that few people ever consciously recognize them— and especially not the would-be privatizers of Social Security. The fact is that privatization could not be economically feasible unless supported by the $44 billion presently supplied by federal tax expenditures every year, but the privatization mavens conveniently choose to forget this fact.

The programs that provide special services to the elderly are appreciated by those who use them, but, predicated as they are on the assumption that all elderly people *need* services, they tend to stigmatize the elderly as a group universally dependent on the larger society.

Medicare, the health insurance program for the elderly, is a troubled enterprise because of its rapidly rising cost, fueled by the escalating cost of medical care and the growing number of participants, and because of the rising deductibles and co-payments that have considerably eroded the value of its benefits. The Medicare Trust Fund is threatened with bankruptcy by the end of the century. Nonetheless, despite the difficulties associated with Medicare, it is likely to continue to be popular because it provides better protection for the elderly at a lower cost than private health insurance does or probably ever can do.

Medicaid and SSI, which are both outright welfare programs, are the least popular. As a result, these programs are poorly funded despite the great need they purport to meet. The requirement that elderly people "spend down" their assets (a euphemism for pauperization) before being eligible for long-term care under Medicaid is almost medieval in its cruelty.

Overall, government provision for the elderly, except for the absence of any program for long-term care other than Medicaid, is roughly comparable to that of most industrialized nations. Nonetheless, it is a patchwork, a jerry-built system leaving much to be desired. Its greatest weakness is on the health care side, where, clearly, the nation would be better off with a system of universal health care insurance. Such a plan was considered back in 1935 by the Committee on Economic Security, a cabinet-level panel created by Franklin Roosevelt, whose report to the president provided the blueprint for the Social Security Act. Roosevelt, fearing the medical establishment's wrath, lost his nerve and excluded health insurance from the Act. It wasn't until 1965 that Medicare and Medicaid were added, and then with such open-ended concessions to third-party providers that future troubles were inevitable.

OASI is by no means a perfect program, but it is certainly one of the best we have. It is administered well and has stood the test of time. Without OASI, more than half of the nation's retirees would be living below the poverty line. It is a fixture of the American retirement landscape, and woe to the politician who dares suggest that its benefits be reduced by any amount for any reason. Paradoxically, Social Security has come under increasing attack recently from several directions.

First, as the largest of the government's entitlement programs, it offers a tempting target as Congress, under the lash of the Gramm-Rudman-Hollings Deficit Reduction Act, faces some extremely difficult decisions. The threat to "violate" Social Security exists in spite of its separate funding structure; in fact, except for a special provision under Gramm-Rudman, Social Security would be off-budget altogether.

Second, because the ratio of Social Security payouts to payroll taxes paid into it favors those presently retired or about to retire over younger people still in the labor force—though it will remain a good proposition even for this last group—the notion that Social Security constitutes intergenerational inequity has gained currency. The old, it is said, are bankrupting the future of the young, ripping them off. There is even an organization, calling itself Americans for Generational Equity, devoted to promoting this divisive concept.

Third, because the overall poverty rate for elderly persons is now, thanks largely to Social Security, slightly lower than that of the general population and because all retirees, regardless of how well off they may be, are eligible for benefits, critics on the far Left and far Right have joined to demand that Social Security be revamped as a means-tested safety-net program. It is outrageous, these critics say, that a millionaire retiree should receive a monthly Social Security check when there are elderly living in dire poverty and when many needs of even middle-class retirees remain unmet.

Fourth, there is another class of critics who believe that Social Security is unfair to young Americans and unsound as a long-term measure for providing retirement security. They claim that while today's retirees receive approximately three dollars in benefits for every dollar they paid in, when the baby boomers (presently aged 28–46) retire in the next century, they will receive only one dollar for each dollar paid in. According to these critics, the Social Security system, which approached bankruptcy in 1983, will be bankrupt when the baby boomers' children retire in the next century. All this is attributable, they say, to Congress's having set retirement benefit levels too high back in the 1960s and 1970s and then having indexed them to Consumer Price Index. They also, and quite accurately, point to a precipitous decline in the ratio of workers to beneficiaries from 16.5 to one in 1950 to just 3.2 to 1 in 1980, a ratio that will further drop to 2 to 1 by the time the baby boomers retire.

The solution to this problem of the fairness and long-term viability of Social Security, these critics conclude, is to phase it out over the next 40 years for people under 50 years of age and replace it with a negative income tax for low-income retirees. Under this so-called reform, only about a fifth of present Social Security outlays would be necessary to ensure that no retirees would have an income below the poverty line. Presumably, all other retirees would depend on present savings and private pension plans, thus effectively privatizing the system.

The weaknesses of this argument are only too obvious. First, once Social Security became a welfare safety-net program, there could be no guarantee that future Congresses would continue to fund it, either through a negative income tax or by direct appropriations, at a level sufficient to meet the needs of lower-income elderly. One has only to look at the miserable funding of SSI to see that. Old age poverty would very likely become a national tragedy once again.

Second, most of the baby boomers, even those in households with two earners, are heavily in debt and are saving little or nothing for the future. If they were relieved of their Social Security payroll contributions in a privatized system, there is no evidence to suggest that they would put this money aside for their old age. Furthermore, there is little to suggest that the baby "bust" generation just behind them will do any differently. It seems likely, then, that when these generations retire, their reliance on the proposed negative income tax will be far greater than predicted by the privatizers, creating a major funding problem and adding significantly to the annual deficit. One of the great strengths of Social Security as now constituted is that it forces all active workers to save for their retirement. We should think twice and twice again before jettisoning the current system.

Third, one of the assumptions that the privatizers make is that the proportion of workers covered by private pension plans will increase. Perhaps we should take a look at what is going on in private employment, where a number of companies are abandoning their pension programs where more and more jobs are part-time and carry no retirement benefits at all, and where increasing numbers of workers are employed on a contract basis, again without benefits. All this should suggest that the private pension movement may have peaked and from here will either remain at current levels or actually decline from the roughly half of all workers now covered, with less than a third having vested rights to their pensions. There are other drawbacks to privatization. Many private pensions are extremely small. They are less available to women workers. We should therefore be very cautious about basing too much of our old age security system on assumptions about private pensions and employer-supplied health benefits. However painful it may be, we must take a realistic look at what may have to happen to the cost of labor if the United States is to hold its own in an increasingly competitive global economy.

The final weakness of the privatization argument is that it overlooks the fact that Social Security provides some very important benefits beyond old age pensions. It also provides disability protection for individuals and families and protects families in the case of the premature death of a breadwinner. The cost of equivalent private insurance would be well be-

yond the reach of most families. Furthermore, virtually no
private schemes provide benefits that increase with inflation.

In thinking about the future, one must consider the enormously complex question of the buildup of the Social Security Trust Fund. As a result of the Social Security rescue oper-
ation of 1983, proposed by the Greenspan Commission and
enacted by Congress, the Trust Fund reserves are now building up rapidly and are projected to reach about $12 trillion by
the year 2030. These reserves, representing the difference between annual payroll collections and annual pension expenditure, are invested in U.S. government securities, which must
be redeemed beginning in 2011, when the first wave of baby
boomers retires, and continuing thereafter until the middle of
the 21st century, by which time most of the baby boomers
will have gone to their rewards. If the reserves are not available when the baby boomers retire, they will not get the pensions they have been promised, creating one of the most ex-
plosive situations the nation has known or will ever know.

The reserves, as they build up, cannot simply sit in a bank,
however. They must be invested in *something*. Presently, they
are being used to reduce the annual government deficit,
which was the reason that the Gramm-Rudman-Hollings Act
reestablished the concept of a unified budget. By 1993, by this
bit of fiscal sleight-of-hand, the annual budget deficit will
seem to have vanished. However, as in any magic trick, the
real deficit will still be there, exclusive of Social Security, to
the tune of $70 billion or more. This will be the case simply
because in that year, 1993, Social Security will be taking in
$70 billion more than it will be paying out.

When we say that Social Security funds are being used to
reduce the deficit, what we really mean is that they are relieving the government of the need to go into the private market
to borrow funds. This is, of course, a good thing because it
should help to lower interest rates by making more money
available to private borrowers and lessening our dependence
on foreign investors. Indeed, sometime after the turn of the
next century, the Social Security Trust Fund may own the en-

tire national debt, presently about $2 trillion but likely to be
much higher by then.
' The big question, then, is whether the government will be
able to redeem its debt to the Trust Fund when the time
comes. Its ability to do so will depend entirely on the level of
economic growth between now and then. That, in turn, will
depend at least in part on keeping the real annual deficit from
exceeding the $70 billion one hopes it will be down to by
1993.

Some analysts suggest that $70 billion is too high for the
permanent annual deficit and that it should be reduced by
cutting entitlements now, thereby allowing the Trust Fund to
build up more rapidly. Another set of calculations, however,
suggest that if the "moderately pessimistic" II B scenario of
the trustees of the Social Security Trust Fund, which envisions a gross national product (GNP) of $54 trillion in 2030,
rising to $161 trillion by 2050, is correct, then the economy
will be large enough to cope with even a long-term deficit of
$70 billion.

One can argue about the precise size of GNP necessary for
coping with a large deficit *and* maintaining entitlements, but
there will be no dispute about the fact that when the baby
boomers retire, the economy will have to support them in
their old age whether under some form of Social Security,
private pensions, individual savings, or some combination of
the three. This means that vigorous economic growth, based
on a growth in productivity, is essential over the next three
decades.

In considering what will spur increased productivity, we
can suggest no viable alternative to investment in the nation's
physical resources, in research and development, and especially in human resources. Right now, we face enormous deficiencies in our educational system and in the functional liter-
acy of millions of workers already in the labor force. The task
we have ahead of us is not just to make steady progress in reducing the deficit. We must also find the money to invest in
people. Many people, myself among them, believe that we can
find these investment funds *without* seriously curtailing our

present system of benefits for the elderly. There are, however, some very influential voices to the contrary. The issue is now before the nation and will be the subject of some major battles in the years ahead.

Certainly, as we move into the future, we must not on any account use any part of the Social Security Trust Fund reserves to increase the present level of benefits or add new benefits. That would simply be robbing the future and would be unwise, to say the least. Where deficiencies exist in the present system, such as in long-term care, we must find other measures to fill them, perhaps by levying new taxes. But if new taxes are necessary, they should not be imposed solely on the elderly, as happened recently in the Medicare amendment to provide catastrophic health care. That would be a clear violation of the principle of collective responsibility. Taxing Social Security benefits as ordinary income is another matter, however, and I have no objection to that. But if a worker is or has been self-employed or has been in and out of the work force, as many women have been, he or she would certainly be justified in objecting to such taxation. The subject is clearly open to debate.

In considering the related questions of economic growth and old age security, I am convinced that the nation must give serious attention to reversing the trend toward early retirement and enabling the many millions of "young old" those aged 65 to 74, to make a greater contribution to the nation's welfare and growth.

It is impossible, given space limitations, to do more than touch on the second largest aspect of government responsibility for old age—health care. Here the public policy questions are truly mind-boggling. The possibilities for extending that responsibility and the attendant costs are virtually limitless. Not only does the matter of health care for the elderly raise troublesome issues about resource allocation between the generations, it also raises the equally difficult ethical issue of what limitations we can properly place on treatment of the elderly.

I have attempted as far as possible to delve into the enormous question of governmental responsibility for old age which, as I have said, is simply one expression of our collective societal responsibility. This responsibility exists despite the lack of any real basis in historical tradition; the responsibility derives from the nature of American democracy and the development of affirmative national government within that democracy.

The question of who will be responsible for my old age is not one that worries me personally. I am already living in that gilded ghetto known as senior citizenship, and as the saying goes, "I'm all right, Jack."

I do, however, worry a lot about the old age security of my children and their children and all of our children and grandchildren. I worry not because I lack confidence in the future of Social Security, but rather, I worry that the conservative forces that are so powerful in this nation today will persuade us to sell our universal compulsory insurance program in favor of a mess of privatized pottage supplemented by a demeaning and perpetually underfunded public old age welfare system. I am uneasy about our capacity as a nation in this myopic and complacent age to make the hard decisions required to deal with our staggering national debt, to rebuild our worn infrastructure, and to upgrade our undereducated and undertrained work force in order to produce the economic growth necessary to finance any adequate system of old age protection in the future. Perhaps time will prove me overly pessimistic on all counts. I certainly hope so.

The Public Sector: Government as Last Resort

11

Mariko Sugahara Bando

I have been asked to discuss government responsibility for the elderly from a Japanese perspective. That's not an easy job, even for a Japanese government official like myself.

In Japan, there are so many policies and measures issuing from so many ministries and agencies that we need a central coordinating office headed by the prime minister just to keep track of them all. The policies for the aged range from medical care to lifelong learning opportunities, as well as novel projects such as the notorious "Silver Colonies." Japanese policies have a long history, changing constantly under the influence of socioeconomic conditions and people's expectations of government.

People outside government often place great emphasis on government's responsibilities toward the elderly, while those in government would rather emphasize individual, family, and private sector responsibility. As is usually the case with golden means, real responsibility should lie somewhere in between. Responsibility for the care and well-being of a nation's elderly should be shared by government and family, individuals and corporations.

Policies and public attitudes on aging have changed several times over the course of recent Japanese history, and we seem to have reached another turning point. For a very long time,

158

the primary responsibility for the care of elderly persons rested with the family. The head of the family—usually the eldest son, who would inherit the family name and property—had a moral obligation to take care of his parents in their old age. (Actually, his wife, their daughter-in-law, was expected to shoulder the entire burden of practical care.) The Japanese government mandated that the responsibility for elder care belonged with the traditional family and was not at all enthusiastic over the prospect of providing public relief.

There have for a long time been pension plans for public service employees, seamen, and some public corporation workers. In 1941, nearly all private sector employees were covered by some pension plan, and some even had health insurance, although the level of coverage provided by these schemes was far from adequate. From the end of World War II until the early 1970s, ambitious improvements were made in Social Security in response to social changes, such as rapid industrialization, urbanization, and the growing number of nuclear families, all of which reduced the ability of the family to take care of old members. Average life expectancy had increased sharply as well. All of these changes forced Japanese to become more dependent on Social Security. In the 1950s and 1960s, government made economic growth its first priority. Japan's enormous economic success made it possible to introduce the idea of a European style welfare state, and it's an idea that has become incredibly popular among the Japanese people.

Both the government and political leaders are increasingly concerned with the quality of life of elderly citizens. Japanese social insurance achieved almost universal coverage by 1961. In 1959, a National Pension Law was enacted to cover the self employed and their adult dependents under 60 years of age. The law's enforcement in 1961 expanded pension insurance coverage to the nation's entire work force. As for health care coverage, the Amended National Health Insurance Law of 1961 provided coverage for all Japanese nationals. And in 1973, all Japanese aged 70 and over were guaranteed free medical care. Health insurance coverage for the dependents of those covered by employee health insurance schemes was raised from 50% to 70% of medical costs. These public health insurance measures provide everyone with access to medical care and increase Japanese longevity and productivity. It should not be viewed as consumption but rather as very productive investment in Japan.

In 1963, the Law for the Welfare of the Aged was enacted, which declared that old people should be respected by every member of society and that they should enjoy a healthy and fulfilling life. September 15 was declared a national holiday honoring our nation's elders.

For many years, the family was the dominant institution in Japan. Other institutions, such as the community or religion, had not been very active in providing for the elderly. These days, we expect the government to share responsibility for the elderly with families. Nevertheless, there has been criticism from some more conservative people; they say that too much involvement by the government might reduce our tradition of family obligation and impair morals. Despite these objections, the years from 1945 to the early 1970s was a good era for Japan.

Now, social and economic circumstances have changed. The radical change in the economy caused by the first oil crisis temporarily pushed Social Security spending up. At the same time, increased costs incurred by Social Security reform in 1973 strained the finances of both national and local government. During the second oil crisis of 1979, the economy settled into a low-growth mode. Government debts began to snowball due to mass issuing of deficit-financing bonds, similar to what is happening in the United States now. Increased debt service gave rise to fiscal austerities.

With a slower stable economic growth, financial constraints on individuals are increasing the costs to the public sector. The need for public measures to meet the needs of the aged are expected to increase rapidly. There were about 5 million people over 65, about 5.5% of the population, in the 1960s. On September 15, 1988 (the day honoring old people, you may remember), it was estimated that there were

13,770,000 people over 65 in Japan, comprising 11.2% of the total population. That number is projected to rise to 31,880,000, or 23.6%, by 2020. Medical care expenditures for the aged was 428 billion yen in 1973 and 4 *trillion* yen in 1985: that's 25% of total medical care expenditures in Japan, which is 16 trillion yen. Medical care costs for the elderly and the general population are increasing faster than the GNP. Annuities are also rising rapidly, and contributions by workers to Social Security will be 35% in 2025, up from 10% in 1986.

An administrative reform program launched in 1986 linked up with fiscal reform efforts, and under strong pressure from the business community, the government began to pursue two objectives: first, to avoid raising taxes, and second, to cut expenditures. In the matter of Social Security, the Second Administrative Research Council's recommendations stressed mutual assistance and self-help on the part of all groups and called for restrictions on total medical spending, reductions in Social Insurance assistance from the National Treasury, restoration of rules requiring the elderly to pay at least part of their medical care costs, a higher pensionable age, unification of pension plans, and a review of the current methods of cost sharing between central government and other institutions. Unfortunately, these recommendations stressed financial efficiency over services and quality of life.

These days, the prevailing opinion in government is that the social protection system should be respected and should encourage as far as possible the self-help efforts of individuals while optimally combining community- and employment-based systems of mutual help with publicly provided support. With respect to cost sharing, social insurance is an effective mechanism for integrating individual effort into an organized framework sustained by a shared sense of civic pride. Within an administrative framework that ensured quality services, individuals with sufficient means would be free to obtain and use services beyond Social Security at their own discretion and cost, while the truly needy could rely on public support. Such options can extend Social Security protection beyond people in low-income brackets to include the general population, encouraging them to be independent and self-supporting.

Under the influence of these recommendations, a lot of reform was effected in Social Security. The Health Law for the Aged of 1982 mandated that elderly patients bear a small share of their health costs; the free medical care policy was ended. Until 1991, costs to the elderly were 800 yen ($6) per month for outpatient services and 400 yen ($3) per day for hospitalization, which included all medicines, food, and other services. Now (1992) it costs 900 yen ($6.50) per month for outpatient care and 600 yen ($4) per day for hospitalization with everything included. Despite this increase, hospitalization is still so cheap when compared to daily living costs *outside* the hospital, that many patients simply prolong their stays. We have many critics of so-called social hospitalization, meaning that many people stay in hospitals for prolonged periods for economic and not necessarily for health reasons. In the United States, the average hospital stay is eight days. Well, in Japan, hospital stays average 42 days, and more than half of hospital patients over 65 remain hospitalized for six months or more.

To remedy this situation, the government has begun developing intermediate facilities, which provide something between hospital and home care. The national government has also begun to cut the prices of many medicines and to push prefectural governments to establish their own guidelines for hospital capacity, length of stay, and so on to reduce costs.

Recently we've seen the promotion of another policy: to raise the retirement age. The Labor Ministry has been making an effort to change the compulsory retirement age from 55 to 60 and to compel corporations to provide job opportunities for older workers. But it is very difficult in Japan to completely outlaw compulsory retirement. Because of the national policies of lifelong employment, seniority, and age-linked wages, many Japanese companies are forced to keep employees until retirement age, with no possibility of layoffs. Therefore, corporations would like to keep mandatory retirement in place so that they can attract newer, younger workers. Many Japanese businessmen view younger workers as cheaper (since they necessarily receive lower wages), quicker to learn new technologies, easier to manage, and less likely to incur high health care costs. Compulsory retirement is very beneficial for younger workers and corporate managers.

But for older people who want to keep working, it can be very difficult to find or keep a job, in spite of their skills and experience. There is a "mismatch" in Japan's labor market, with plenty of job opportunities for a smaller pool of young workers and not enough jobs for a growing population of older workers, especially in the manufacturing industries. The Labor Ministry is now making an effort to encourage businesses to provide job opportunities for workers in their early sixties. Fortunately, Japanese workers—or at least Japanese *men*—don't want to retire early. They prefer to work as long as they can, perhaps because there's no room for them at home. Government should continue to create job opportunities for the elderly, provide job training, and postpone the pensionable age so that people will be encouraged to keep working as long as they can.

Public pension plans were also reformed. In the late 1970s critics of public pension policy began to point to problems in the system, such as the widening benefit gap among different pension plans and the inadequate pension schemes for employees' spouses, especially wives. They also pointed to the increasingly precarious financial base for pension plans in a nation with a rapidly aging population. The Japanese pension system was based on a number of independent pensions, including (1) the contributory national pension plan for the self-employed and free-lance worker; (2) the general employee pension insurance and seamen's insurance for private sector workers; and (3) four mutual aid association pensions for national and local public service employees, private school employees, and agricultural, forestry, and fishery employees. The problems of this kind of system included benefit gaps among the different plans and fund shortages in some of the plans.

One factor that has an enormous bearing on the financial

basis of old-age pension insurance is the ratio of total beneficiaries to total contributors. Some pension systems with extremely high beneficiary/contributor ratios went into effect.
This problem, caused in part by structural changes in industry, was too complex to be dealt with effectively by individual
plans. The dependency ratio of people over 65 as a percentage
of the working age population is expected to increase from
15% in 1985 to 39% in 2020. Consequently, the number of
workers supporting each pension-age person will decrease
from 6.6 to 2.5, resulting in a heavier burden for each worker.
The upward trend of the age of dependents will mean a corresponding rise in the cost of pension payments. If the contribution rate goes up too fast too soon, working people will be
keenly aware of the burden they must bear and may begin to
resent old people. Government is faced with the problem of
designing policy that will maintain a proper balance between
the disposable income of the labor force and the living standard of pensioners. The Japanese Constitution mandated a
minimum standard of living for all citizens in 1947, but it is
difficult to define just what that minimum standard consists
of. The burden of contributions and the disbursement of benefits should be equitably distributed within and among the
generations. Without such a balance, we will not be able to
ensure the kind of long-term stability essential to support the
social protection system now in place.

To resolve these difficulties, the pension reform introduced
in 1986 established a new two-tiered pension system, which
ensured more equitable benefits and the integration of financial resources for the base proportion of the various pension
systems. Under the new system, the lower tier is represented
by the National Pension, which now covers *everyone* in Japan
between 20 and 60 years of age, assuring each individual a basic retirement income. An employee's company pension, pro-
portional to his or her salary, is now part of the second tier,
over and above this basic benefit. Government encourages
companies to set up their own private pension plans, providing some tax deductions as an incentive. And individuals are
encouraged to prepare for their own retirements by partici-

pating in a private insurance scheme, further reducing federal expenditures.

Welfare services have also been reformed. The scope of welfare services for the aged has expanded enormously and continues to expand, mostly because of the increase in the numbers of bedridden and demented elderly. One measure for those elderly requiring daily care has been the establishment of residential institutions such as nursing homes. In 1986, 128,000 people were cared for in 1,743 government-subsidized nursing homes. These homes were not established to care for the elderly poor but to care for the bedridden and those suffering from dementia, whatever their income. Residents pay the cost of care on a sliding scale according to their income. There are special homes set up to care for the poor elderly. The government has also begun to emphasize domiciliary support systems: home helpers are dispatched to the homes of families with bedridden elders who cannot care for them without some kind of help. Until recently, this type of service was limited to low-income families, but since 1982 home helpers have been available at a nominal cost to all families in need of this service. The cost is about $2 an hour. There is, however, a severe shortage of available home-help workers. There are an estimated 222,000 people in Japan aged 54 and over who have been bedridden for six months or longer, but there are only about 15,000 home helpers.

In some cases, families may find themselves temporarily unable to care for an aged family member. To meet this need, a certain number of beds were reserved in the national homes for the aged to accommodate bedridden elders for short stays, usually seven days or less. Day care is also available to handicapped elders living in their own homes; they can either go to a local day-care center or be cared for at home by visiting nurses. Visiting nurse service includes physical rehabilitation for the aged person and instruction on proper bathing and feeding for family caretakers.

Special public housing for the elderly is provided by the Ministry of Construction as part of its public housing program. In 1971 public housing eligibility rules were changed, making housing available not only to low-income elderly but also to those with higher incomes. The Ministry of Health and Welfare, to encourage families to share living space with their elderly relatives, instituted a program that lends funds to families that will allow them to obtain adequate housing for this purpose. There are also tax reductions for those families with elderly relatives living with them.

There are many ways for elderly persons to find self-fulfillment and participate in social activities in Japan. Just one example is that of a group of men and women aged 60 and over who have joined a voluntarily organized neighborhood club, through which they can plan and conduct various activities, including volunteer work. Government assistance is provided to these clubs, many of which are federated at the national and local regional levels. In 1986 there were over 128,000 clubs for the elderly, with 8 million members. The government also subsidizes many sporting and cultural events designed to encourage increased participation of the elderly in society.

There are other measures designed to give more meaning to life for the elderly. For instance, there are 1,826 welfare centers for the aged, 3,834 community-based rest homes, and 67 recreational homes located in resort areas. Rural elderly have not been forgotten; the Cultural Ministry has established a number of community-based homes in rural areas, where there are many elderly people living alone. The Educational Ministry has mandated opportunities for life long learning, and several colleges and universities have opened their doors to the elderly, offering them a chance for continuing education regardless of age. Other services are offered by the prefectural and municipal governments, such as free transportation passes, and sometimes gifts or cash awards to celebrate the birthdays of those who have reached a very advanced age.

Government is beginning to understand that the services and benefits provided under the Social Security system should be designed specifically to meet the general needs of the beneficiaries, while other provisions, *not* covered under Social Security should be left optional, available to individuals who choose to receive them at additional cost. But the government cannot be expected to meet every possible need of every elderly citizen, especially in times of budgetary constraints. Nor, given the increasing affluence of many of the elderly, would such public funding be greatly appreciated by the taxpayers. Certainly, the elderly might like ready access to goods, services, and information specifically designed to meet their every need, such as newspapers in large print or radio and television broadcasts geared toward those with declining visual and aural acuity. Products and services designed for easy use by the elderly would not only be convenient but would help to integrate more old people back into the larger society, making them feel independent and useful once again.

But who should pay for these special benefits? As the demographic structure has shifted upward toward higher age brackets and as pension systems have begun to provide more reasonable income levels for the elderly, more and more old people have enough property and/or savings to support them comfortably in their later years. The Research Institute on Aging has estimated that in the year 2000 the average yearly expenditures for households whose members are over 50 years old will be about 80 trillion yen, while savings for these same households will be about 512 trillion yen. Opinion surveys also reveal that more people are saving their money to finance their retirements than to leave large legacies for their children. Where market principles are applicable, then, nonprofit or profit-making institutions should be encouraged as much as possible to provide in-kind services. The social protection system is increasingly less able to respond flexibly and efficiently to the changing needs of the population. Even in a country like Japan, where the primary responsibility for providing such services rests with the public sector, not only is the private sector better able to serve many such needs; it can also help to prevent excessive drain on the public sector's resources and thereby prevent a loss of the nation's economic vitality. Such goods and services may well evolve into a very attractive commercial market for companies seeking to expand.

Government is willing to help the private sector share responsibility for social welfare. In fiscal 1989, the Japanese government extended public financing to nonprofit and joint-stock corporations that set up regional projects supplementing public efforts, such as domiciliary care services and special housing for the elderly. The government has also prepared the infrastructure by building large parks and public transport systems, making it easier and cheaper for the private sector to set up projects, such as cultural and sporting events, for the elderly. Government has also encouraged research and development in bioindustrial and high-tech companies that may better meet the needs of sick and disabled elderly persons now and in the future.

Much has been done, and much needs to be done still. But resources are limited. It is therefore necessary that we think hard about setting our priorities. First, we must maintain a high rate of economic growth. While we continue to grow, we must also provide employment opportunities for those older workers who wish to keep on working. There has been a great deal of public debate over whether to raise the pensionable age to 65. I believe that the time has come to do just that. Until 65, everyone should be able to keep his or her job or have the opportunity to move into a new job. The government should provide administrative guidance, job training, and subsidies to those corporations that employ elderly workers, and so on.

Second, it is imperative that we improve the quality and efficiency of services for the elderly. In the past, the government has concentrated on building nursing homes to care for those most in need. Now the government is emphasizing the availability of home care services for the elderly, encouraging families to stay together in their own neighborhoods and reduce their reliance on the government for the health care needs of older family members.

Third, the mental and physical well-being of a nation's people is vital to *national* and *economic* well-being. Under the Comprehensive Health Program for the Aged, the government will place more stress on health care management that incorporates prevention and rehabilitation. Japan has also introduced the idea of intermediate care facilities for the aged—something between hospital and home—that will help to reduce dependence on hospitals and shorten the average hospital stay.

"Aging" is now a key word in nearly every government document and policy paper. Even the recent tax reform, introducing the consumer tax in Japan, was imposed to help the country prepare for an aged society. There is a consensus in Japan that we can no longer attempt to escape from the serious problems presented by the prospect of an aging population. Japan's policies on aging are the target of a great deal of criticism from a great many pessimists. But I think that these social pessimists are forgetting that the new longevity and the aging of our population are reflections of Japan's social, technological, and economic success. Longevity is a blessing. We're always hearing about the great numbers of bedridden and demented elderly placing an enormous strain on the health and resources of their children and the whole society. But let's not forget that 95% of people over 65 can take care of themselves and do so very successfully. The time has come for us to change our perceptions of aging and encourage our older citizens to share in everything our society has to offer, including the responsibilities. The government is merely a supplement to the efforts of individuals, communities, and the private sector, and it should always remain the last resort for the elderly.

The Private Sector: The Gift of Time

12

John L. Steffens

Nothing can be of greater concern to us than the personal security and prosperity of the most valuable resource we have in Japan and the United States: our human resource—*people.*

We are two nations that care deeply about our citizens. We nurture the young, we develop the talents of those actively enjoying midlife, and we celebrate the experience and wisdom of our elders. These are natural, noble, and necessary responsibilities we share as members of the human race.

I was asked to write on the economic enterprise (business, the company, the corporation) and its role and responsibility in the social phenomenon we are calling the new longevity. I am by nature an optimist, defined in the dictionary as "one who habitually expects a favorable outcome." I once heard another great optimist, the comedian George Burns, who at 93 years of age said, "You can't help getting older—everybody does that. But you don't *have* to get *old!*" He was, of course, referring to the importance of maintaining a positive outlook throughout one's lifetime.

The issues that challenge us as we move into the 21st century—the sheer numbers of elderly, the medical complexities, the social burdens that could stop us dead in our tracks—these issues sometimes seem to overwhelm us. Clearly, we won't—and can't—allow that. We must assume that we will solve these problems. We must adhere to the spirit of true optimism and not expect anything less than a "favorable outcome."

I have three themes that I would especially like to address. First, we must remember that *quality of life* is what brings value to life. There's nothing to be gained by merely living longer if the quality of life we've been living cannot be sustained through our later years. There are four basic elements that make for a "quality" life: physical health, psychological well-being, financial security, and social engagement. Modern medicine, new technologies, and impressive advances in scientific research have brought us far along in all four areas, especially in the first two. People are staying sound, physically and mentally, years longer than had ever been thought possible in the past. We need to equal that progress in the areas of financial security and social engagement. We must ensure that the elderly can live free from worry about financial problems and that they are surrounded by active communities of caring people.

Second, we must begin now to take action, committed, spirited action, to make the most of the "gift of time": time to develop solutions and time for financial solutions to grow and compound over the years. This will make all the difference as we strive to conquer in the battles that lie ahead.

Third, we must make a united effort among all the nations of the world that confront these problems and concerns. We in the United States and Japan must lead a unified push to victory over the threat to one of our most precious national and international treasures: our aging populations.

It can be difficult to determine just what relegates a person to the ranks of the elderly. My father-in-law, for example, is an active golfer, playing 18 holes three times in an average week. He doesn't think of himself as old, even though he's 85. By the year 2000, folks like him will be the rule rather than the exception. We're fast approaching the day when it will be conceivable that more than just a few people will live to be 110 or even 120. By the year 2030, it's estimated that there will be over 2 *million* people over 100 years old in the United States alone.

As a representative of the American business community, I naturally take a special interest in what is probably the single most important milestone in the aging process and the one that people are often least prepared to deal with, and that's retirement. Most of us delay planning for this part of our lives, conveniently putting it aside to deal with more pressing problems, such as getting into a good college, finding the right job, starting a family, buying a house, getting your *kids* into a good college, etc. Then, finally, after every other need has been met, we turn to our retirements and too often find that we've lost the opportunity to plan for these years. We've started too late and saved too little.

Retirement, for many people, is the first time they see themselves as "old." Their routines may change dramatically, and they may find themselves for the first time standing outside the circle of activity that defined their lives. Americans thrive on doing and having; these are our motivation and reward for living our lives.

Then retirement comes along, and we have to learn what it means not to work. For some people, it may mean being "out of the game," segregated from mainstream society like a second-class citizen. Some people keep active by doing volunteer work but may still have trouble considering themselves as vital and contributing members of a work community, as they once were. These are stereotypes and negative ones at that. We do have the power to replace these negative perceptions with positive convictions. And do it we must.

People used to think of retirement as part of the life cycle's final plunge. They were "riding out" their lives between retirement and death, segueing into the end of life. Now it's time to change the way we look at the life cycle. Perhaps the old way made sense at the turn of the century, when average life expectancy was 47 years and only 4% of the population ever made it to 65. Today, average life expectancy has jumped to 75, with predictions that it could rise to 90 by the year 2040. Far more of us are living long lives. The over-65 population of the United States is growing by about 50,000 people every *month*. The over-85 segment of the population is the fastest-growing in America. For many of us, retirement no longer marks an end. Rather, it is a beginning to a long, potentially productive, and exciting phase in the life cycle.

We're fast approaching a time when many people spend as many years in retirement as they did working at their careers. Every one of us must think about how we can make good use of the time between retirement and age 100. We must plan for a kind of productivity that will carry us through the "extra" 25 or 30 years we have, courtesy of the new longevity.

This new longevity is a phenomenon like no other that we've experienced. It's not going to go away. Therefore, we must leap into the fray of the "longevity revolution." But the greater revolution must occur within ourselves so that we prepare for our own old age and welcome it.

In America, private enterprise has the foresight, power, and influence to champion the cause of a good retirement. We can help our employees provide for their retirements and plan for the kinds of lives that financial security makes possible. The challenge is twofold: We must develop the instruments and programs that enable our employees to take charge of their financial futures, and we must motivate and direct both the private and public sectors to pay attention, get involved, and prepare for the social, psychological, and medical realities of the century to come. The responsibility starts here with us, and the future is now.

Let's take a look at the situation in the United States. In 1989, 31 million people, or 12% of the population, were aged 65 or older. By the year 2030, only about 40 years from now, 64 million people, or 20% of the population, will be over 65. Our elderly population will actually double in the next 25 to 30 years. We've got the baby boom generation, 75 million strong, monopolizing the work force entering their peak earning years. But in the next century they will require the care and funding necessary to support their old age.

Let's also take a look at the money being set aside today to fund tomorrow. In 1989, private pensions totaled $2.2 trillion.

American businesses paid about $150 billion into Social Security, which is held by the government as part of the worker's future financial safety net. Throughout the 1990s, the "after payouts" surplus in the Social Security Trust Fund is expected to grow to over $100 billion annually, and by the year 2030, we expect a staggering $12 *trillion* surplus. Will this be enough to support the increasing number of elderly? And how can we create for our senior citizens the means with which to live quality lives, happy and productive?

Most people would like to maintain the standard of living they enjoyed during their working years into retirement. Studies show that retired people require 60% to 80% of their preretirement income to meet this standard. Typically, they need less cash income for fewer daily expenses and enjoy special tax advantages that lower their income taxes. But the need for health care services increases and, with it, expenditures for health care.

If we were to take a snapshot of today and freeze this moment in time, we might look at it and think we were in pretty good shape. But in order to see the picture more clearly, we must focus on the issue of providing long-term care for the elderly. A major public policy debate is currently raging over just who will pay for this care. In the United States, $42 billion is spent on long-term care annually. Medicare pays for less than 2% of this, and private insurance companies pick up another 2%. That leaves the rest, more than 95%, to be covered by out-of-pocket expenditures by the individual or family or, in the case of welfare recipients, by Medicaid. While the elderly population will double over the next 30 years, the cost of long-term care will triple. It is glaringly obvious that government and private insurance are not meeting many of the health care needs of the elderly today. Existing programs are not likely to be able to meet the higher costs of the future. In the absence of any new programs, out-of-pocket expenses can be expected to rise, and individual savings will have to rise to keep up.

I may be an optimist, but I'm a realist as well. I certainly believe that we should all "live for today," but that's *only* if we also "plan for tomorrow," guaranteeing that future todays will be *worth* living for.

How must the American worker plan today for the financial tomorrow? Well, the responsibility for that planning lies in three places: with the private sector, with the government, and, clearly, more and more with the individual worker.

Americans have, by and large, neglected to plan for their retirements through personal savings. We've gone from the old ethic of "a penny saved is a penny earned" to a new and not-so-improved ethic of "a dollar I can borrow is a dollar I can spend." The personal savings rate in the United States has fallen below 4% a third of Germany's and a quarter of Japan's. The baby-boom generation is most affected by the new ethic of consumerism. They work hard and earn more than their parents did, but they put away far less toward their futures.

Those of us who work for companies with pension programs tend to assume that everyone does. But that's obviously not the case, and even those programs that exist often don't provide very much, especially for the new breed of worker who changes jobs frequently. While pension plans are and will continue to be an important part of many people's retirement mix, only about 40% of American retirees receive pension benefits. And, on average, they derive only about 20% of their total retirement income from this business-based source.

The government's contribution, through Social Security, amounts to about 40% of income for most retired workers and up to 75% for low-income workers. These three primary sources of retirement income—personal savings, employee pensions, and Social Security—forge a tripartite relationship among individuals, corporations, and the government. This strategic triad will become increasingly critical as we watch our snapshot of the present fade away over the next few years. We've already got a rapidly aging population and a lengthening life span. We've been producing fewer babies since the early 1960s and 1970s, but those we produce, to put it in crude industrial terms, are lasting longer. Today's babies are lasting longer because they get better maintenance. And for that, we must thank modern medicine.

But good maintenance costs money. Medical and other health care costs in the United States are skyrocketing. In 1988, costs reached $500 billion, up 9.8% from 1987. The biggest consumers of health care are those over 65, and long-term care alone is suffering under the current system.

If we look ahead to the year 2010, when the first baby boomers begin to retire, the numbers of those needing medical and long-term care will rise sharply, and costs will soar. Over the subsequent 25 years, until about 2035, as more and more baby boomers become pensioners rather than earners, the effect on benefit systems and savings will be rather like having all of a ship's passengers move to the starboard rail. The balance of workers to retirees will begin to shift soon. As more people live into their eighties and nineties, we will be challenged to deliver whatever it takes to maintain the quality of life over longer and longer retirements.

The demographic trends of increasing longevity and the aging of the baby boomers will converge in the next century, each compounding the impact of the other. Either of these trends alone would represent a major demographic shift. Together, they signal climactic social change for this country, and unless we prepare now for the impact, it will hit us with the force of a hurricane. But because these two trends are clearly visible to us, we have the rare luxury of time to prepare, that "gift of time" that I mentioned earlier.

It's crucial that the private and public sectors lead the crusade for the elderly. Leaders in both business and government must engage in a public policy debate focusing on the critical issues of aging. Historically, the economic enterprise has played a role in providing support for individuals' old ages. People used to work right up to the time they died, literally carried out with their boots on. The concept of retirement is relatively new in this country. It developed early in the century, with the help of the Social Security Act of 1935. Workers no longer worked after age 65, but business continued to pro-

vide income, matching the Social Security contributions employees made during their working years.

There are two basic ways of paying the costs of retirement,
prefunding and pay-as-you-go. Social Security began as a pay-
as-you-go system but it has shifted in recent years, at least in
part, to a prefunded system. As a result, there is a set of staggering numerical projections for Social Security looming over
the entire universe of retirement planning.

When the Social Security system was introduced during
the Great Depression, when jobs were scarce, one of its aims
was to get older people to leave the labor force to make room
for younger workers. These days, the Social Security calculus
is changing. We have proportionately fewer workers available
over the next several decades to support ever-increasing numbers of retirees. In 1942, there were 42 workers for every beneficiary in the Social Security system. Today, there are just
over three workers for every beneficiary, and by the middle of
the next century, there will be fewer than two to one. The new
boosts in the Social Security payroll tax were designed to
keep the system solvent until the middle of the next century,
but between now and then, the graphs charting the Social Security Trust Fund look like the Space Mountain roller coaster
at Disneyland.

On the way up the roller coaster, the surplus is enormous—
an expected $12 trillion. But as American business people like
to say, there are no free lunches (or free rides) and, at least in
this case, some very serious catches. First of all, around the
year 2030, the roller coaster will start its downward trend. By
then, most of the baby boomers will have retired. By the year
2025, Social Security will be paying out $10 billion *a day*! By
2050, the entire $12 trillion surplus will be gone, and the sys-
tem will need to be revamped. Of course, most of my generation won't be around to see this, so it's easy for us to think it's
not our problem. But we have to ask ourselves just how proud
we'll be to have left such a legacy.

Second, the $12 trillion isn't real money but an accounting
entry on the federal government's books. By law, the excess
funds Social Security collects are given to the Treasury in ex-

change for interest-bearing (but nonmarketable) Treasury
IOUs. For example, 1989's $40 billion excess went to help pay
the expenses of Agriculture, Defense, and other federal departments. In other words, this "cooking" of the fed's books
masks some of the deficit so that instead of having a deficit of
$198 billion, we appear to have a deficit of "only" $158 billion. And all the Social Security system gets is those IOUs.

Third, that tantalizing $12 trillion is out there in full view,
where everyone in Congress can see it. Already the halls of the
Capitol ring with proposals for spending that "extra" money.
We might pay off the national debt, or fund new health care
or education programs, or increase the benefits for the current crop of retirees, or bail out the hospital insurance portion of Medicare. New ideas for spending the surplus will
continue to flow into congressional committees. And that
brings us back to the issue of long-term health care. Many
politicians look at the needs of elderly citizens for long-term
care and say that it's up to the government to meet those
needs. This means providing a new federal entitlement program and imposing new taxes to pay for it. Perhaps the taxes
will just be tacked onto Social Security. But there may be a
better way.

Non-means-tested entitlement programs are already out of
control. The Social Security roller coaster can carry only so
many riders. If we are to preserve Social Security—and we
must, since it remains *the* retirement foundation for the majority of Americans—we've got to resist any temptations to
load new entitlements on it.

Right now, we have a terrific opportunity to initiate new
policies for the long term. Living well longer entails dealing
with a range and a variety of related issues. We must look at
retirement and all its financial ramifications as a whole. We
must have leaders and policies that will encourage savings at
all levels: personal, business, and government. The present
administration must address the critical problem of a mas-
sive budget deficit in order to elevate our standard of living
and increase our rate of economic growth. The current budget
deficit reflects our alarmingly low national savings rate—

2.8% of the gross national product, down from 7.2% a decade ago—which, if reversed, would spur new investments in physical plants and equipment and lead to higher national productivity and income. Ironically, the current American tax structure actually discourages individuals from saving. Government must redirect policy and give the American public incentives to save.

In past years, the pendulum has swung toward increased reliance on government innovation to respond to the problems confronting our nation. But government alone can't defuse the demographic time bomb set to go off in the 21st century. The job is too big for government to handle on its own. It requires a new popular attitude and a new partnership, one in which the public and private sectors work together to help individuals help themselves. We don't need a crystal ball to see the kind of society we face in the next century and what kinds of policies and innovations are demanded. We have all the numbers we need right in front of us.

First, individuals must be encouraged to take charge of their economic lives and actively plan for their futures. There's no better or sounder reason for people to save than to guarantee high-quality retirements.

Second, the government must adjust its tax policies regarding employee benefit programs and individual savings to allow this kind of forward planning, while continuing to maintain the social safety net for those who cannot provide for themselves.

And third, the private sector must use its ingenuity, talent for innovation, and insight into the American public's needs and desires, to design and market imaginative new savings and investment plans that will encourage new savings and take full advantage of all the incentives that government can provide.

As the Social Security equation changes, we must come up with a new "social recipe" for the new times. We won't be able to rely on the "two parts government, two parts corporation, one part individual" recipe much longer. In its place we will need a balanced equation of one part each of government, corporation, and individual. And if the individual is able to contribute two or even three parts to the financial equation, the long-term positive results in the way of increased benefits for all could be phenomenal.

If government provides incentives that enable corporations to get employees to save, we will have, not an arithmetic, but a geometric savings progression over time. We have seen the emergence of employee-directed savings/retirement plans, or 401 K programs. An employee's take-home pay is reduced to put aside tax-deferred money with which to "buy" a better and richer retirement. This may be accomplished through a defined contribution plan that permits savings to grow when market conditions are favorable. These days, employer-sponsored pension plans and medical benefits packages face increasing restrictions and, in some cases, even termination, shifting more of the burden of retirement planning to the individual. 401K plans or the new IRA-like accounts represent a kind of "self-insurance" for individuals and should be developed and expanded to further benefit employees who participate in them. Ultimately, individuals must change their economic behavior in order to take advantage of these plans.

But try telling a 25-year-old man or woman of the 1990s to forgo a ski vacation in Colorado and set the money aside for his or her retirement. Let's suppose that ski vacation costs $2,000 today and that a young man puts that same $2,000 into an Individual Retirement Account (IRA) this year. Over the next 40 years, compounding tax-free at an average of 9%, that $2,000 will grow into $63,000 in retirement assets. That vacation, taken today, will actually cost the young man $61,000 in the long run. IRAs and Keogh Plans, by offering tax-deductible contributions and tax-deferred growth, appeal to workers of all ages, putting time to work for them.

Furthermore, money placed in retirement plans doesn't just sit idly, like money stashed in a cookie jar. It funds the country's economy and helps keep America productive. For the individual saver who multiplies his money, this is another "gift of time." For the nation, that same gift helps to reverse the drain on capital and spurs capital building.

Studies conducted by the National Institute on Aging have shown that when people enjoy financial security they live longer, better, and healthier. And you just can't put a price tag on the kind of peace of mind that comes from controlling your own retirement.

Small changes in government policy can sometimes yield big results. The IRA is a good example. In the four years following the 1982 liberalization of the tax laws regarding IRAs, $250 billion poured into these accounts, 80% of it net new savings. How can we create *new* structured programs of asset accumulation that can meet the needs of the next century?

There's no shortage of ways to address the challenge. We have to give this challenge the platform it deserves in the economic policy arena. That priority can come only from a united front formed by government, corporations, and individuals. Therefore, our first priority must be to unite in this cause.

Government should make use of the innovative, creative genius of the private sector. American business and the public sector must engage in open and ongoing dialogue on the issues of aging and retirement in this and the next century.

The private sector looks to both the individual and the government for support in pursuing a sound social policy and a sensible plan for the future. We intend to work with Congress and the administration in Washington to provide such incentives for savings as the restoration of full tax deductibility for IRAs and similar savings vehicles; the creation of new tax-advantaged plans for retirement asset accumulation that would permit tax-free exchanges for the purchase of health care insurance or services; a realistic realignment of the laws on pension and defined contribution plans, as well as insurance and annuities, with the projected needs of the next century; the stimulation of a private market for long-term care insurance, especially group insurance; and long-term stability of tax and economic policies in order to enable time to work its compounding miracles. For its part, the private sector must aggressively create and market the financial instruments that will turn today's savings into tomorrow's secure retirement.

Industrial corporations across the United States are already getting a preview of what we can all expect in the next century in terms of worker-beneficiary ratios. Some of these companies actually support more people on retirement than they have working for them at present. We may all face different economic challenges in the next decade, but we must learn from each other and work together toward a common goal.

Individual companies, especially those like Merrill Lynch that have large employee bases, will have to structure benefit systems that do more. Employees are demanding more in the way of benefits, and employers will have to meet these demands in order to remain competitive and attract and hold the best talent. At Merrill Lynch, we've designed a long-term care model that combines the asset accumulation of savings with the pooled risk of insurance. It will be financed through employer and employee contributions, with tax-deferred internal buildup; the assets spent on health care after retirement are tax-exempt. Merrill Lynch is not yet marketing this plan, which is still in the prototype stage, as it requires new legislation in order to work. We do expect that it will be a model for other programs designed to meet the needs of the nation's elderly. Our model is predicated on the idea that what we want from the government is not payment for all services for the elderly but rather new policy initiatives that will enable working people to provide for themselves in old age. This approach would help the government to better allocate its resources to provide for the poor.

Many companies now refuse to consider long-term care benefits as part of their employees' retirement package. A recent survey by Merrill Lynch shows that *most* corporate benefits managers feel that their companies simply can't afford to provide this kind of benefit and have no plans to do so. But the survey also showed that the overwhelming majority of preretirees view long-term care as a major retirement problem. One wonders if employers can afford *not* to consider some of their employees' more critical needs and anxieties.

This kind of thinking is comparable to that of the driver in the famous "pay me now . . . or pay me later" commercial. The driver refuses to buy a $3 oil filter from the service station attendant and, as a result, has to come back to the same station for a new engine to replace the one ruined by driving with a dirty oil filter. He ends up spending about $900. Well, we can face up to the retirement needs of the future now, or we can wait for the government to meet these needs later at greater expense to us all. We can pay now, . . . or we can pay later.

Peter Drucker, the noted American authority on business management, once said, "Long-range planning does not deal with future decisions, but with the future of present decisions." It's no secret that we're heading toward an age-neutral society. People will retire earlier, live longer, have more time to fill, and more years to pay for. The real trick is not in adding years to life but in adding life to those years. All the elements that contribute to a person's physical, mental, financial, and social health, happiness, dignity and grace—these comprise that "quality of life" that we must claim as our birthright. It is on this birthright that we must base the decisions we make now.

Fears can blind us to the joys to be found in the continuum of the life cycle. People are often more afraid of living through old age than they are of dying. They—we—fear the poverty, loneliness, debilitating illness, and emotional exile that have come to be associated with old age. So we turn away our eyes, preferring to take the easy route of denial and dismissal, at least for the short term.

I urge you: Look again. There are a lot of older people out there determined to live well—and they prove it by *living* every day. They begin second and even third careers after retirement. Some take up jogging, even run marathons; others travel around the world. They publish papers, help deliver babies, manage their investments. They know how to have the time of their lives.

What role will the economic enterprise play in the future of an aging population? The private sector must share that role in harmony with government and individuals in a three-way partnership whose efforts will prove that the whole can indeed be greater than the sum of its parts.

It's time we joined forces, as individuals, families, employers, and government officials. We must reach out across oceans and continents to our foreign neighbors. We must dedicate ourselves to putting back into life some of the knowledge and experience we have gained from it, thereby ensuring a "favorable outcome" for the optimist in each and every one of us.

There's no dream too grand when we brave the challenges presented by the aging of our populations. The test of a dream comes when we awaken and take charge of the *new* reality, when we *act* upon the dream with courage and resolution. I look forward to victory on the battleground we have seized and to meeting all of you in celebration of our longevity.

The Private Sector: The Silver Plan

13

Toshiyuki Kato

Throughout the industrialized world, large corporations must deal with the rapid aging of populations. The new longevity that has accompanied our rapid economic and technological development presents new challenges to the business enterprises's commitment to continued growth. Since more and more corporations "go multinational" every year, each attempt to deal with the challenges of the aging of the labor force—aging that, we must remember, does not bypass managers and CEOs—takes on an international dimension. There is no company in any nation that cannot learn from other companies in nations with different cultural experiences.

Before I go on to tell you how my company, Mitsubishi Electric, and its union are meeting the challenge of aging and retirement, I should provide a little background. Japanese trade unions are composed of "enterprise-based" unions, unions whose memberships are composed of all the employees of a company. Every employee, from the president to the most recently hired worker, is automatically a member of his company's trade union. I am employed by the Mitsubishi Electric Company; therefore I am also a union member. For this reason, Japanese labor unions have great influence on corporate policy, and union members have extremely strong ties to each other and to management. Japanese labor-management rela-

185

tions are conducted on the basis of the dual role of the Japanese worker. Unions regard workers as union members, while management regards them as company employees. Since every employee has an interest in the union *and* in the company, negotiations take place within a climate of mutual trust.

In many cases, those enterprise-based unions within an industry will federate into industrial unions, which will then combine to form national centers. For instance, each of the large electronics corporations, such as Mitsubishi, Toshiba, Panasonic, and Hitachi, has its own separate union; these unions are then amalgamated into an industry-wide electrical trade union association. According to a survey by the Ministry of Labor, there were 166 industrial unions in 1989.

Labor in Japan is in the middle of a historic movement toward full unification. In November 1988, the unified body of private sector trade unions, known as the Japanese Private Sector Trade Union Confederation, or RENGO, was inaugurated as a national center. Despite such moves toward unification, enterprise-based unions are likely to remain the basic unit of organization.

The right to collect union dues from individual workers rests, for the most part, with the enterprise-based union. There are exceptions: a few industrial unions, such as the seamen's unions, have the authority to collect dues from their members; and some enterprise-based unions allow their branches to collect dues at the factory level and send them on to the union headquarters.

As to human resources, enterprise-based union officers, most of whom serve on a full-time basis while registered as company employees, are assigned to industrial unions and national centers as officers, and they exert considerable influence on Japan's national labor movement. Enterprise-based unions have in this way acquired an enormous amount of control over economic and personnel policies in Japan.

One of the principal responsibilities of enterprise-based unions is to work directly with management to improve working conditions, primarily by increasing wages. Union officers and management enter into negotiations during the annual nationwide spring labor "offensive" while remaining in close contact with the national centers and industrial unions. The union officers are also responsible for conducting industry checks and for presenting suggestions on intracompany activities, including the actual structure of business management. Once management has carried out the union officers' demands for improved working conditions, the union officers may then work with management to come up with strategies for successful competition with other companies.

Enterprise-based unions share responsibility with business enterprises for their contributions to the larger society as well. With management, they work to ensure a high rate of employment and a supply of first-quality goods and services and to prevent illegal and unethical practices among managers, union officials, and workers. They also contribute to the public's awareness of the kinds of social problems facing Japan today and in her future. One of these problems is the rapid aging of the Japanese population and the concomitant rise in health care and retirement-maintenance costs.

According to an awareness survey that I conducted in 1986 among trade union leaders, 79% of those polled felt that the environmental change most seriously affecting their unions was the aging of employees. To reach this conclusion, these union leaders had conducted interviews with 2,107 members of the leading private enterprise unions.

When I asked these union leaders what they planned to emphasize in the near future, 38.6% answered that they wished to formulate "full-fledged countermeasures to ensure a comfortable life for workers' twilight years, including retirement allowances and pensions."

With regard to the actual introduction of education for employees in order to better prepare them for retirement, 12% of union leaders responded that their companies had already implemented such education, while an additional 7.4% responded that their companies planned to introduce such educational programs in the near future. However, nearly 80% of those polled said that their companies had no plans to introduce any such program in the foreseeable future.

Nearly 70% of the union leaders polled came out in favor of such retirement-preparation education programs and said that they have stressed the need for this kind of program in labor-management negotiations. Twenty-three percent said that while they approved of such programs, they would not be adaptable to their particular type of companies. About 7% opposed such programs.

From these figures, it would appear that union leaders, particularly those who have kept in regular touch with members through routine activities, face a serious problem of corporate consciousness about issues of aging and retirement. It also appears that many union leaders have not yet reached the stage of real dialogue over concrete countermeasures for aging workers and that few of them are taking substantive action on these issues. Since union members themselves usually focus their demands on issues of working conditions and wages, their officers tend to concentrate on these problems as well. Despite this, we know that union members in general are very much interested in their own post-retirement lives, particularly where economic security and medical care are concerned. RENGO recently sent a questionnaire to younger union members, asking them about their concerns. Of workers under 30, 61.6% replied that they were quite concerned about old-age care issues. If that many young workers are worried about their welfare in later years, how many more workers must be concerned as they themselves get closer to retirement age?

At the time of my survey (1986), all union members were covered by public pension plans, with average monthly pensions of about $1,300. Company employees are also enrolled in highly advantageous health insurance plans during their employment. After they retire, they must be covered by the national health insurance system. Except in a few areas in Japan, people over 70 must enroll in the Old People's Health Insurance Scheme. Because of the way the system is set up, people between 60—the regular retirement age—and 70 bear a greater share of the burden of medical expenses.

Pensions and health insurance are issues of great concern

to the working population of Japan. Many people entertain very high expectations for the upgrading of such systems. What can the labor unions do to ensure that their members will be able to live out their retirement years in full economic and medical security while also helping Japan to maintain a high rate of economic growth and a high standard of living for all workers?

Here are some of my proposals for the role of labor unions in planning for a better retirement for all. My plans are based on the existing structure of labor unions in Japan today. No radical changes in labor-management relations are mandated.

First of all, the national centers should focus their strategies and activities on the role of central and local government. Some of the issues and problems that need to be addressed are the formulation of comprehensive countermeasures (i.e., long-term policies) for our aging society; increased employment for elderly people, with job sharing as a basis; medical and health countermeasures, with an emphasis on disease prevention; facilities and policies designed to support the social activities of older people; ability-development projects aimed at developing lifelong vocational abilities for the population as a whole; basic study of the problems of aging; and a full-fledged, comprehensive pension system.

Of course, responsibility for solving the problems of aging in our society does not rest solely with the government, but it is important that the government create the climate for dealing with the issue by extending guidance and help to businesses, trade unions, families, and individuals. The government should also be responsible for enforcing the policies it implements on a long-term and comprehensive basis.

Industrial unions should support the efforts and activities of the national centers and assist in communicating and explaining the issues to the affiliated trade unions. Industrial unions must also see to it that industry-wide standards are implemented and enforced, especially with regard to retirement systems, pensions, and the employment of older workers. Where inequities exist, the industrial unions' leaders must work with union members and management to achieve industry parity. Industrial unions should also implement intracompany education programs and assist in the development of life-style programs.

Enterprise-based unions must act as watchdogs and enforcers, seeing that management properly and fairly carries out negotiated programs and policies. Programs such as vocational ability development, retirement-preparation, health insurance for middle-aged workers separated from their jobs, and health maintenance education should be the province of the enterprise-based unions.

Enterprise-based unions should also act as educators for the workers, helping union members to understand the effects of aging on family life, physical and mental well-being, and social and vocational status. They should help members consider dispassionately the problems they may face as they age; provide information and resources for intelligent consideration and management of such problems; and extend positive and concrete assistance to help workers with their own solutions, worked out in their education programs, to the problems of aging and retirement.

Every enterprise-based union can establish effective programs and policies for coping with the aging of the work force. Branch union officers must hone their personal relations skills, since they will be working most closely with individual workers, interviewing them about their needs and counseling them about their problems. Finally, it is the responsibility of every union *member* to participate in and support these programs and to do all he or she can to make them bear fruit. We need funds and facilities to support ideas and policies, but we also need *human* resources in order to make ideas become reality for everyone.

At the 19th regular union rally in 1972, Japan's labor unions organized a committee whose job it was to develop effective countermeasures for the problems facing middle-aged workers. Until 1975, the committee conducted a variety of activities, including surveys and panel discussions involving middle-aged union members, in order to discover where problems were greatest and in what direction the countermeasures should proceed.

At the 24th rally in 1977, the Silver Plan was approved by the unions, and studies began on the drafting of retirement-preparation programs and of a system for developing jobs for middle-aged workers separated from the workplace and for unionizing such workers.

Such were the birth pangs of the first Silver Plan, which was finally introduced in 1987. But what were the conditions that led to its conception?

My company, the Mitsubishi Electric Company, had traditionally maintained a personnel affairs system that separated office personnel from factory workers. In 1968, Mitsubishi eliminated such institutionalized differentiation and instead introduced a new system of qualifications and wage scales. This placed senior workers at a considerable disadvantage in the conventional seniority-based wage system and caused widespread dissatisfaction. In those days, Japan was enjoying a period of very high economic growth, and the new technologies that were being introduced into the workplace further weakened the status of senior workers. The union at Mitsubishi decided to look into the situation and do something about it.

In December 1978, a labor-management committee formed to study problems involving middle-aged workers. Their findings were described a year later in a joint labor-management report, "Recommendations by the Committee on the Study of Problems Involving Middle-aged Workers." The main points of the committee's report included recommendations for maintaining and improving productivity, enhancing the physical and mental fitness of employees; and establishing a spirit of self-sustenance through the implementation of life-style programs requiring the combined input of government (in the area of social security), management, union leaders, and individual workers.

As a result of the committee's work, the union put the Silver Plan into action. The Silver Plan is a life-style program for all workers 40 years of age and older and is primarily administered by the union. Mitsubishi's Golden Plan, a retirement-preparation program, is carried out largely by the company with the cooperation of the union. These two plans are part of a continuum of life-style planning at Mitsubishi, helping 47,000 workers of every age in 36 locations throughout Japan to make the most of their working and retirement years. The very youngest members of the trade union, those in their late teens and early twenties, participate in what we call the Fresh Plan. At age 30, they become eligible for the Human Plan, at age 40 for the Silver Plan, at age 45 for the Redesign Plan, and at age 55 for the Golden Plan; finally, at age 59, just before retirement, workers are enrolled in the Diamond Plan. I'm happy to say that the name Silver Plan has become famous in Japan, with nearly the same status as a brand name like Coca-Cola.

The Silver Plan is designed to help 40-year-old union members design their own plans for the rest of their lives. They do this by means of group activities that center on seven themes, including work, family, social life ("There's life beyond work"), health maintenance (not just medical care but proper diet, exercise, and a balanced outlook), life-cycle issues, the best way to use one's time, and even the meaning of life itself. Workers also perform regular self-checks, engage in discussions with friends and family members, and participate in studies and inspection trips. There are fees for participation in some of these activities, but the union bears much of the cost.

Silver Plan workers use a textbook to help them plan their lives. Other activities include lectures after work and on weekends and holidays, discussion groups, dinner get-togethers, and courses. Some progressive branch unions have introduced programs allowing workers' spouses to participate. Spouse participation, by the way, is an important distinguishing feature of the Golden Plan for union members 55 to 59 years of age.

One of the first questions we ask of new Silver Plan participants at their first meeting is this: After retirement, how will you spend your days? Do you have something planned for every hour of the 24 in a day? We give them a piece of paper with a 24-hour clock drawn on it and ask them to write in an activity for each hour. Naturally, the average Silver Plan participant can take care of eight hours easily enough—that's the time spent sleeping. And then there's an hour for breakfast, one for lunch (after retirement, that is, since Japanese workers are notorious for their five-minute lunch breaks), and one for dinner. After writing that, most of them put down their pencils. Oh, a few might add such things as an hour for walking or a few hours for watching television. Some write down that they plan to play golf. "Every day?" we ask them. Can you possibly see yourself with the strength or even the desire to play golf *every day*? The point is this: most workers simply do not know how to spend the hours that will be left empty by retirement from their jobs. Some might counter that they will spend more time on hobbies. Fine, we say. What hobbies? Will you really be ready to spend all your leisure time on your hobbies? *Now*, not after retirement, is the time to think about these things.

An awareness of the family's life cycle is also important to planning for the 24-hour clock. Some male worker might write down, for instance, that he will spend a great deal of time engaged in conversation with his wife and children. So we ask them: Are you quite sure that your wife will *want* to spend a lot of her time talking to you? Are you really that charming? Will your kids have the time to spend talking with you? For participants in the Golden Plan, we invite their spouses, usually their wives, to write down *their* 24-hour schedules. What a revelation! The men can barely fill in the time not spent sleeping, while their wives are writing furiously. Their husbands ask them, "When did you get these hobbies, these activities? *I* never noticed." So their wives mention classes, singing clubs, aerobics—things their husbands know nothing about. While the men have been working, the wives have been out making their own plans, living their own lives.

We also ask participants about their finances. How much

have they saved, what will their retirement bonus be, what investments have they made, what do they think their savings cut-off will be, etc.? We often find that while a lot of them have made good plans for their children's educations, they have not made what we call "life-cycle plans" to account for their old age.

Family relationships have often suffered during an employee's work years. So we do what we call an "interfamilial relationship checklist," offering examples from case studies and asking participants what they might do in such cases. For instance, we use the example of a 15-year-old daughter who stays out all night. How does the worker respond? Most likely, a male worker tells us that he would punish the daughter, or punish the wife, who is supposed to be responsible for the daughter and for everything else that happens in the home. Some even say that they would have the girl committed to a psychiatric hospital. So we ask them, "Aren't *you* also responsible for your children, for your home?" (Some men really have their minds in the old Edo period when men were absolute rulers in the home and women had all the family responsibility.) Then we ask them if they can name any of their children's friends or tell us what books their children are reading or what sports or hobbies they might engage in. The answers these participants give are revealing to us—and to them.

We also have Silver Plan participants look at their relationship to their own communities. After all, that's where they will be spending most of their time once they retire, and they may find themselves more and more dependent on the community for care as they get older and more frail. Some participants, in much the same spirit as when they discussed hobbies, say that they plan to do volunteer work when they retire. Remember that Japanese attitudes toward volunteering are very different from American attitudes. We ask participants if they think it will be easy to just jump in at age 60 and start doing volunteer work. Many people in your community might wonder where you've been all those times before when you were needed. Are you sure they'll accept your help now? We also take participants around to see the various facilities and institutions for the aged. We take them to the "Old-Age Clubs," where seniors go to socialize and engage in various activities. We also take them to the workshops that help seniors get involved in small businesses and earn some money. They may visit some of the nursing homes and facilities for incapacitated elders. Then we may have a discussion period where they can meet and talk with municipal leaders. What we're engaged in is giving our employees a healthy dose of reality so that they can see for themselves the kind of world they may be living in after they retire.

The Silver Plan has been in effect for 13 years now and has gained widespread approval among workers. There are, however, some union members who stubbornly refuse to participate. Many of them say that the required activities take up too much of their time, that they're busy enough as it is. I'm afraid that many of them are really scared to confront the fact of aging. No employee can be forced to participate in the Silver Plan against his or her will, but I hope the day will come when every worker in Japan will have the opportunity and the desire to take advantage of what plans like this have to offer them for the present and for the future. We need the cooperation of every politician, business manager, union leader, and worker to achieve that goal. Let me tell a Japanese version of a famous American legend. One morning, George Washington's father observed to his son that a big tree was obstructing the view from his house and that it would have to be cut down right away. Later that evening, he returned to see that the tree was still standing and that George seemed worried. "Why hasn't this tree been cut down yet?" he asked his son. George began crying. "This tree is so big, and the bark is so hard that I just couldn't cut it down!" His father replied, "My son, I asked you to *cut* down the tree, but I never said that you had to do it alone. To cut this tree down, you need to ask this one for the right saw, that one for help in drawing the saw through the wood, and another for help in carting away the lumber." Getting old well is indeed the responsibility of the individual, but other people must also be a part of your endeavor. Your wife, your children, your neighbors, your community, company, union, city, and nation will all have to get together to help you clear the view for a brighter future.

The Public Sector: The Golden Plan

14

International Leadership Center on Longevity and Society

How may long-term care for elders be financed while keeping costs controlled and family members in the labor force? This question challenges policymakers around the world. In Japan, after decades of debate, the Ministry of Health and Welfare has issued its answer: a 10-year national health care and welfare plan for the elderly known as the Golden Plan. Throughout the plan, there is strong emphasis on promoting the interests of the elderly, providing them with appropriate care, and ensuring them a high quality of life.

The plan proposes a major shift from long-term institutionalized care to home programs and geriatric rehabilitation in the community, reflecting the calculation that the cost of home care can be generally lower than hospital or nursing home care. Japanese policymakers regard rehabilitation as a major cost-reduction measure as well. The ambitious objective is "complete elimination of bed-fastness among the elderly." Now some 700,000 Japanese, or 4.6% of those aged 65 and over, are so severely disabled that they are bedridden or require constant supervision. Of

Reproduced here with the permission of the International Leadership Center on Longevity and Society of the Department of Geriatrics and Adult Development, The Mount Sinai Medical Center.

these, 42% are in geriatric hospitals, 20% in skilled nursing homes, and 36% at home. In 10 years under the plan, these proportions would change to 12%, 24%, and 35%, respectively. The biggest move is out of geriatric hospitals and into newly created geriatric rehabilitation centers. To accommodate the expected one million severely disabled elders requiring long-term care by the year 2000, the plan proposes the construction of rehabilitation centers with a total of 280,000 beds. In addition to the provision of geriatric rehabilitation centers, the plan mandates that each municipality provide enough outpatient rehabilitation facilities to serve any older person desiring the assistance. The FY 1990 budget covered the cost of 1,054 specially equipped buses to transport elders to and from rehabilitation centers.

A notable feature of the plan is the emphasis on decentralization. The government feels that the municipality is more suited than the larger prefectural unit (in U.S. terms, a prefecture is equivalent to a state) to design programs to meet local needs. While the national government finances most of the programs proposed by the plan, the implementation will be undertaken on the municipal level. Each city, town, or village will establish a semigovernmental authority to implement the plan by providing home-care services and making certain that disabled persons receive adequate assistance. Low-interest loans or subsidies to those applying to build geriatric facilities, such as hospitals and nursing homes, will be provided through a variety of channels.

The emphasis on home-care programs capitalizes on families' ability to provide that care, but, at the same time, the Japanese government recognizes that families need substantial support to continue as effective providers of care for the disabled aged. To relieve or supplement family caregivers (typically, the wife, daughter, or daughter-in-law of the patient), the plan proposes a three-fold increase in government-employed visiting home helpers, a 12-fold increase in respite care centers, and a 10-fold growth in

*adult day-care centers. Ten thousand Emergency Home-
Care Centers will be established to provide immediate
help on such problems as wandering Alzheimer's disease
patients and caregiver burnout. Staffed by two nurses and
eight volunteer counselors, the typical 24-hour center will
serve an area with about 2,100 elders.*

*The Golden Plan, which will cost the government
around $40 billion over the next 10 years, was developed
out of the need to increase services to a rapidly aging society and to contain costs. In the context of the long-term
care policy debate in the United States, it is encouraging
to see a long-term care plan proposed, accepted, and budg-
eted. Perhaps the Golden Plan can help guide us in the
United States as we struggle to resolve similar issues.*

JAPAN'S RESPONSE TO A CHANGING DEMOGRAPHY

Japan enjoys the longest average life expectancy in the
world. A baby born in Japan today is expected to live some 80
years. In the 21st century, Japan will become an extremely
aged society in which a quarter of the population is 65 years
or older. In light of these demographic changes, the country
wishes to develop an infrastructure that can accommodate
the particular needs of an aging society, especially in the areas of health care and social services.

Several general goals underlie the development of a plan to
make the Japanese economic and social systems suitable for a
longer life expectancy in a country whose population will
comprise a greater number and proportion of older people in
the future. In implementing measures to achieve each of these
goals, emphasis will be placed on dividing responsibilities
among individuals, families and communities, government,
and the private sector, as well as considering and respecting
the regional differences that exist in Japan.

General goals for an aging society:

- To create an economic and social milieu in which older and
  disabled people may lead full and healthy lives while living at

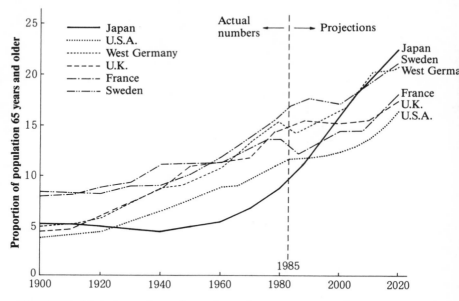

FIGURE 14.1 Actual and projected proportion of population 65 years and older in selected industrialized countries.

Sources: For Japan: "Census," Statistics Bureau, General Affairs Agency. For other countries: UN Population Studies. Projections: Institute of Population Problems, Ministry of Heath and Welfare.

home and continuing to contribute as productive members of society for as long as possible.

• To have in place a network of proper institutional care for those people who cannot live at home or those who could live at home if rehabilitative care were provided.

• To encourage community-based, voluntary, intergenerational support, as well as self-reliance.

• To provide a variety of financial and social supports to families caring for children and/or older family members, particularly in light of the rising rate of employment of women and single-parent households.

• To expand employment opportunities for the aged as well as guarantee income after retirement through a unified public pension plan.

- To promote health throughout the entire life span and enhance affordable health care and social services for the older population.
- To develop a lifelong learning system through existing educational and other institutions.
- To increase opportunities for volunteering.
- To improve housing and housing standards.
- To increase research and development efforts.

GOALS OF THE GOLDEN PLAN

The Golden Plan is Japan's 10-year strategy to prepare for the expansion of the older population during the next century. During this last decade of the 20th century, specific measures will be implemented to enhance medical and social services, adjust social institutions and the environment, and increase research and development, all in anticipation for imminent demographic changes.

Presented to the Diet in late 1988 and agreed upon by the three ministries of Health and Welfare, Finance, and Home Affairs in December 1989, the Golden Plan called for the expenditure of approximately $2.4 billion during 1990, its inaugural year. Expenditures will steadily increase over the following nine years, with an expected total project expenditure of about $40 billion or more. This is the first time in Japan's history that the areas of health and welfare have established such long-term goals on such a large scale. In contrast, during the past decade (1980 to 1989), only about $11.3 billion were spent on these same areas.

The specific goals of the Golden Plan are described below.

Goal 1: Increasing services for older people who live at home
Through this project, home-care services will be significantly increased by the year 1999.

- The number of *home helpers*, who provide assistance with activities of daily living and housework, will be augmented to 100,000.

- The number of beds in *temporary-stay facilities*, such as nursing homes that care for the bedridden aged for a short time in place of their families, will increase to 50,000.
- Comprehensive *day-care centers* will total 10,000.
- *Domiciliary care support centers*, which provide counseling and referrals for appropriate services, will be developed, with the goal of 10,000 such centers by the end of this century.

As part of its efforts to expand home services, the government will establish in 708 municipalities model communities where old and disabled people are enabled to lead active and healthy lives.

Goal 2: Reducing the number of bedridden aged

Precautionary measures to keep people from becoming bedridden will be instituted. Plans to achieve this goal include the following:

- *Rehabilitation centers* instituted in all municipalities.
- A system of *stroke information centers*. Through this system, the facility in which a stroke patient was hospitalized will be able to give the municipality where the patient lives relevant data on the patient so that he or she may get proper services upon returning home.
- Improved *health education* to prevent disease and disability.

Goal 3: Establishing a Social Welfare Fund for security in old age

The *Social Welfare Fund* provides for home-care services, improvement of the environment to meet the special needs of elderly and disabled people, and research on the improvement of social services for the elderly who live at home. Through *social services corporations*, resources from the public and private sectors will be combined with the energies of community volunteers to promote productive aging and the highest possible quality of life for the elderly on a regional level. Social services corporations have been increasing in recent years. The Musahino City Social Services Corporation is a representative example of this kind of organization.

Goal 4: Expanding institutional facilities for older people who cannot live at home

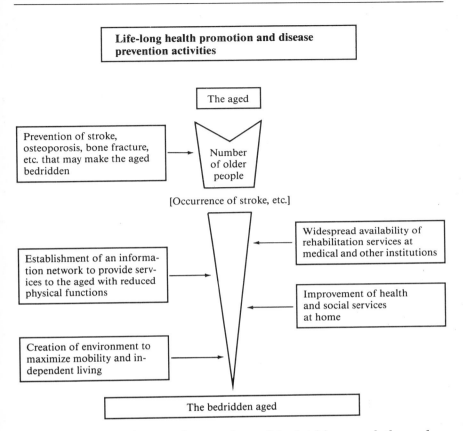

FIGURE 14.2 Reducing the number of bedridden aged through a series of interventions.

Institutional care will be expanded considerably to provide services to many more people on an as-needed basis. By 1999,

- *Nursing homes* will be able to accommodate 240,000 older people who need constant care and cannot live at home.
- *Rehabilitation centers*, that is, facilities for the elderly who need functional training and nursing care for rehabilitation purposes, will be expanded to serve 280,000 persons.
- *Retirement homes* designed so that older people may live independently with the help of wheelchairs and/or home helpers will be increased to house 100,000 persons.

- The number of *multipurpose senior centers* developed in depopulated areas of the country will rise to 400.

Goal 5: Promoting productive aging and maintaining high quality of life for the aged
Efforts to promote productive aging, continuing health, and high quality of life will be undertaken on three levels: national, prefectural, and municipal.

- At the national level, the *Foundation for the Social Development of Senior Citizens* will conduct research, disseminate information, and act as liaison among prefectural organizations. It will hold seminars for group leaders who work with senior citizens' groups. It will promote national movements and the *Nenrin pic* (the *National Health and Welfare Festival for the Aged*), which was held for the first time in Hyogo Prefecture in 1988.
- At the prefectural level, *organizations to promote a prosperous old age in society* will be created to influence public awareness about aging, train leaders to work with senior citizens' groups, and promote activities leading to better health and more productive and active lives for older people.
- At the municipal level, communities will be designated each year to serve as models where activities for older people, such as volunteering, creative endeavors, continuing education, etc., are supported and promoted.
- Corporations and individuals who make donations to the Foundation for the Social Development of Senior Citizens get preferential tax treatment through a deduction for their donations.

Goal 6: Promoting a national agenda for research on aging
The national agenda for research on aging includes studies on the processes of aging, diseases and disabilities of old age (particularly the dementias), preventive and treatment methods, and nursing and other clinical care of the aged. Toward this end *the Foundation for the Promotion of the Science of Old Age* has been established. It will support both public and private research on aging in Japan through the *National Research Center for the Science of Old Age*, as well as interna-

TABLE 14.1 The Golden Plan: First Year (1990) Goals Compared to Base Year (1989)

Efforts	1989	1990
I. Help at home		
1) Helpers for older people living at home	31,405 helpers	35,905 helpers (+4,500)
2) Beds in temporary stay facilities	4,274 beds	7,674 beds (+3,400)
3) Day care centers	1,080 centers	1,780 centers (+700)
4) Domiciliary care support centers	—	300 centers
5) Model communities where older and disabled people are enabled to lead active and healthy lives, and where community and intergenerational support is urged.	Newly created in 30 municipalities	Newly created in 50 municipalities
II. Health promotion, disease prevention, and rehabilitation		
1) Rehabilitation sites	3,849 sites	4,316 sites (+467)
2) Vehicles to transport people to and from rehabilitation sites	—	1,054 vehicles
3) Development of "stroke information centers" in locations throughout the country	—	10 prefectures*
4) Funds to improve preventive health education	$117.5 million	$118.5 million
III. Social Welfare Fund Funds to promote productive aging and highest possible quality of life for the elderly	$66.6 million	$400 million

TABLE 14.2 The Golden Plan: First Year (1990) Goals Compared to Base Year (1989)

Efforts	1989	1990
IV. Institutional Care 1) Nursing home beds	8,000 beds	10,000 beds (+2,000)
2) Rehabilitation centers	150 centers	250 centers (+100)
3) Number of people living in "care houses" (i.e. retirement homes)	200 persons	1,500 persons (+1,300)
4) Establishment of multipurpose senior centers in depopulated areas	—	40 centers
V. Promotion of productive aging 1) Model projects that implement measures to encourage productive aging (e.g. continuing education, creative activities, senior sports, etc.)	152 municipalities	304 municipalities (+152)
2) Regional administrative offices to oversee and coordinate projects	15 prefectures*	30 prefectures*
VI. Research Funds for research on aging	$3.4 million	$6.7 million
VII. "Furusato 21"** Funds to aid municipalities and institutions in developing facilities and community services for the aged	$400,000	$400,000
*Prefectures = States **Furusato 21 = "My Home Town" in the 21st century		

tional collaborations with such institutions as the U.S. National Institute on Aging.

In addition to the above, lifelong health promotion and disease prevention techniques and interventions will be supported and taught to young children so that they may eventually enter adulthood and the later years with their health intact and with the promise of a fulfilling and productive old age.

Goal 7: Developing comprehensive institutions for the aged

Under the program called *Furusato 21* ("My Hometown" in the 21st Century), efforts will be speeded up to establish comprehensive institutions for the health and welfare of the aged. Taking advantage of regional characteristics and existing resources, Furusato 21 will help develop communities so that their older residents will be able to live full, active, and healthy lives. Help will come in the form of support for public community-development projects, as well as aid to private facilities such as nursing homes, domiciliary care support centers, and senior centers.

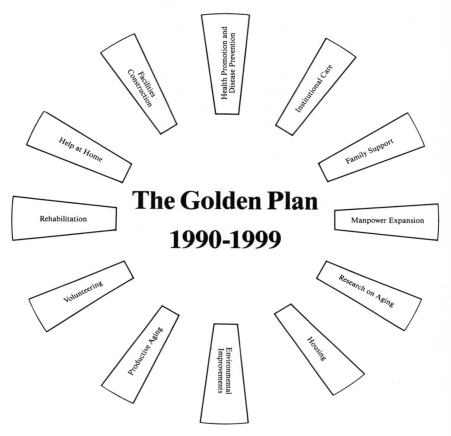

FIGURE 14.3 The Golden Plan 1990–1999.

Afterwords

Your Tomorrow: Requirements for Japan

15

Yoshio Gyoten

In every society, throughout history, people have pursued the dream of longevity. We all, somewhere deep within us, long after that utopian vision of eternal youth combined with the wisdom that comes with long years—for immortality.

Since the turn of the 20th century, the developed nations have begun to experience the rapid "graying" of their populations despite the fact that the actual percentage of old people in the entire world is very small indeed. Japan first became a part of the "longevity revolution" in 1970; since then, its population has been aging so rapidly that, if the current rate of population aging is sustained, by 1995 over 14% of Japan's people will be over 65. This rapid aging of a nation's population is unprecedented in human history. Despite the persistence of the utopian vision of longevity, the rapid aging of Japan's population is generating bewilderment, confusion, and premature anxiety among its citizens. The problems of an aging society threaten to overwhelm the Japanese people and their leaders. As reaching old age becomes an attainable dream for the many, societies must shift gears and start dealing materially with the aging of nations. For too many of our leaders and people, the prospect of coping with the costs and challenges of a large aged population has transformed the utopian dream into a forbidding reality.

211

Traditionally, the Japanese have not regarded old age as a problem. In the past if someone lived long enough to retire from active life and work, that person became the central figure in the family, cared for and revered by the members of the younger generations. One faced one's death in the shelter of one's family home, surrounded by loved ones.

This way of life has come to an abrupt end in Japan. These days, with the increased social and geographic mobility of families, the rising dominance of the nuclear family, and the unprecedented participation by women in the work force, a person must cope with old age and death on his or her own, without the assurance that family members will provide much needed support. People know that they will no longer be able to depend on their families for support, yet at the same time they are hesitant to rely on the larger society. More people, therefore, have begun to deal with the issues of health and medical care, economic security, and death. As a result, these issues have emerged as a dominant element of social discourse.

Many of us in Japan are aware of the propensity of the Japanese people to ignore difficult social questions and problems until they reach the point of crisis. Therefore, in order to impress upon people the need to prepare themselves for the inevitable realities of old age, a program was broadcast over NHK (the Japan Broadcasting Corporation) in 1981. The program depicted the current state of long-term care for the bedridden elderly in Japan (one title card read "Medical Care—Your Tomorrow"), taking the camera inside nursing homes and intermediate care facilities, as well as into homes where bedridden elders were cared for by the combined efforts of family members (usually daughters or daughters-in-law, often aging themselves) and home care workers. Grim scenes, showing long rows of beds occupied by immobile elderly men or women, spoon-feeding, intravenous feeding and medication, stacks upon stacks of adult-size diapers, were juxtaposed with scenes filmed in an old age hospice in Connecticut in the United States. There the elderly were entertained and comforted, and a great effort was expended on rehabilitating the elderly person and restoring him or her to a measure of independence. In Japan, despite the recognition that we must offer some alternative to nursing homes and family care, we do not yet have anything that compares favorably with the kind of hospice care available in the United States.

I'd like to stress that although this film was made in 1980, the many and varied issues addressed by it are still very much with us. Many hospitals and nursing homes devoted to caring for the frail elderly suffer from chronic financial problems. The hospitals are reimbursed by the national health insurance according to the number and types of treatment procedures offered. So while the doctors, nurses, and other staff members may try to provide care fine-tuned to the needs of each individual, it is often the case that the government will not pay for many innovative procedures, such as individualized physical therapy and rehabilitation. As an example, the hospital will find it more profitable, as well as easier, to feed all the patients intravenously, rather than spend time and money on actual meals. But patients on intravenous feeding recover more slowly from their illnesses, spend more time in the hospital, and are less likely to ever regain any measure of independence. Without more aggressive and individualized therapy, aimed at rehabilitation and reintegration into family and community, the frail elderly will only become more of a burden on the health care system and the economy.

When an elderly patient is cared for at home, the cost of care falls largely on the individual or his family; the emotional, physical and economic toll on the household can be enormous. Some families find that the only way to reduce their burden for even a little while is to put the elderly relative in the hospital, where the bulk of the cost of care will be covered by the government. Such inequities in long-term health care coverage ought not to persist in any society, especially one as advanced in its health-care policy as Japan.

At present, the Health and Welfare Ministry estimates that there are over 980,000 elderly Japanese living alone. It is estimated that that number will increase to over 2 million by 2010. If the Japanese government insists that families take on more of the costs and responsibilities of caring for the elderly, who then will be responsible for the well-being of those who have no family members willing or able to care for them?

This is not to say that there has not been any innovation and creativity in the field of health care for the elderly. In many areas in Japan, newly established intermediate care facilities and networks of visiting nurses and home health care workers have allowed many Japanese elders to recover more quickly and return home to their families from the hospital. Increasing attention is given to the psychological well-being of the elderly patient and the family as a whole.

But these innovations, and others like them, have yet to be implemented on a nationwide scale. Many elderly still spend long months or even years in hospitals; many others live alone or with spouses or children unable to give them the care they need. There are even households composed solely of bedridden elderly husbands and wives. More and more elderly face lonely deaths in silent hospital rooms, while their grieving families look on, wondering if there is no better way to spend one's "golden years." I'd like to share with you a letter from a young woman who recently lost her father:

> Even when the doctors informed me that my father was likely to die in a very few hours, the nurse would not allow me to stay at his bedside. I was forced to wait for his death in the waiting room, not at his deathbed, where I belonged.
>
> Throughout his stay in the hospital, my father was tied up to several machines giving him medicines intravenously. Tubes were inserted in his nostrils and his body was connected to several life-support machines. On top of all this, I was not even allowed to be at his side when his last moment came. "Your father has just passed away," I was told. "Please come right away."
>
> I looked at my father, at last free of tubes and needles. He looked human now, in peace after his long suffering.
>
> With all our technological know-how, with the most advanced medical system in the world, my last farewell to my father was still a heart-breaking experience.

Father, please forgive me.

The situation described in the letter above is becoming increasingly common in Japan. As more and more people end their lives in hospitals rather than at home, doctors and medical workers rely more and more on advanced life support technology, such as respirators and machines for intravenous feeding, hydration, and medication, to prolong life. But we have to ask ourselves, what kind of life are we prolonging? Are we sacrificing quality of life, ignoring the emotional, social, and even spiritual needs of the very ill in order to add a few days, weeks, or months of existence?

Shouldn't there be a different kind of care for the patient whose death is imminent? The biggest advances in quality-of-life issues for the dying has been done with patients with terminal cancers. Japanese medical researchers have recently spent time in the United States, visiting several hospices for terminal cancer patients. In these facilities, doctors, social workers, and other professionals meet with the patients and their families to discuss the kinds of care available. Choosing a particular type of treatment is a group decision. Emphasis is on rehabilitation, integration into the family and community, and, finally, acceptance of and preparation for the patient's death.

By admitting that there are occasions when medicine is powerless to prolong life and instead concentrating on making the life that remains worth living, medicine may truly find its heart.

We can no longer depend solely on doctors and hospitals to care for the very ill, the very old, and the dying. Families, communities, and the government must extend warm and helping hands to those who depend on others for care. We cannot wait—the future has arrived. Every one of us—young, middle-aged, retired—must ask ourselves, who is going to care for me tomorrow and what kind of care would I like to have? We must reach into our hearts today to find the answers for tomorrow.

Reanimating Old Age 16

Claude Pepper

The challenge to this generation from the generations that will follow us is a great one. Among our priorities should be the realization of the dream of the poet Alfred, Lord Tennyson,

> . . . the war drum throbbed no longer, and the battle flags
>   were furled
> In the Parliament of man, the Federation of the world.

Surely everyone of us hopes that we will all live to see the time when the nations of the world spend less money on nuclear weapons or other instruments of death than they spend on health, education, housing, and the welfare of all. We have seen, in the past five years, enormous progress toward a real and lasting peace between the Soviet Union and the United States. But there is still so much more to hope for. We witness the troubling diffusion of nuclear weapons among the nations of the world. How can this present generation stop the spread of the tolls of destruction, reduce the growth in the sheer numbers of warheads? How can we bring all men and women together in fellowship and peace? This is the great challenge to our generation.

It is also the responsibility of this generation to see to it that all who are born on this beautiful earth shall find their natural environment so unimpaired that their lives shall not be threatened, their very existence shall not be jeopardized, by anything that we do. This means that we must not pollute our streams with dangerous wastes, or fill our air with foul chemicals, or strip the earth of its life-giving minerals, or deplete the ozone layer—and we must not provide others with the encouragement or incentive to do so either. We want a world in which our children can be safely born and grow up in good health and happiness. This means that we must also see to it that we enhance our earth's natural beauty, not diminish it. This is the second great challenge to our generation from the generations to come.

We must work to transmit to our children and their children, here in the United States and in every nation, a political structure that will assure that every man, woman, and child enjoys every natural, human, and civil right, with all the benefits that spring from these rights. We must establish the kinds of institutions that will foster a society in which people all respect, indeed love, one another and work together for the common good.

I'm often reminded, in this context, of one of the most dramatic illustrations of the contrast between the kind of world we live in and the kind of world we want to build. One of our astronauts was just lifting off in his space capsule from the surface of the moon. Suddenly, 250,000 miles ahead of where he sat, he saw a tiny blue orb, like a glittering marble hanging in space. That, he knew, was Earth—*home*. No matter where else he looked in that vast immensity of sky, he could find nothing else, no moon, no star, no planet in all the universe that was quite like that tiny blue marble. From there he came, to there was he bound. How marvelous, how very *miraculous* it seemed to him then—of all the worlds that we've explored and photographed, only on that blue marble are there living creatures, plants, animals, people. What a miracle that is and what a wonder. How grateful must we all be for the privileges we enjoy on this earth. Then, reflecting upon the miracle, he realized that, rather than spending our lives in grateful appreciation and nurture of our planet, we spend so much of our energy and resources in figuring out new ways to kill one another. What a sobering thought for that distant observer, there in the moon's orbit, watching the earth rise.

One thing that we have great hopes of successfully transmitting to the future generations is an order of society and economy that allows humans to work and function as they were designed to. In 1978, we in the United States Congress changed the law regarding mandatory retirement. You see, until that time, if you worked for the United States government, when you reached seventy, you faced a little scene like this:

"Well, we're really sorry to have to tell you this, but you have to go now."

"Why? What have I done?"

"Well, for one thing, you're seventy years old now!"

"Is that a crime? Have I broken any law?"

"Not broken, but the law *does* say that you can't work here anymore. I'm afraid you'll really have to go."

Well, we changed all that. Now you can work for the United States government until you're as old as Methuselah (or at least, as old as he's said to have been), and no one can fire you—excuse me, *retire* you—on account of age. More and more, we're making age irrelevant in the private sector as well. While the laws regarding discrimination based on age are not as effectively enforced as they should be, it is the law of the land. You can no more consider age than you can consider race, sex, or religion as a criterion for employment or continued employment.

We are currently entering a new phase, which I call the era of the "reanimation of the elderly." It's really just a whole new way of looking at retirement. Instead of retiring altogether and entering a prolonged period of leisure—you might find yourself wishing you could retire from so much retirement—you would have a range of options. You might go to your employer and say, "Well, I'm sixty-five now [or seventy-five, or eighty], and if you don't mind, I believe that I'd like to remain in my job and work half-time." Someone else might say, "I'd like to share my job with a fellow-worker so that we can each adjust our work schedules to suit our needs for work and leisure." President Ronald Reagan once called me to congratulate me on my birthday. I said, "Mr. President, I think we need more seniors running things around here, don't you?" He agreed (naturally enough). I mentioned to him my idea about the reanimation of the elderly. I told him that we should find ways to encourage business to provide opportunities for part-time or shared-time employment for people who have officially retired. It's already happening all over the country, even without government incentives. I was playing golf with three gentlemen in San Francisco not too long ago. As we sat down to lunch, I said, "Well, I guess you fellows are all retired. Are you?"

One of them said, "Well, yes and no. I *did* retire. Several of my colleagues in my company are now retired. After a while we decided we wanted to go back to work and go back into business. We formed our own, new company. We started all over again."

Elderly people are some of the best-qualified working people in America. They are punctual. They are responsible. They are good people to have working for you. Just remember that those retired people out there, only a few years ago, were the ones who were running things in America. Someday, we'll reach a time when there will be no "retirement" period in anyone's life. Perhaps you might change your level of activity, for example, the amount of time you put in at work; perhaps you'll divide your time among a variety of activities. Whatever you decide to do, you must *never* think of yourself as retired from society; you must continue to contribute to the growth and progress of your country and to the well-being of its citizens. Government will have its place in promoting the sort of economy that will support employment for everyone who wants it. But in the end, the decision remains with each and every one of us, to reanimate life and work after "retirement."

Youth Speaks on Old Age   17

Daiseku Teraguchi

People think that teenagers never think about aging. And I have to admit, that it's usually true—we don't. Before I was invited to speak at the symposium called "Who Is Responsible for My Old Age?" I never thought about growing old and retirement. I'm sure that my Japanese and American friends haven't given it much thought either. If we discuss aging at all, it's when we get together and talk about how great it must be to be over 21 and able to walk right into any bar and order a drink, legally. A lot of teenagers smoke, drink, and use various kinds of illegal drugs. It sometimes seems that we're doing our very best to ruin our health. We tend to be careless about such things, focused on the present and the immediate future, never thinking about what life will be like *after* we've had our fun.

But coming here to speak to you about youth's responsibility for old age, I have come to realize how important it is to take care of one's body, to assure that one will have a healthy old age, both physically and mentally. But our responsibility isn't just for ourselves. We—young people of all countries—ought to care more about old people and respect them. In turn, old people must take responsibility for themselves.

I haven't seen my grandparents, who live in Japan, in several years. I really envy kids who get to see their grandparents more often. When I was six years old, I was sent to live with my grandparents for a time. I learned many things from them that I would never have learned from my parents. It is very important for a family to maintain strong relationships among the generations, especially between grandparents and their grandchildren. It's a great idea for us to come together and discuss the problem of aging in the modern world, for aging is something that we will all face. By the time my generation has to face old age, I'm confident, or at least hopeful, that the present generation of adults will have solved some of the economic and social problems that surround aging. It will be up to us to continue to work on the problems of old age—and the larger problems facing our world—not only for ourselves, but for the generations to come.

Appendix
Japan–U.S. Comparisons

The following pages have been adapted from Almanac on Aging: Japan–U.S. Comparison *by Charlotte Muller, PhD, and In Huh, M. S. (1992). Portions of that document are reproduced here with permission from the International Leadership Center on Longevity and Society (U.S.), which commissioned the almanac.*

International comparisons are necessary in the modern world because it is important to determine whether countries differ, and to what extent, in needs, resources, and approaches to social and economic problems. The comparisons are a tool in the process of developing common initiatives toward the solution of worldwide problems threatening individual well-being and social and economic stability. Improvement in international comparisons will help lead to more efficient and effective policy decisions.

This general observation is very applicable to the field of aging. Those countries that have solved, through industrialization, the basic problems of sustaining their populations and extending their life expectancy are facing another set of problems: how to integrate the elderly into economic and social life and how to minister to the frailties and functional losses that afflict a portion of this age group. Those countries that have not fully achieved desired industrialization and are burdened with poverty in the general population still have to provide a decent standard of life for their elderly. Family systems that maintained their stability for centuries are changing through urbanization and modernization, and public confidence in the family's ability to shoulder the burdens resulting from longevity has been weakened. There is, therefore, a growing interest in how well countries are equipped to adapt to the changes that longevity brings and in what these countries have achieved in this area already.

JAPAN–U.S. COMPARISONS

Projection of the Total Population by Age and Sex, 1990–2010

The total number of persons age 65 and older in the United States is expected to increase by 7.8 million—3.5 million men and 4.3 million women—by the year 2010 (Table A.1) At that time, men 65 and older will comprise 11.8% of all men; women 65 and older will comprise 16.0% of all women. Although this is a substantial growth (24.7%), the comparable increase projected for Japan will be 88%. The number of men will grow by 1.3 million and the number of women by 1.7 million, raising the percentages of men 65 and older to 18.9% of all males; of women 65 and older, to 25.0% of all females. Social adjustments to a longer-living population will be a challenging task for both countries but especially for Japan.

Average Expectation of Life in Years, 1960–1988

Life expectancy at birth for both sexes increased 7% in the United States between 1960 and 1986, compared to 16% in Japan in a similar time period (1960–1988; Table A.2). Although the improvement rate was the same for males and females, the expected length of life at the end of the period was greater

TABLE A.1 Projection of the Total Population by Age and Sex, 1990–2040

Age and Sex (Age in Years)	Population (1,000)						Percent Distribution					
	1990	2000	2010	2020	2030	2040	1990	2000	2010	2020	2030	2040
United States												
Total	249,891	268,266	282,575	294,364	300,629	301,807	100.0	100.0	100.0	100.0	100.0	100.0
0–14	54,070	54,232	51,509	52,311	51,210	49,898	21.6	20.2	18.2	17.8	17.0	16.5
65 and over	31,560	34,882	39,362	52,067	65,604	68,109	12.6	13.0	13.9	17.7	21.8	22.6
Male total	121,775	131,191	138,333	144,035	146,543	146,454	100.0	100.0	100.0	100.0	100.0	100.0
0–14	27,692	27,800	26,424	26,836	26,254	25,567	22.7	21.2	19.1	18.6	17.9	17.5
65 and over	12,852	14,273	16,372	22,430	28,594	29,235	10.6	10.9	11.8	15.6	19.5	20.0
Female total	128,116	137,076	144,241	150,329	154,086	155,353	100.0	100.0	100.0	100.0	100.0	100.0
0–14	26,378	26,431	25,085	25,476	24,956	24,332	20.6	19.3	17.4	16.9	16.2	15.7
65 and over	18,708	20,608	22,991	29,637	37,010	38,874	14.6	15.0	15.9	19.7	24.0	25.0
Japan Total	124,225	131,192	135,823	135,304	134,067	131,646	100.0	100.0	100.0	100.0	100.0	100.0
0–14	23,132	23,591	25,301	22,327	23,009	23,798	18.6	18.0	18.6	16.5	17.2	18.1
65 and over	14,819	21,338	27,104	31,880	31,001	31,738	11.9	16.3	20.0	23.6	23.1	24.1
Male total	61,054	64,543	66,861	66,543	65,950	65,933	100.0	100.0	100.0	100.0	100.0	100.0
0–14	11,856	12,104	12,981	11,456	11,806	12,211	19.4	18.8	19.4	17.2	17.9	18.8
65 and over	5,971	9,056	11,745	13,925	13,442	13,994	9.8	14.0	17.6	20.9	20.4	21.6
Female total	63,171	66,649	68,962	68,761	68,117	66,713	100.0	100.0	100.0	100.0	100.0	100.0
0–14	11,276	11,487	12,320	10,871	11,203	11,587	17.8	17.2	17.9	15.8	16.4	17.4
65 and over	8,848	12,282	15,359	17,955	17,559	17,744	14.0	18.4	22.3	26.1	25.8	26.6

Source: From Projections of the Population of the United States, by Age, Sex, and Race: 1988 to 2080, series 14 (middle series), U.S. Department of Commerce, Bureau of the Census, Jan. 1989; and *Japan Statistical Yearbook* (1989), table 2-2.

TABLE A.2 Average Expectation of Life in Years, 1960–1988

Age and Sex	1960	1970	1980	1985	1986/ 1988
United States					(1986)
At birth					
Male	66.8	67.0	70.1	71.2	71.3
Female	73.2	74.6	77.6	78.2	78.3
At Age 20					
Male	49.8	49.5	51.9	52.7	52.8
Female	55.6	56.6	59.0	59.3	59.4
At age 40					
Male	31.4	31.5	33.6	34.3	34.5
Female	36.6	37.6	39.8	40.1	40.2
At age 65					
Male	13.0	13.0	14.2	14.6	14.7
Female	15.8	16.8	18.4	18.6	18.6
Japan					(1988)
At birth					
Male	65.3	69.3	73.6	74.8	75.5
Female	70.2	74.7	78.8	80.5	81.3
At age 20					
Male	49.1	51.3	54.6	55.7	56.4
Female	53.6	56.1	59.7	61.2	62.0
At age 40					
Male	31.0	32.7	35.5	36.6	37.2
Female	34.9	37.0	40.2	41.7	42.4
At age 65					
Male	11.6	12.5	14.6	15.5	16.0
Female	14.1	15.3	17.7	18.9	19.5

Source: From *Statistical Abstract of the United States* (1990), Table 104; Japan, Health and Welfare Statistics Association, *Indexes of Health and Welfare: The Trend of National Health, 37*, 423, 1990.

for females. A boy born in the United States in the late 1980s could expect to live 72 years; a girl, 79 years. For Japan the corresponding figures are 76 and 81 years, respectively.

A 65-year-old male in the United States could look forward to 14.7 more years of life; a woman of similar age, to 18.6 years. In Japan, the figures are higher: 16.0 years for men and 19.5 years for women.

The sex differences in both countries foreshadow widowhood and concomitant economic and social disadvantages for women whose husbands had been the principal wage earners. These problems can be forestalled by laws protecting surviving spouses against pension loss and other appropriate social policies, including those addressed to improving the economic position of younger women so that they can better prepare for retirement.

Marital and Family Status and Living Arrangements, Persons 65 and over, 1980–1988

The projection of future living patterns is an important part of planning for an aging population and of adapting social and health programs to fit needs (King, 1988).

In both Japan and the United States over half of the elderly are married, and most of the rest are widowed. The percentage who are widowed is higher in Japan than in the United States (38% vs. 34%), but the percentages who are single or divorced are lower (Table A.3).

Almost all of the elderly in both countries live in households rather than institutions but more of the U.S. elderly live alone (30% vs. 11% in Japan) and in two-person households (54% vs. 26% in Japan).

In the United States, elders with functional problems often combine households with an adult daughter or son, but there are many older persons living alone who are in or near poverty and have few personal supports.

Living arrangements of the elderly in the United States tend to be quite different from those in Japan, where elders traditionally share their household with children (especially the eldest son) and grandchildren.

In the United Sates, the number of one-and two-person households has increased since 1960. In Japan, too, the family unit has changed, although more slowly. Okazaki (1990) notes that in Japan the percentage of elderly living with children and grandchildren declined from 87% in 1960 to 66% in 1985. The elderly in Japan increasingly rely on social security for

TABLE A.3 Marital and Family Status and Living Arrangements, Persons 65 Years and Over, 1980–1988

	Total		
Characteristic	1980	1985	1989/ 1990
United States			(1989)
Total (millions)	24.2	26.8	29.0
Marital status	Percent distribution		
Single	5.5	5.2	4.9
Married	55.4	55.2	56.4
Widowed	35.7	35.6	34.3
Divorced	3.5	4.0	4.4
Family status			
In families	67.6	67.3	67.4
Nonfamily householders	31.2	31.1	31.3
Living arrangements			
Living in household	99.8	99.6	99.7
Living alone	30.3	30.2	30.5
Spouse present	53.6	53.4	54.3
Living with someone else	15.9	15.9	14.8
Not in household	0.2	0.4	0.3
Japan			
Total (millions)	10.6	12.5	14.9
Marital status	Percent distribution		
Single	1.1	1.4	1.8
Married	54.5	55.1	57.5
Widowed	41.9	41.3	37.6
Divorced	1.9	2.1	2.4
Family status			
In families	88.6	87.6	85.4
Nonfamily householders	11.5	12.3	14.7
Living arrangements			
Single person	8.5	9.3	11.2
Aged couple	19.6	23.0	25.7
Living with unmarried children	16.5	16.7	17.8
Living with married children	52.5	47.9	41.9
Other	0.2	0.2	0.2

Source: *Statistical Abstract of the United States* (1990), Table 42; "The population census in Japan, 1980, 1985, 1990." Management and Coordination Agency; Comprehensive Survey of Living Condition of the People on Health and Welfare, Ministry of Health and Welfare.

economic support rather than on children in a shared household. If chronically ill, the elderly rely more on institutional care than on family caregivers.

Factors besides culturally preferred living arrangements may influence the probability of intergenerational households as well as the probability of an elderly person's living alone. Adult children of divorced elderly parents may not have close relationships with the noncustodial parent. Disability of an elderly parent motivates decisions to share households so that more help with daily living can be provided (largely by female relatives). If a particular birth cohort is large because of more children, aging members may have more surviving siblings with whom they can live if unable to live with children. Adequate income makes it possible for widows or widowers to maintain their own household and to purchase paid help with activities of daily living if they are functionally limited. But many elderly who have no surviving children, or whose children are poor, are obliged to live alone.

Comparison of Economic Strength of the United States and Japan, 1978–1988

Japan and the United States are both world leaders in the value of their GNP, as shown in Table A.4, but the economic activity of the United States is more concentrated in tertiary industry, that is, the financial and service sectors (72.2% vs. 62.8% for Japan). In 1988, Japan's per capita GNP was 18% higher ($23,382 vs. $19,813 for the United States). Steel and motor vehicle production grew in Japan while declining in the United States and the Japanese output now exceeds the U.S. output. The United States has more automobiles per 1,000 persons (including imports), but the growth of automobile ownership has been more rapid in Japan. The pattern for telephones is similar—more common in the United States but more rapid growth in Japan. A higher percentage of young people in the United States are enrolled in higher education than in Japan. Japan has a far higher population density than

TABLE A.4 Comparison of Economic Strength of the United States and Japan, 1978–1988

	United States		Japan	
	1978	1988	1978	1985/ 1988
GNP (US $100 million)	22,497	48,806	9,717	28,669
Rank in market economies	1	1	2	2
GNP (per capita US $ current prices)	10,107	19,813	8,456	23,382
Private final consumption (% of GNP)	62.5	66.3	58.6	56.3
Government final consumption (% of GNP)	16.2	17.6	9.7	9.3
Gross domestic fixed capital formation (% of GNP)	20.1	16.5	31.6	31.9
Percent of domestic income by industry				
Primary industry	3.3	2.3	4.5	2.3
Secondary industry	32.4	25.5	36.6	24.9
Tertiary industry	64.3	72.2	58.9	62.8
Household savings rate (% of disposable income)	8.3	7.7	20.8	14.8
Tax burden rate (% of national income)	27.9	25.6	21.3	28.2
Social security burden rate (% of national income)	(77) 7,1	(87) 8.8	(77) 8.4	(87) 10.9
Tax burden and social security burden rate (% of national income)	34.6	35.2	27.8	38.3
Steel production (1,000 metric tons)	123,888	90,012	102,096	106,680
Motor vehicle production (1,000)	12,876	11,226	9,240	12,714
Petroleum consumption (per capita liters per day)	13.5	11.2	7.1	5.8
Telephones in use (per 1,000 persons)	(75) 637	(82) 759	(75) 353	(85) 552
Motor vehicles in use (per 1,000 persons)	507	561	164	236
Education (number enrolled in higher education as % of population)	(77) 5.2	5.1	(75) 2.0	2.9
Ratio of paved roads to total roads (%)	(75) 48.3	90	37.1	(87) 1.6
Surface area (1,000 hectares)		937,261		37,780
Population (1,000)		246,330		122,610
Population density(persons per square kilometer)		26		325
Rate of working-age population to elderly population		5.4		6.4

Source: From *The International Comparative Statistics of Japan and Other Countries* (pp. 3–4) by Research and Statistics Bureau, The Bank of Japan, 1990, Japan Credit Check Company Ltd.,

does the United States. Although Japan's population is about half that of the United States, its surface area is only 4% as great. Population density may make it more difficult to maintain quality of life. However, Japan may enjoy economies of scale relative to the United States in distribution of public services and dissemination of health information.

Total Labor Force, Unemployment Rate, and Earnings in Manufacturing, 1980–1988

The labor force participation rate for persons 65 and older has been fairly stable over time in both the United States and Japan, but it was more than twice as high in Japan (Table A.5). Japan has a lower unemployment rate, which undoubtedly makes it easier for elders to find gainful work. For males, the transition from full-time work to retirement is managed and experienced differently in the United States and in Japan. Men in the United States tend to choose early retirement before age 65 with actuarially reduced social security benefits, and they did so even in the 1970s, before mandatory retirement was legally forbidden. In Japan, however, where guaranteed "lifetime" employment ends in almost all firms by age 60, there is no general exit from the labor force. Employers retain some of their older workers at lower wages, a practice not forbidden by labor law, and transfer another portion to subsidiaries or related firms. Some of the workers not retained or reemployed in this way find jobs with their old firm's suppliers or customers or through personal search, while others remain unemployed. It has been found that the wage drop after expiration of the "lifetime" contract is least for those men staying with their first employer, with larger firms, and in their primary occupation (Rebick, 1991). Pension rules about permitted earnings provide an incentive for men to seek part-time rather than full-time work and for bonuses to be used frequently by employers as a mode of payment.

TABLE A.5 Total Labor Force, Unemployment Rate, and Earnings in Manufacturing, 1980–1988

	1980	1984	1985	1986	1987	1988
United States						
Civilian labor force (millions)	106.9	113.5	115.5	117.8	119.9	121.7
Labor force participation rate (%)						
Total	63.8	64.4	64.8	65.3	65.6	65.9
65 years old and over	12.2	10.5	10.4	10.3	10.5	11.2
Unemployment rate	7.1	7.5	7.2	7.0	6.2	5.5
Number of work hours per week	39.7	40.7	40.5	40.7	41.0	41.4
Average wages per hour						
Current dollars	7.27	9.19	9.54	9.73	9.91	10.18
Constant dollars (1985 prices)	9.49	9.51	9.54	9.55	9.38	9.26
Rate of year-to-year changes in						
real hourly wages	−4.3	−0.2	0.3	0.2	−1.8	−1.3
Japan						
Civilian labor force (millions)	55.7	58.5	58.8	59.4	60.0	60.9
Labor force participation rate						
Total	63.3	63.4	63.0	62.8	62.6	62.9
65 years old and over	26.3	24.8	24.3	23.7	23.6	23.8
Unemployment rate	2.0	2.8	2.6	2.8	2.9	2.5
Number of work hours per week	38.8	41.1	41.7	41.1	41.0	41.3
Average wages per hour						
Current dollars	5.28	5.91	6.04	8.79	10.41	11.74
Constant dollars (1985 prices)	6.05	6.03	6.04	8.74	10.34	11.58
Rate of year-to-year changes in						
real hourly wages	−0.6	1.5	1.1	1.0	1.9	4.0

Source: From *Statistical Abstract of the United States* (1990), tables 42, 660, 1461; *Japan Statistical Yearbook* (1989), Tables 3-1, 3-2.

Annual Income and Living Expenditure of Elderly Households, 1987 (in U.S. Dollars)

See Table A.6.

Social Security Programs, 1989

A simple but crude measure of the adequacy of public old age pensions is provided by the ratio of the average pension to

TABLE A.6 Annual Income and Living Expenditure of Elderly Households, 1987 (in U.S. Dollars)

	United States		Japan	
	Amount	Percent	Amount	Percent
Total income	15,775		15,710	
Total expenditure	16,526		17,340	
Food	2,538	17.1	4,596	26.5
Alcoholic beverages	289	2.0	b	b
Housing	5,243	33.7	3,024	17.5
Apparel	790	5.1	900	5.2
Transportation	2,334	15.0	1,308	7.5
Health care	1,643	10.6	720	4.2
Other expenditure[c]	3,689	23.7	6,792	39.1

Source: From Statistical Abstract of the United States (1990), Table 715; Japan, Statistics Bureau, Management and Coordination Agency.
[a]U.S. data are based on the Consumer Expenditure Survey and refer to consumer units with reference person 65 +. Japan data are based on "households led by (aged) jobless people 65 +."
[b]Not shown separately.
[c]Includes life insurance, personal care, entertainment, reading, education, cash contributrions, tobacco and smoking supplies, and miscellaneous expenditure.

the average wage in manufacturing for 1986. The values for the United States and Japan are virtually the same (Table A.7). In both countries the public pension value is just over two-fifths of the wage level. However, the current wage may not be the best standard for judging pension adequacy. It has been shown that the wage-replacement rate for subgroups of the retired varies according to the number of years of earnings and other definitions used in calculating replacement rates, as well as the work history and marital status of the re-tirees (Grad, 1990). In general, the decline in income level upon retirement is marked, even though elders tend to sup-port fewer persons out of one income than do younger house-holds. A 40% replacement rate in Japan in 1990 is cited as a reason for higher labor force participation after age 60 (Re-bick, 1991).

Projection of the Total Dependency Ratio, 1990–2010

See Table A.8.

Health Expenditures: Total, Per Capita, and as Percentage of GNP, 1970–1987

A huge growth of health expenditures occurred between 1970 and 1987 in both Japan and the United States. If exchange rates are used to convert yen to dollars, total outlays in 1987 in current dollars were 17.9 times those in 1970 for Japan and 6.7 times for the United States in the same period of time (Table A.9) Much of this increase was due to population growth. The use of per capita expenditure adjusts for this effect. Per capita health expenditures in 1987 were about 15.2 times higher than in 1970 for Japan and 5.7 times higher for the United States. Expressing health expenditures as a percentage of GNP controls for the effect of general inflation and economic growth. By this measure, Japan and the United States were similar in expenditure growth rates, with the percentage of GNP going to health care increasing by 50%. However, the U.S. figure was more than twice that for Japan— 11.1% versus 5.2% of GNP going to health.

Substitution of statistics based on purchasing power parity reduces the change between 1970 and 1987 in Japan's expenditure to 8 times (total health outlays) and 6.9 times (per capita outlays). Growth was thus more similar to U.S. rates.

Ten Leading Causes of Death, Age 65 and Over: Number of Deaths and Death Rates (per 100,000), 1988

Heart diseases and malignant neoplasms are by far the leading causes of death in the U.S. elderly, amounting to 61.4% of all deaths; the death rate for diseases of the heart is twice that for cancers (Table A.10).

For the specific age groups 65–74, 75–84, and 85+ in the United States, there is continuity as to the top causes of death: the same 10 are the leaders in each age group, with a

TABLE A.7 Social Security Programs for the Elderly, 1989

	United States	Japan
Type of system	Social insurance	Dual: universal and social insurance
Qualifying age	65 (62–64 with reduced benefit)	(1) 65, reduced benefit if retiree is 60–64; (2) M 60; F, seamen, miners 56
Government contribution	100% of special benefit for those 72 before 1968 and means-tested allowance	(1) 33 1/3% (2) none
Old age cash benefit	Up to $899 for workers retiring at 65 in 1989 and increment for deferral 65–69; cost of living adjustment (COLA)	(1) 627,200 yen/yr. and increment for extra contribution (>40 months) if self-employed (2) .75% of indexed monthly wagep × months of coverage up to 420
Coverage	Gainfully occupied, including self-employed	(1) residents 20–59; voluntary for residents 60–64 and for citizens living abroad 20–64 (2) industry and commerce
Public employees	Separate; coverage under Social Security is available for state and local employees	Separate
Old age benefit/average wage (manufacturing industries 1986)	43.1%	42.1%

Source: Social Security Programs Throughout the World—1989, US DHHS Research Report #62, May, 1990; Chouju Shakai Taisaku Kankei Shiryoushuu, p. 106, March 1990, Section of Aging, General Executive Office.

single exception. It is chronic liver disease and cirrhosis, which constitutes the eighth cause for those aged 65–74, dropping to a lesser rank (and to a much lower number of deaths) in the older groups. One reason for this is that the liver damage developing after years of heavy alcohol use has

TABLE A.8 Projection of the Total Dependency Ratio, 1990–2010

Age Group (Years)	1990	2000	2010
United States		% distribution	
0–17	25.6	24.5	22.2
18–64	61.8	62.5	63.9
65 and over	12.6	13.0	13.9
		Dependency ratio	
0–17	41.4	39.2	34.7
65 and over	20.4	20.8	21.8
Total	61.8	60.0	56.5
Japan		% distribution	
0–14	18.6	18.0	18.6
15–64	69.5	65.8	61.4
65 and over	11.9	16.3	20.0
		Dependency ratio	
0–15	26.8	27.4	30.3
65 and over	17.2	24.7	32.5
Total	44.0	52.1	62.8

Source: From Statistical Abstract of the United States (1990), Table 18; Japan, Section of Aging, General Executive Office,. Data for a Long-life Society; (p. 1) March 1989.

TABLE A.9 Health Expenditures Total, Per Capita, and as Percentage of GNP, 1970–1987

Year	Total (billion $)		Per Capita $)		Percent of GNP	
	U.S.	Japan	U.S.	Japan	U.S.	Japan
1970	75.0	7.0	349.0	67.4	7.4	3.3
1975	132.7	21.8	591.0	195.1	8.3	4.3
1980	248.1	52.9	1,055.0	451.4	9.1	4.9
1985	419.3	67.6	1,696.0	554.8	10.4	5.0
1987	500.3	125.0	1,987.0	1,022.1	11.1	5.2
1987/1970	6.7	17.9	5.7	15.2	1.5	1.6

Source: From Statistical Abstract of the United States (1974) Table 99; (1990) Table 134; Japan, Ministry of Health & Welfare.

TABLE A.10 Ten Leading Causes of Death, Age 65 and Over, Number of Deaths and Death Rates (Per 100,000), 1988, United States

	65–74			75–84			85+		
	Deaths	Death Rates	Rank	Deaths	Death Rates	Rank	Deaths	Death Rates	Rank
Diseases of heart	176,126	984.1	1	242,116	2,542.7	1	209,252	7,098.1	1
Malignant neoplasms	150,824	842.7	2	125,049	1,313.3	2	48,314	1,638.9	3
Cerebrovascular diseases	27,694	154.7	3	52,716	553.6	3	50,335	1,707.4	2
Chronic obstructive pulmonary disease	27,185	151.9	4	29,806	313.0	4	11,623	394.3	6
Diabetes mellitus	11,02	62.0	5	11,907	125.0	6	6,548	222.1	8
Pneumonia and influenza	10,713	59.9	6	24,481	257.1	5	33,149	1,125.4	4
Accidents and adverse effects	8,971	50.1	7	10,145	106.5	7	7,880	267.3	7
Chronic liver disease and cirrhosis	6,266	35.0	8	—	—	—	—	—	—
Nephritis, nephrotic sydrome and nephrosis	4,590	25.6	9	7,467	78.4	8	6,396	217.0	9
Septicemia	4,292	23.9	10	6,732	70.7	9	5,862	198.8	10
Atherosclerosis	—	—	—	6,679	70.1	10	11,677	396.1	5
All causes	488,545	2,729.8	—	601,914	6,321.3	—	459,710	15,594.0	—

Source: From *Monthly Vital Statistics Report*, 39 (7; suppl); *Advance Report of Final Mortality Statistics*(1988) Table 9, pp. 24–25.

most of its impact on the affected persons before age 75. After age 75, atherosclerosis enters the ranks of the top 10 causes, replacing chronic liver conditions (it is 10th for those aged 75–84 and 5th for those aged 85 and over). Within the 10 leading causes of death there are some shifts in rank with advancing age, but heart and cerebrovascular diseases and malignancies are in the top three in all of the elderly age groups. The data suggest that further improvement in life expectancy is likely to be highly dependent on control of circulatory disease and cancer.

The leading causes of death for all elderly (65 and over) in Japan are also heart diseases and cancer, but their shares are about equal (Table A.11). The death rate from heart diseases after 65 is more than twice as high in the United States as it is in Japan—2,006.4 per 100,000 (combination of the deaths from the three subgroups in Table A.10, divided by the 65+ population) vs. 946. The rates for neoplasms are much closer (only 15% higher in the United States).

Certain causes of death are likely to be preceded by lengthy periods of illness requiring health care services or by severe functional disability requiring aid with personal care and household management. Other causes of mortality may impose no such prior burdens on family and social systems. (In fact, both situations are possible for different individuals within a single diagnostic group such as stroke). Future reduction of mortality, therefore, does not necessarily imply that social costs associated with aging will be lower.

REFERENCES

Grad, S. (1990). Earnings replacement rates of new retired workers. *Social Security Bulletin, 53*(10), 2–19.

King, M. L. (1988). *Changes in the living arrangements of the elderly, 1960–2030.* Washington, DC: United States Congressional Budget Office.

Okazaki, Y., Tsuji, T., Otomo, E., Hayakawa, K., Ibe, H., and Furuse, T. (1990). Social factors behind the aging of society. In T. Okazaki et al. (Ed.), *Responding to the needs of an aging society* (pp.

TABLE A.11 Ten Leading Causes of Death, All Ages: Number of Deaths and Death Rate (per 100,000, 1988, Japan)

	All Ages			65+			80+		
	Deaths	Death Rates	Rank	Deaths	Death Rates	Rank	Deaths	Death Rates	Rank
Neoplasms	205,470	168.4	1	127,461	928.4	2	39,232	1,496.8	3
Cardiovascular diseases	167,920	129.4	2	129,900	946.2	1	72,951	2,703.3	1
Cerebrovascular diseases	128,695	105.5	3	106,914	778.7	3	59,071	2,276.7	2
Pneumonia	82,914	51.6	4	58,049	422.8	4	36,204	1,381.3	4
Accidents	30,212	24.8	5	11,418	83.2	7	4,565	174.2	8
Senility	26,400	21.6	6	26,390	192.2	5	24,038	917.1	5
Suicide	22,705	18.7	7	—	—	—	—	—	—
Hepatocirrhosis	16,992	13.9	8	7,377	53.7	9	—	—	—
Nephritis	15,891	13.0	9	13,167	95.8	6	6,835	260.8	6
Hypertension diseases	10,258	8.4	10	9,583	69.8	8	6,780	258.7	7
Diabetes	—	—	—	7,062	51.4	10	2,818	107.5	10
Circulatory diseases	—	—	—	—	—	—	3,368	128.5	9

Source: From Japan, Ministry of Health & Welfare.

7–14). Tokyo: foreign Press Center. (Reference Reading Series 21)

Rebick, M. C. (1991a, October). *Finding jobs for older workers—the Japanese approach*. Paper presented at the Conference on New Jobs for an Aging Workforce, Ithaca, NY.

Rebick, M. C. (1991b). Job loss in the land of "lifetime" employment: Unemployment among older Japanese men. Unpublished paper.

Index